Endorsements

Written with courageous and confident insight, "A Better Way" addresses one of the greatest challenges in the Christian church today ... loving others as Christ loves us. The church is full of people who talk about grace and support; but when tragedy strikes or we suffer deep pain, more often than not, the hurting or helpless encounter judgment and betrayal. Having endured great sorrow, David shows us there is another way ... "A Better Way" ... it is the way of love as Christ loves. It means to love purely ... to love without condition, to give without expectation, to embrace the rejected, to seek those misunderstood, and in every way, to walk humbly with one another.

Colleen Swindoll-Thompson
Director of Special Needs Ministry, *Insight for Living*

"A Better Way" is not a book! No, these pages you hold in your hands are a wakeup call that will sound the alarm to the global church for a better way ... the way that Jesus intended it to be all along. In these chapters, David Glover gives voice to often a neglected and often misunderstood people in God's family who are often sidelined. As the radical leader of the PURE movement, David reminds us to embrace the diverse tapestry of God's kingdom and then equips us with a strategy on how everyone in God's army has a place to belong and serve."

David Nasser, Senior Vice President for Spiritual Development,
Liberty University, Lynchburg, Virginia

Love compels us to obey our beloved Lord who loves us. It motivates us to emulate Him by loving others, all others, in His name. In "A Better Way" David Glover illustrates love in action while calling from us a loving response for the "whosoever" in our sphere of influence. All persons have limitations, but the capacity to receive love is universal. The only thing comparable to receiving love is giving it. "A Better Way" shows what is a better way of showing love. It is an exhortation to share love with "the least of these." It is sure to warm the cockles of your heart and open your eyes to opportunities you might tend to overlook.

Dr. Nelson L. Price, Pastor Emeritus
Roswell Street Baptist Church, Marietta, Georgia

David Glover is a gift to the Body of Christ! His insightful wisdom and compelling passion are expressed in his book – "A Better Way." We are shown how to be

Christ's hands and feet as we minister to those who are so very precious in the Lord's sight.

Jeff W. Crook, Senior Pastor
Blackshear Place Baptist Church, Flowery Branch, Georgia

Out of the crucible of his own experience, David Glover offers practical encouragement and inspiration to the church to become aware of and sensitive to the needs of individuals and families with disabilities. After reading this book I am more conscious than ever of my need to show the love of Christ to "pure people" who have the capacity to make us more like Jesus. Every church leader, indeed, every Christian, should read "A Better Way" in order to awaken to God's calling for His church to minister to a very special group of people who make up 15% of our population. This is a ministry that will change you and change your church.

J. Robert White, Executive Director
Georgia Baptist Convention, Atlanta, Georgia

Need a book on practically demonstrating Christ's love, read this one. When one considers that ministering to the least of these is in turn ministering to Jesus, it becomes the deal breaker. Read and then obey.

Pastor Johnny Hunt, Senior Pastor
First Baptist Church Woodstock, Woodstock, Georgia
Former President, Southern Baptist Convention

David Glover reminds us of the Lord's teaching in Matthew 22:37-40 in which He says that to love the Lord is the first and greatest commandment and to love our neighbors is the second. It is from this that David and PURE Ministries derive their mission: To strengthen and build relationships with God and fellow Christians to become better Christian ourselves. It is this principle that guides my life and work. By reading "A Better Way" you will see how David shows us the path to become true and ardent agents of transformation for the Church in the 21st Century.

Lynn Westmoreland, Honorary Member,
PURE Ministries Advisory Board, Grantville, Georgia

"A Better Way" and PURE Ministries present the heart of the Gospel to the Church for implementation. We are all called to reach out to "the least, last and lost." "A Better Way" instructs us in the process. It's powerful, compassionate ministry in action! It makes the church, the church.

Dr. Randy Mickler, Senior Pastor
Mt. Bethel United Methodist Church, Marietta, Georgia

Every person, believer and non-believer, should read this insightful book. Look around you. What do you see? The blinders that we often wear unknowingly can be removed and your life will be changed. I encourage you to pick up a copy of "A Better Way," read it and then share it with a friend.

Dr. Richard Lee, Founding Pastor,
First Redeemer Church, Cumming, Georgia

A BETTER WAY

WHERE LEAST
IS MOST

DAVID ZACHARIAH GLOVER

WESTBOW
PRESS®
A DIVISION OF THOMAS NELSON
& ZONDERVAN

WestBow Press books may be ordered through booksellers or by contacting:

WestBow Press
A Division of Thomas Nelson & Zondervan
1663 Liberty Drive
Bloomington, IN 47403
www.westbowpress.com
1 (866) 928-1240

ISBN: 978-1-5127-2705-0 (sc)
ISBN: 978-1-5127-2707-4 (hc)
ISBN: 978-1-5127-2706-7 (e)

Library of Congress Control Number: 2016900696

Print information available on the last page.

WestBow Press rev. date: 01/14/2016

In loving memory

My dad, Melvin Glover,
My daughter, Katie Emerson
My son, Gabe Glover,
My grandson, Zachariah Emerson,
and my dear PURE Ministries friend, Laura Vandiver:

We'll talk about all this someday.

Special authors note about Katie Glover Emerson

We never dreamed that when we published this book originally in the beginning of 2013 that the Lord would call home our precious Katie, the mother of Zach, in October of that same year. From when I introduce her in the beginning of the book in the preface to the very last page, Katie is all over this book and remains all over our hearts. She was truly a remarkable person, our firstborn, and a special gift from God. As each day passes since she left this earth, we miss her terribly – her humor; her God-given wisdom and counsel she often and freely shared with me, her Dad; the so very close relationship with me; her very presence bringing calm to all those her called her friend; and, forever, her beautiful smile. At the same time, her mother and I can only thank God that we had her for 39 years and that He chose us to be her earthly parents. Yes, we miss her, but her legacy lives on in her children. I smile each time that I think of the joy she now knows each minute in the presence of her Lord, now holding her precious Zach. I would never have known a better way without your gift of Zach. His presence, though brief, changed us all for the better.

In gratitude

Anna Lee and Jeff Walding:

> Your constant encouragement, steadiness, and counsel have helped me more than you'll ever know.

Dr. Jim Pierson:

> Since I met you in 2004 as we first started *PURE Ministries*, you have been my good friend, consistent encourager, and great source of godly wisdom. Much of what is contained here is but a just little of the wealth of knowledge you so graciously shared with me.

Lori Millwood

> Since we met for the first time at respite at Blackshear Place Baptist Church many years ago, you have been my hero. I have admired your great abilities in ministering to people and families affected by disability. God has blessed you with a unique talent of relating to virtually every PURE person He has brought your way. I believe this talent is surpassed only by your obvious passion and love for these folks. It has been my opportunity and blessing to simply observe and learn from you as you love on people. I am inspired each time I hear you share your consistent message to these PURE children and adults, alike, "God loves you just the way you are." I can assure you that God loves you as well, just the way you are.

My many friends and family:

> Many people have helped me in the writing of this book, some directly and others, indirectly. I want to thank my many godly friends and mentors (and "mentoresses" or "mentorettes" or

whatever the feminine term might be for godly women!) that God has given to me in my life. I'll not try to name you all, but God has blessed me greatly over the years and I am forever thankful to Him for you. Without your guidance, affirmation, encouragement, and many prayers, I would never have even attempted to write this book.

PURE Ministries team and Board of Directors:

Thank you for your friendship and support: Jacque and James Daniel; Diana and Billy Duncan; Dianne and John Reynolds; Lynne and Tommy Davis; and *PURE Ministries* Board, I thank you for doing the day-to-day work it takes to keep *PURE Ministries* running so that I had time to write this book.

Editor and proof reading friends:

Some of you special friends were kind enough to help me edit, re-edit, and then edit again the manuscript for this book. The most amazing thing is that you were sweet enough not to laugh in my face one time or ask if I really wanted to put my thoughts on paper! You encouraged and inspired me and, with your wise advice, helped me make the book what we all prayed it would be. I can only assume we could have kept editing forever, but we had to go to print sometime! I especially thank these folks: good friend, editor, and "grammar extraordinaire," Pat Chennault; our PURE Ministries Foundation Relationships Director, Lynne Davis, who has been beyond patient and helpful in her many readings and editing of the manuscript; sweetest sister anyone could have, Lynda Dean; long-time, great friends Helen Heard and David Sitton; and my sweet brother and sister in Christ who constantly encourage, inspire, uplift me, and now PURE parents themselves, Jeff and Nan Rice.

Lee

To my precious wife, Lee, who has had to listen to me preach and had to read and edit more of my writings than any human ought, all done with more love and devotion than any man ever possibly deserved. I love you.

But we preach Christ crucified, to the Jews a stumbling block and to the Greeks foolishness, but to those who are called, both Jews and Greeks, Christ the power of God and the wisdom of God. Because the foolishness of God is wiser than men, and the weakness of God is stronger than men. For you see your calling, brethren, that not many wise according to the flesh, not many mighty, not many noble, are called. But God has chosen the foolish things of the world to put to shame the wise, and God has chosen the weak things of the world to put to shame the things which are mighty; and the base things of the world and the things which are despised God has chosen, and the things which are not, to bring to nothing the things that are.

I Corinthians 1:23-28

Contents

Foreword

We first learned about PURE Ministries when David Glover approached us in 2010 to get involved with the ministries' first "PURE Celebration" in Atlanta, Georgia. As parents of a son with special needs, we were immediately drawn to the ministry's heart to change the church and open the eyes of others to the amazing gifts "PURE" people bring to those around them.

Zachary, our son was injured early in his life, resulting in a traumatic brain injury and legal blindness. Despite his physical limitations, however, Zack is one of the happiest and most content people you will ever meet. He brings perspective to our family in a world fixated on beauty, fitness, money, and power. But watching the outside world miss the treasure inside Zack brings emotional pains far greater than any physical trials. As parents, it is heartbreaking to see Zack sitting alone or apart from the group. Throughout his years in school his peers enjoyed the "normal" life, while he was left out of birthday parties, overnight sleepovers, youth league sports, and so many typical childhood experiences with others. For years Zack worshipped next to us in church without much interaction from those around him.

While Zack was in high school we started a disability awareness program through our First Things First Foundation called CHEER (Consciousness Helps Encourage Equal Respect) using Zack's high school for the pilot program. As students' eyes were opened to see Zack beyond his disability a new world began for him, one with birthday parties and school dances. And those who welcomed Zack into their lives told us he had changed their worlds too. We firmly believe if the church's eyes were opened as well, all would benefit from the new relationships built with PURE people and their families. It is for this reason David has written *A Better Way*.

In this book David does not sugarcoat the lives of PURE people or attempt to mitigate the challenges of being PURE in a world that often dismisses them as without value or worth. *A Better Way* is not a "Christian instruction manual" of steps to be taken by a local church to do a better job of reaching out to PURE people and their families, though a greater awareness of PURE people and perhaps better church ministries will undoubtedly be an effect of the book.

From our perspective, David has attempted to do two things with this book. First, he has addressed questions about PURE people and God's plans that confound all of us – even PURE parents - every day, if we are honest: questions about the very existence and value of certain people and of the God who created them. David challenges readers to move from an inability and reluctance to accept His ways that we can't understand or fathom to embracing our loving Father for His gift of PURE people on this earth. The questions posed and the clear, undeniable, and biblical answers will make you think and more importantly we hope will cause you to act. Having lived with Zack, we can bear witness that God does use PURE people in ways that will undoubtedly change our lives. Zack has taught us more about God and His love than we could have ever learned any other way.

Secondly, the "better" way described within these pages is crucial to truly understanding the treasure inside PURE people. Whether we can grasp it or not, God is moving in and through this world in various ways to accomplish His purposes. David details here that, if we are willing, God is moving and working through the "least of these," PURE people, to change us. As you and I change, His church is transformed.

As you read this book, we challenge you to move from merely accepting PURE people to truly seeing the God-imputed worth He has placed in them. Further, we hope you will come to realize we are all called to become more like PURE people in order to impact our world for Christ. As a result of understanding that He not only uses PURE people to change us individually as we observe and love our PURE friends and family members, we also discover the truth that God is using the "least of these" to transform the church in America to a place where "least *is* most." The profound truth of *A Better Way* is simply this: If we allow Him, God does use people to change us and thereby change His church to have a real impact for Him on this earth!

Be prepared to think, be blessed, and enjoy discovering a "better way" to live for Christ where you would least expect to find it.

Kurt and Brenda Warner
PURE parents,
NFL Football legend and devoted wife and mother,
and Founders of Treasure House, a supportive living community for
adults with developmental disabilities
www.treasurehouse.org

Preface

The lady was just too nice. When we entered the small office, she exclaimed, "Mr. Glover! Have you seen it yet?" My confusion was obviously apparent. Embarrassed, she followed with, "Oh, I guess not." I had made arrangements with another lady in the office before and hadn't met the lady who now scurried before me. She smiled too much, knew too much, and was too anxious to get my business completed and my wife, Lee, and me out of the office. She even knew my name before she should have. She giggled with excitement and smiled broadly as we walked out the door.

Without the foggiest idea of what was happening, I signed the final papers for our funeral plots at the small cemetery in Cumming, Georgia, and left the office. Lee and I had been asked by our daughter, Katie, and her husband, Kyle, to meet them at the grave of our grandson, Zachariah, who had died a month before. To tell you the truth, I wasn't all that excited at seeing the new grave marker, but Katie and Kyle were, so I put up a good front. They had talked about it in hushed tones for the last few weeks and called us to come over to the cemetery as soon as the grave marker had been installed.

As you will learn in detail later, Zachariah, our first grandson, had been born 4 ½ years earlier with a host of disabilities. He faced many challenges during that short time, but God blessed through it all and taught all of us who knew him amazing things about Zach, ourselves, and God Himself. He died unexpectedly while he was recovering at home from one of his many brain surgeries. Yes, I say *unexpectedly* because, even though Zach had significant medical issues, we had never considered the possibility that God would take him home so soon. Life for Zach and our family was always busy with frequent doctor visits, hospital stays, therapists, and seemingly never ending, new diagnoses.

I can remember dreading returning to the little grave. It was still winter in Georgia and the grass, I knew, had not had time to repair itself. Like all of us, the ground around the grave would still be deeply scarred. Katie and Kyle stood out by the grave as we drove up. Ben, Zach's two year old little brother, was playing and toddling around the empty cemetery nearby. Katie had a very contented, satisfied look on her face, as we walked up. As I looked down, before me was the new grave marker for Zachariah Kyle Emerson.

Completely unaware of their intentions, my sweet daughter and son-in-law had chosen to grace me with what was then, and will always be, the greatest honor of my life. They had taken my favorite picture of me holding Zach in my lap, his smiling face next to my smiling face, with my hand holding him close and somehow had it made into a three dimensional bronze relief on the marker. This image was forever captured in bronze along with his name, birth and death date, and a description of his life, "An example to live by - a smile to treasure." Zach's smile was vibrantly alive and you could even see the veins in my hand and ribs in the sweater I was wearing. As I gazed, I knew everything had changed. This moment was a game changer for me. Life was not ever going to be the same.

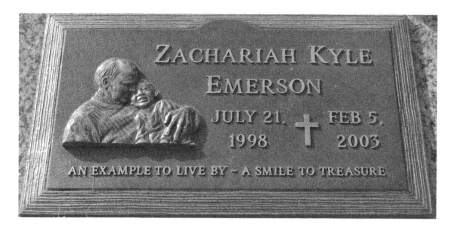

By definition, and even in the current vernacular, a game changer is an event that changes the game – the entire game. Similarly, a life changer is something that forever changes our life. These are not events that simply cause things to change for a day or a week or a month. Game changers change everything for good and in many cases, forever.

We've all had them, these *life changers*: a marriage, a car wreck, the birth of a child, a diagnosis, in a courtroom a sentence is pronounced, a divorce, or a betrayal. If you are reading this and you are a Christian, at the moment you submitted your life to Jesus, you experienced the most significant *life changer*. Conversely, if our lives didn't really change radically when we became a Christian, then we probably really didn't in fact become one! How could we have encountered the God of the Universe in the person of His Son, Jesus, have the Holy Spirit live within us, and remain the same? Impossible.

You see, *game changers* or *life changers*, change everything and they can change everything eternally. Our individual life changers may all be different, but they are all the same in that our lives are irrevocably changed by them - permanently. We all have them, but we all don't respond the same. As illustrated by the sample list of common life changers above, most are not pleasant or happy events. We'll talk about this in the book, but some we even call *tragedies*, at least from the human perspective.

So, is God out to get us with these life changers or does He have a different agenda? Since God is sovereign, I believe He does indeed have a different agenda. We crave earthly pleasures, while His desire for us is drastically different: He wants us to become more like Him. We desire pleasure, He desires compassion; we want comfort, He desires contentment; we want security, He desires dependence; we want relaxation, He desires growth; we want things to make us happy, He desires joy; we want the familiar, He desires change.

In one instant I came face to face with a profound truth staring back at me in bronze: I was different; I had been changed; my very identity was now something else. Yes, I knew it had been happening for the last 4 ½ years, but now I could see it concretely (or rather "bronzely"). What had happened? It hit me like a ton of bricks: God had used a person, though deemed of very little or no value or worth based on worldly standards, to change me. Now, the ball was in my court: how would I respond? Zach was a life changer. Would I be? Would my life make one bit of difference to others?

I am not so naïve as to think that the book you are reading will be a life changer for you. However, I do know the Lord works in strange and mysterious ways. If I can simply initiate some reflection, I'll be satisfied. If reading any of this will cause reflection on what He has done for us and is doing with those He has placed around us in our families, churches, and communities, then I will consider myself to have succeeded. If hidden on some page, the Lord speaks to you, and your game and life changes, praise only Him.

While contemplating this book and in the actual process of writing it, I have wrestled with just who you, the reader, will actually be. Not just everyone will pick up a book and read about heavy subjects – subjects which this book undoubtedly addresses. I realize that today we are more of a "quick fix, put it in the microwave, let's get going" type culture than a contemplative or "crock pot slow" one. But who is my "target" or audience, if you will?

When people ask me about what we do at *PURE* Ministries[1], I always tell them we simply try to awaken the average Christian to the blessings and needs of PURE people and their families. People at this point normally ask, "What does PURE mean?" Until we explain it later in detail (see page 68), when you read PURE, think:

> **P** erfectly created by a loving sovereign God, designed for His purpose
> **U** nique in his or her own gifts, blessings, talents, desires, and contributions
> **R** eceptive and responsive to our communication, touch, and acts of love
> **E** ternal, because there are no *disabled souls* in God's eyes

I know this may sound strange at this point, but trust me. It will make sense later. I tell them we do three things at *PURE Ministries*: *compel* Christians to listen to the needs of families affected by disabilities and awaken them to ministry opportunities; *inspire* Christians to see how

---

[1]   See SPECIAL NOTE 1. below at end of this Preface for explanation of "PURE".

they can be involved and blessed; and *equip* Christians to act in their communities through their church. By the way, I realize this ain't rocket science! So there you have it - if you're reading this book right now (and you keep reading!) you're most likely an average Christian and that's great - depending on your definition of average! What I mean by average is best exemplified by myself before my grandson, Zachariah, was born. Before he was born, I considered myself a "sensitive, involved, serving, and loving Jesus with all my heart" type Christian. Or at least, that was what I thought I was. Though God had saved me and I did love Jesus, I was content in my selfishness and self-righteousness to simply label myself these things. In retrospect, I was none of these. Not even close.

With Zach's birth, God got my attention as only He can do. By introducing me to and immersing me in the world of special needs, God opened my eyes in ways that I could have never comprehended otherwise. Zach was a game changer, too. Though God is certainly not through with me nor am I today what I need or want to be, I am much more because of my experience with Zach. What God did, as I like to explain to those who ask, is this: God put His arm around me and said, "David, I know you love Me and think you are close to Me, but I'm going to give you something special to really draw you closer to Me in a way you would never believe. Hard? Yes. Joyful? Yes. And, you'll thank Me forever for it."

He did this through Zach, by teaching me a better way to live. He did it by removing the quotes from how I previously described myself above. I'm still average or below in most ways, but I'm a little more than that now in some significant ways, especially in my love for people. Again, I am not there yet by any measure or standard nor am I anything to write home about, but God is working on me. He is making me more of something I am not naturally. He has made me more sensitive to people who are hurting, giving me more of a servant's heart, and providing opportunities for me to be involved more with people than with programs, organizations, or things. I love Jesus today with what I believe is a larger and deeper heart; all things I am not by nature or in my own power. And, I truly believe God primarily used a little boy who could not talk, walk, or do so many things we think necessary to have value, to begin this real change in how I think and live.

In a sense we're all average if the sampling is large enough, so please don't be offended. What I have to offer you in the pages that follow is the story of how God used a little boy, who this world would not consider of much value, to change me and to literally start a movement in our culture: the PURE movement. In this book, you will find my story, our family's story, and most importantly, the story that is being written today and for the future. Hopefully, you'll find words of encouragement, based not only on my own limited experience, but also that of countless others I've met along the way. But, most importantly, we will examine the Scriptures and learn what God has to say about PURE people and their role in His divine plan. Maybe, just maybe, God will open your eyes as He did mine some years ago, to this new world most of us never see, of which we are little aware, and perhaps about which we don't even want to think. Everybody is not going to be blessed as I was to be a granddad of a PURE child. You may not even have a PURE person in your immediate family, but that doesn't mean you have to miss the special blessing that God has placed in PURE people in your church, your neighborhood, and your community. Read, contemplate, and let God speak. My prayer is you won't be average when you finish the book.

Also, I have been constantly reminded that PURE ministry is no more *ministry* than one might call "marriage" or "family" a ministry. That is to say, authentic PURE ministry is simply *relationship*. Of course PURE ministry involves programs, events, and services, but like marriage, family, and friendship, PURE ministry can be condensed simply to relationship. PURE ministry is not so much what we do, but who we are. It is not some place or plateau or level we reach or a variety of programs we offer in ministry, but rather it is how we choose to live and interact with those around us.

So with that background information and history, what is the purpose of this book? First, the purpose is to make aware, encourage, inform, and inspire the average Christian of the need and blessing of PURE ministry. If we become more lovingly aware of and sensitive to those around us, God will profoundly change us. As the apostle Paul states in *Romans*:

> *I beseech you therefore, brethren, by the mercies of God, that you present your bodies a living sacrifice, holy, acceptable to God, which is your reasonable service. ² And do not be conformed to this world, but be transformed by the renewing of your mind, that you may prove what is that good and acceptable and perfect will of God.*
>
> *Romans 12: 1-2*

It is reasonable, based on what God has done in His unspeakable gift, for us to be a *living sacrifice* for Him. Paul goes on to say that we do this by not being *of* and *conformed* to this world around us, but by being *transformed* by the renewing of our minds - we must think differently. Though we obviously cannot do this with perfection, the *renewing of your mind* here means that we are to be transformed into thinking like our Heavenly Father. Perhaps in no better way can we emulate the Lord than in caring for and loving those around us who are marginalized in our culture - PURE people - just like He did.

Second, this book is intended to give the reader a foundation on which PURE ministry, specifically in the reader's personal life, can be built. As PURE ministry grows in individual hearts and becomes an integral part of the lives of Christians, PURE ministry permeates the local church. It is a simple one-by-one process of awareness, followed by personalization, then understanding, and, finally, a life change that can and will revolutionize the church of Jesus Christ. It is not only a change in our perception of and involvement in PURE ministry, but also of *when* we catch the vision. Then there is a change in our perception of and involvement in all ministry as Jesus intended!

The third reason for my writing this book requires that I must make another confession. In the very beginning, my humble intent was to write the definitive book on disability ministries for churches. It didn't take me long to realize that not only was I not qualified to do this, but also it became quite evident that such a book would probably be impossible to write anyway. With this in mind, I took a different tack. I have written this book to encourage and inspire Christians as to *why* and *what* PURE ministry is from a Scriptural perspective. I hope, though, in this book you will discover some practical information and suggestions on how to relate and reach out to people and families with disabilities. There is much more to share about how churches can go about implementing meaningful ministry. We at *PURE Ministries* pray that God will give us opportunity to more fully address these topics in a follow-up book now being developed.

This book is an attempt to call Christians, individually and collectively as the body of Christ, the church, to PURE ministry. I pray that it will be used by God as a motivation, reason, and inspiration to begin ministry. However, it is certainly not the definitive work on disability ministry. It is intended to awaken the typical Christian who is simply unaware of the need of a group of special people all around them, but with whom most have little, if no, involvement. In fact, most of the principles discussed here can and should be applied to our reaching out, with the love of Christ, *to any person* He brings across our path -- particularly any hurting person. It is our hope and prayer that this book simply opens people's eyes and hearts to immeasurable PURE ministry possibilities. True PURE ministry should never be thought of as something we do only at church, but rather it must become a vital part of who we are as Christians, wherever we are.

Finally, be warned as you read. I make some rather controversial statements and observations about the church in America today. I certainly don't mean to make anyone upset, but I do hope these things will at least make you think. Some of what is said may very well make you uncomfortable or even mad at me. However, I think we have patted ourselves on the back entirely too much in recent days, and it is high time that we take an objective look at the current state of the church in America in regard to our influencing our world with the message of Jesus Christ. Church membership (and more importantly, baptisms) in most all denominations in the U.S. continues to decline and our Christian impact on our culture is undeniably waning. I truly believe now is the time that some of these things presented here need to be debated, thought through, and acted upon by Christian leaders while we still have time. Also, please understand that when I am referring to the "average Christian" in this book in what can be interpreted in a negative way, I am primarily referring to *me*, for I am, without question, the best *worst* example I know – and I do know me well!. I have not tried to be judgmental, but rather honest and objective. My only request is that if you become troubled with something said, please first reflect, meditate, and most importantly, pray about the essence of *A Better Way*. If you do take exception or disagree with anything said here within these pages, please feel free to contact me via email or phone and we can talk about it. My current contact info can be found on www.pure-ministries.com.

Humbly, I hope and pray that the Spirit in which this book is written will help you and your church in your reasonable service to our Lord in loving Him more and loving others that He brings into your path. Transformational change is in the air in the church in America today and God is using PURE people in many ways to bring about that change. It is where least is most. A better way and divine appointments await - and we will be changed forever.

David Glover

SPECIAL NOTES

1. We will fully explain in the course of the book the deeper meaning of the term "PURE." We will use PURE throughout the book (in fact, we've already used it!) instead of the more commonly used terms "special needs," "disabled," and "disability." For example, rather than referring to someone as "a person with disabilities" or "a person with special needs," we might simply use "a PURE person." Another example would be to use "PURE ministry" instead of the more common "special needs ministry." As part of The PURE Ministry Project, we are attempting to change the terminology of disability in our

culture and especially in the church. We hope that through its use here on these pages, the reader will gradually, subtly, and perhaps even unwittingly, become accustomed to using PURE instead of the older, negative words. There is method to our apparent madness, but you'll have to read on to discover what it is.

2. A potential point of confusion as you read this book is "PURE ministry" as opposed to *"PURE Ministries."* "PURE ministry" (special needs ministry), which is our reaching out individually and corporately to people and families affected by disability, is in many ways the focus of the book and is used repeatedly and often throughout the book. *"PURE Ministries,"* however, is the actual ministry organization that encourages and promotes PURE ministry to Christians. It is used less frequently and is not in any way the focus of the book. To alleviate any chance of confusion and to make sure the reader easily differentiates the two terms, I will use "PURE ministry" (lower case "m" and singular "ministry') always when referring to ministry and *"PURE Ministries"* (in *italics* and plural *"Ministries"*) for the organization.

3. Finally, I have chosen to use the term "normal" when referring to people without special needs or disabilities. Use of this term in this way is somewhat controversial. Among some in the disability community, its use would imply the converse, "abnormal," as the logical label for PURE people. I certainly do not intend for anyone reading this book to walk away with that understanding, but I find *normal* much more explanatory and descriptive than the more politically correct "typical." With your permission and understanding as the reader, I will, therefore, use normal, without quotes and not in *italics*, from this point forward to describe "non-PURE" people.

An Introduction to PURE Ministry

For You formed my inward parts; You covered me in my mother's womb.[14] I will praise You, for I am fearfully and wonderfully made; Marvelous are Your works, And that my soul knows very well.

Psalm 139: 13-14

Explaining the Title: A Better Way — Where *Least* is *Most*

Has this ever happened to you? While perusing books in a bookstore, you come across a title that really intrigues you. You pick it up, start looking through it, and perhaps even buy it. But, even after reading the entire book, no matter how hard you try, you can't understand the title and how it relates to the book! It's happened to me, but it won't be happening here to you - at least not in this book.

It is imperative at the very beginning that I share with you the underlying premise of this book as it relates to PURE ministry in the church in America today. If we don't understand this basic principle, reading the remainder of this book would be a waste of your time.

I must tell you that from the very moment God inspired me to write this book, the main title has always been, *A Better Way*. However, the subtitle has changed from my original choice to what it is now. The subtitle modifications and other changes have come as a result of my being given some great advice by people much smarter than this author. I learned that people read books basically for two main reasons: 1) the author or 2) the subject or plot of the book. In other words, people will buy virtually any and every book if written by an author they have come to like or is popular or maybe even controversial. Others will choose their reading material more along the lines of subject matter or plot themes. When told this by my advisors, I knew immediately I was in trouble. I was "0 for 2," to use my baseball background terminology. People don't have any idea who I am and I know for a fact that most people are not interested in PURE ministry because that's one of the main reasons for my writing the book in the first place!

Furthermore, people advised me that the first page of any book must catch the eye and capture the typical book browser. This made sense to me, for it is exactly what I find myself doing at the bookstore or library. The cover of the book must summarize and encapsulate the book in such a way that it will compel the reader to look inside. Most importantly and depending on the type of the book, it should cause the reader to *want* to read that book.

My desire, as you read this book, is that you, too, will begin to see this better way where *least* is *most*. I originally hesitated to use the word, *least*. Often, when we speak of the *least of these,* it is said implying pity and sadness. That is not my intention. In fact, you will see how God is using the *least of these* to accomplish great things for Him. It is clear to me and I pray it will be to you as well after you read this book, that though perhaps *least* intellectually or physically, God has chosen these same people to be *most* critical in His Kingdom. In a very real way, the *least*, as normally viewed by society, are the *most* precious in God's eye. It is worth our time to learn why.

My original subtitle, *Divine Appointments for the Disappearing and the Invisible*, is the topic of a message I often preach in churches about PURE ministry. I still think it best describes what God is doing through PURE ministry. However, it must be explained and you simply can't do that on the cover of a book. It normally takes me thirty minutes to do this in a sermon and I never feel that I do it adequately.

One thing I do know is that God is using the *least* in *most* significant ways. He is using the *least*, that is, PURE people and their families, to transform us and, therefore, transform the church in America. This statement begs the question, *"How?"* *How* is God doing this? I know it is presumptuous of me to even try, but I will spend the rest of this book trying to explain my perspective of this delicate topic. If we open our eyes just a little, I believe we see God moving in a new and exciting way, though not new and exciting to God, it is new to us! He is moving in and through people and situations most of us would rather not even think about, but *He* is moving. He is moving for our good, if we are truly the called, and for His glory. I will attempt here to share my experiences and similar experiences of others drawn into the PURE world to help us see this. On the other hand, I am not so foolish as to try to explain *why* God is doing *what* He is doing. The very fact that He is God and loves us more than we can ever comprehend is sufficient for me. I'll just leave the why to Him; He need not explain it to me. As I once heard a person respond to the deep theological question, "Do you think we can change God's mind in prayer?" The answer was, "Why would you *want* to?"

The original title, *Divine Appointments for the Disappearing and the Invisible*, though at first may seem mysterious or provocative, was not chosen to be so. Rather, it was chosen because it not only accurately describes the Scriptural picture of real ministry that Jesus would desire of us, but also describes the context in which we are to minister in relation to PURE people in our midst. In fact it is through the mystery of this obscure statement that we begin to see how God is doing what He is doing. Hopefully, after the following brief explanation of the subtitle I did *not* use, you will begin to see the how God is moving in this way and at this time. More importantly, I pray you will agree with me on the truth, relevance, and application here of the statement, *A Better Way*.

Let's work our way *backward* through the unused subtitle – I think it will make things a bit clearer.

Who Are the *Invisible*?

We will get to the *disappearing* next, but let's first address the *invisible* group. Very simply, the *invisible* are people in our culture who have special needs or disabilities - people that we refer to as PURE people. The *invisible* are not only the actual persons with a disability, but in most cases and in most ways, also their immediate families that are somewhat invisible as well.

You may say, "I see people in wheelchairs and other people with disabilities when I'm out in public, sometimes - why would you say they are invisible?" Good question, but as we will see later, we do not see them in the same numbers as they are statistically represented in our culture. People with disabilities constitute over 15% of the United States population. Could any of us honestly say that 15% (over 50 million of the U.S. population of 300+ million people) of the people we see in public are PURE people?

The operative word in our physically observing people with disabilities in public places is *sometimes*. We sometimes see people in wheelchairs, we sometimes see a child with Down syndrome, and we sometimes see a person that just doesn't appear normal to us and we make an assumption: "That is a person with some kind of disability." Again, we don't see a lot of these people and certainly not as many as we know statistically are living in our neighborhoods. There are two good reasons for this, and more importantly, these reasons explain why people with disabilities in our culture are essentially invisible.

The first reason that people with disabilities are invisible to us is simply that, in many cases and situations, it is just too difficult for PURE people to go out in public very often. Yes, laws have been passed that make all public places physically handicapped accessible, but these laws and the access they provide do nothing to help the PURE person and their parents or caregivers do all the things necessary, that the rest of us take for granted, simply to leave home and go out. For example, if we take that person we see in the wheelchair and try to identify with all that they must do to go out in public, we will understand more why PURE families will often just say, "It's just too hard; we'll just stay home." In this example, if we understood what is required for that PURE person simply to go to the grocery store, we would probably stay home too. First, the PURE person may need help dressing. Second, he or she most likely will need help physically getting out of the home or building. Third, if the family is not fortunate enough to have a van which will accommodate a wheelchair, the PURE person must be lifted and placed into a seat in the car and the wheelchair must be loaded and stored in the car. Fourth, if a van is used, the PURE person in a wheelchair must be securely locked into the van. Fifth, upon arrival at the store, steps 3 and 4 must be repeated in reverse. Sixth, after maneuvering through cluttered aisles, heavy doors, and high shelves, shopping is complete and steps 2 through 4 must be repeated again to drive home. Seventh, upon finally arrival back home, steps 1 through 4 must be repeated once again in reverse!

The wheelchair example, though physically demanding for the parent/ caregiver and the PURE person as well, is but one common situation with which many of us can identify. At least temporarily, if we have ever had a broken foot or leg or other types of surgery, those of us who have found ourselves in wheelchairs have survived the experience, but we do gain a better appreciation for people who literally live their lives there.

Another common example of our only sometimes seeing that PURE person in public frequently is that many disabilities are not so readily apparent or noticeable -- for example, a child with autism. Though it may not be as physically taxing to take this child to the store, for the parent/caregiver of a PURE child with autism, every venture outside of the home is always a new experience and frequently not a pleasant one. Because a child with autism rarely responds to a given situation in an expected way, the shopping excursion for the mom and/or dad is often filled with great anxiety and apprehension. And, like in the wheelchair example, in resignation, and after several embarrassing situations in the checkout line perhaps, the PURE parent often simply decides that staying home is much easier and less stressful.

So, one reason that we see fewer PURE people in public is that it is very difficult for them to get out. Indeed this invisibility of PURE people and their families is no more evident than in the church. In countless interviews with PURE families I have been told so often that it is just not worth the effort to go to church. This simple fact should sadden all of us as Christians and should challenge all of us to make our churches more welcoming to PURE people and their families. A growing, vibrant, alive church should always be a place all of us want to go, even if it *is* difficult to get there!

The second reason that PURE people remain invisible to us is much more subtle and insidious to us as Christians. If you are reading this book and have had little or no experience in the world of disabilities other than observation at a distance, that is, you have had no real relationship with a PURE person, you most likely will be shocked by the second reason. Even if you have had some experience with PURE people, the second reason may be surprising as well.

Years ago, I felt God was leading me to begin the ministry called *Zachariah's Way* (which has now become *PURE Ministries*) and employ a new approach in spreading the message of disability to the church.

He provided an eye-opening and revealing experience that was not only a confirmation to my calling, but also the realization of who I had become after living with Zach for 4 ½ years. While shopping with my wife in a large, full-service Wal-Mart on vacation in Florida, I saw a group of developmentally disabled adults and their chaperones enter the store and begin shopping in the food section. The first realization that came to me as I saw these sweet people was that before my grandson, Zach, was born and I understood little about disability, I would literally not even have seen them! Oh, they were physically there all right, but I understood for the first time that I had taught or conditioned myself not to see them - for all intent and purpose, they were *invisible* to me! I remembered how I used to feel in my "pre-Zach" life (i.e. before God had opened my eyes to the blessings of PURE people through the gift of my PURE grandson) and what I had told myself to feel better. Thoughts like, "The situation makes me feel sad, I don't know what to say or do to these people, and besides what difference does it make?" But now in my "post-Zach" life (i.e. after God took Zach home to Heaven), I am literally drawn to PURE people, and, before I realized it, I was talking and laughing with the sweet people as they began their trek through the store that night.

It was at this point as I recall, that I felt God clearly leading me to watch what was about to happen in that Wal-Mart that evening. I began walking, at a distance, behind the small group of PURE people as they pleasantly went about their shopping. What I observed as I followed this group was the second reason PURE people are invisible in our society: because of the discomfort and awkwardness we feel, we have literally *taught ourselves not* to *see* them! As the group made their way through the store, I observed people starting down an aisle, catching a glimpse of the group, and then hurriedly turning around in quick, and often frantic, retreat to another aisle. In fact, I stayed with the group until they checked out of the store, and besides myself and the checkout clerk, who had to engage them slightly while helping them pay, I never saw another person interact with them. How unbelievably sad and how unbelievably revealing! In this Wal-Mart, I had just observed an excellent real-world illustration of this second reason for the invisibility of PURE people in real life. God impressed something else on my heart. I realized I had been an excellent example of this troubling phenomenon myself before God changed me with Zach. Yes, I was a Bible-believing follower of Jesus, thinking myself sensitive to hurting people around me, and yet, I was virtually blind to people with disabilities around me! How could this happen?

Before you judge or criticize me too harshly, let me state that I think my blindness to PURE people was, and is, not unique to me. Most likely, if we are honest with ourselves, we can all remember situations involving PURE people in which we have simply chosen not to see them. Proof of this statement is the overwhelming absence of PURE people in our churches. If we as Christians were seeing PURE people in our communities, we should be seeing more of them in our churches. If we were engaging and evangelizing them, we would be counting more of them as our brothers and sisters in Christ. Our inability, or rather our unwillingness, as Christians, to choose to see PURE people in our midst is by far the greatest barrier we face in PURE ministry becoming a reality in our churches. We must re-teach ourselves to see PURE people so that they are no longer invisible.

In most cases, there is little that we can do to remedy the first reason for PURE people's invisibility. Of course we can help some families be more mobile in certain situations, but we cannot make the difficulty in getting out for these families go away. On the other hand, we can do much if we can learn to really see them as we move about in our daily lives. The real intent of this book is to help the reader *extend* his/her comfort zone by interacting and befriending PURE people and their families. Our comfort zones, the ways we define them, and how we extend them is one of the major themes of this book and we will talk in detail about comfort zones throughout. Note that I say *extend our comfort zones* rather than the more common, *getting out of* our comfort zone. Getting out of our comfort zone naturally implies that we later also *get back into* our comfort zones - PURE ministry, like all true callings from Jesus Himself, requires much larger comfort zones! I believe that God desires that we actually enlarge our comfort zones to include PURE people and their families, not just occasionally leaving our comfort zone only to return to a more limited one. We must earnestly and seriously ask ourselves this question, "Can we continue to allow our discomfort or sense of awkwardness in relating to PURE people keep us from ministering to them and being blessed by them?" If we answer "yes" and stay comfortable, PURE people will remain invisible to us. If we answer "no" and allow God to permanently expand our comfort zones, He has something very special awaiting us.

Who are the *Disappearing*?

We are not told in Scripture of the early life relationship of Jesus and His cousin, John the Baptist, or even if there was a relationship at all. The first encounter we see between Jesus and John is recorded in the first chapter of the Gospel of John. John is baptizing in Bethabara when he sees Jesus coming:

> *The next day John saw Jesus coming toward him, and said, "Behold! The Lamb of God who takes away the sin of the world!*
> *John 1:29*

No, we do not know for sure whether Jesus and John had even ever met before this instance. What we do know is that John the Baptist immediately recognized who Jesus was - the Messiah! A few days later, John the Baptist is being questioned by some of his disciples and the Jews as to exactly who *He who was with you beyond the Jordan, to whom you have testified*, that is, Jesus, really was. John the Baptist quickly replies that he, himself, is not the Christ, but that *I am sent before him*. John the Baptist assures them that Jesus is the Messiah and Savior of the world.

However, John the Baptist continues and forever changes the perception of man in relation to a Holy God. John goes on to say to those who listened then and to us who listen now:

> *He must increase, but I must decrease.*
> *John 3:30*

In a single statement, John forever summarizes and crystallizes the perspective of any Christian. Here we have John the Baptist, of whom Jesus said, *"Among those born of women [that is, of all the people in the world], there is none greater than John,"* clarifying his relationship with Jesus: *"He must increase, but I must decrease."*

The Greek word for increase is *auxanō* and means to cause to grow, become greater, or to grow. The tense of the verb is significant in that it is in the present, active infinitive. The present tense represents a simple statement of fact or reality viewed as occurring in actual time. The active voice represents the subject as the doer or performer of the action. The Greek infinitive mood in most cases corresponds to the English infinitive, which is basically the verb with "to" prefixed, as "to increase." What John is actually saying is that Jesus is to become preeminent in our lives.

Conversely, the Greek word for decrease is *elattoō* which means to make less or inferior or to decrease in authority or popularity. The tense of the verb, decrease, is perhaps even more important to us here and we find it in the present, passive infinitive. Again, while the present tense represents a simple statement of fact or reality viewed as occurring in actual time and the infinitive mood corresponds to the English infinitive, the passive voice represents the subject as being the recipient of the action e.g., in the sentence, "The boy was hit by the ball," the boy receives the action. As opposed to becoming something more, John is telling us that in relation to Jesus, he is being made to be less or inferior – i.e. he is willingly reckoning himself to *be* less. When we consider this statement with other passages, the concept of our *disappearing* becomes plainly evident. Paul states in *Galatians 2:20*:

> *I am crucified with Christ: nevertheless I live; yet not I, but Christ liveth in me: and the life which I now live in the flesh I live by the faith of the Son of God, who loved me, and gave himself for me.*
> *Galatians 2:20 (KJV)*

Again, Paul confirms in *Romans*:

> *Or do you not know that as many of us as were baptized into*
> *Christ Jesus were baptized into His death? ⁴ Therefore we were*
> *buried with Him through baptism into death, that just as Christ*
> *was raised from the dead by the glory of the Father, even so we*
> *also should walk in newness of life.*
>
> *Romans 6:3-4*

John the Baptist is obviously not saying that he is physically disappearing or that he is less of a person as he decreases or disappears. Rather, he is now and will forever be living in and through Jesus - he has been crucified with Him and his life is now found only in Him - as are we who call ourselves Christians. What this means in a very real sense is that *we are to be disappearing* and that when people look into our eyes and feel our touch and are warmed by our love, they in actuality are seeing, feeling, and being loved by Jesus Himself! When we fade, Jesus flourishes through us. The more we surrender to Jesus, the more He becomes predominant in our attitudes, words, and actions - people should see more of Jesus than they do of us.

In the 15th chapter of John, Jesus explains who we are in Him as well as who we are if we are *not* in Him:

> *I am the vine, you are the branches. He who abides in Me, and*
> *I in him, bears much fruit; for without Me you can do nothing.*
>
> *John 15:5*

Jesus stated earlier in this same chapter that God is the gardener and here declares that Jesus is the vine and we, though we are to be disappearing in one sense, are the branches that are to bring forth fruit. In the matchless humility found only in Jesus, He chooses to remain in the dirt and lift us up to bear fruit. However, and we can never forget this, it is only through the vine, Jesus Himself, that we are able to do anything - for without Him, *"we can do nothing."*

Practically, what does it really mean to disappear? It's much too easy here to pridefully say to myself, "Why, I'm already doing this; I'm disappearing!" While at the same time, I remain content with living half-heartedly and lackadaisically for God. *Surrendered* somewhat, but not yet *totally*. Committed, in a *limited* way, but with some *reasonable* reservations. I disappear as I understand it, occasionally, but much more frequently am very visible and quick to receive the credit or shift the blame. Is this just me, or does it describe you as well? Does it describe most of your Christian friends? Most likely it does, as I believe it fairly accurately describes most churches in America today. How else can we explain the scarcity of real impact of our churches today by other than our willingness to remain "somewhere in the middle?"

Mark Hall, Student Pastor at Eagles Landing First Baptist Church in McDonough, Georgia, south of Atlanta, but perhaps better known as the songwriter and leader for the wonderful Christian music group, *Casting Crowns*, describes my condition more honestly than I ever could. Mark is a masterful artist and in one of his very best songs, he describes me as living "*Somewhere in the Middle*":

Somewhere in the Middle

Somewhere Between The Hot And The Cold
Somewhere Between The New And The Old
Somewhere Between Who I Am And Who I Used To Be
Somewhere In The Middle, You'll Find Me
Somewhere Between The Wrong And The Right
Somewhere Between The Darkness And The Light
Somewhere Between Who I Was And Who You're Making Me
Somewhere In The Middle, You'll Find Me
Just How Close Can I Get, Lord,
To My Surrender Without Losing All Control?

Fearless Warriors In A Picket Fence,
Reckless Abandon Wrapped In Common Sense
Deep Water Faith In The Shallow End And We Are Caught In The Middle

With Eyes Wide Open To The Differences,
The God We Want And The God Who Is
But Will We Trade Our Dreams For His Or Are We Caught In The Middle?
Are We Caught In The Middle?

Somewhere Between My Heart And My Hands
Somewhere Between My Faith And My Plans
Somewhere Between The Safety Of The Boat And The Crashing Waves
Somewhere Between A Whisper And A Roar
Somewhere Between The Altar And The Door
Somewhere Between Contented Peace And Always Wanting More
Somewhere In The Middle You'll Find Me
Just How Close Can I Get, Lord, To My Surrender
Without Losing All Control?

Lord, I Feel You In This Place And I Know You're By My Side
Loving Me Even On These Nights When I'm Caught In The Middle.[1]

The words of this song nail me. I don't want to be in the *middle*, I don't like to be in *middle*, but that's probably where you'll find me. What bothers me most, however, is that too often I am content to be *somewhere in the middle*. I frequently find myself possessing what I believe to be *deep water faith*, but am perfectly satisfied to stay in the *shallow end*. Armed with biblical knowledge, material blessings, and wonderful opportunities I am truly a *fearless warrior*, but scared to venture beyond my *picket fence* made of sticks of desire for comfort, security, and pleasure. Sometimes, sensing God moving within me and compelling me to live with *reckless abandon*, I stop and reconsider. *Wrapped in common sense*, I retreat to my cozy place in the *middle*.

Choosing to disappear is far more complex that we can ever realize, yet as simple as listening as Jesus speaks to us and doing both the little things and the big things that He tells us to do. It is telling someone about Jesus when we would rather not. It is stopping and really listening to our child or grandchild. It is working in the nursery when we would rather be in worship. It is going on that mission trip to Africa even though we're scared to death. It is starting that neighborhood Bible study we've talked about for years. It is forgiving the one who hurt you so. It is lovingly confronting that friend who is going down a dark road. It is befriending that certain someone at church, school, or work that everybody else avoids. It is getting out of the way and doing whatever He tells us to do. It is doing these things when He tells us without delay. It is having no concern about ourselves, our reputation, or how others perceive us. It is being what God requires of us and doing whatever He asks – with no reservations. It is living life the way God intended it to be lived: in Him.

This type of *disappearing* means simply loving God so much that we actually do what He says do: allow the Holy Spirit to literally take over our lives! I admit it is easier said than done, but you can be assured that when we put others before ourselves in the name of Jesus, we will slowly be fading from view and Jesus will be more visible to those around us.

At the heart of PURE ministry for each of us is a personal decision. What we must ask ourselves is whether we are willing to surrender – not partially, but totally - and *disappear* and allow Jesus to work through us. The question is crucial and supremely important. How we respond defines and determines not only our effectiveness in ministering to PURE people, but also more importantly, our usefulness to our Lord at all.

Divine Appointments?

Matthew 25 is one of the most dramatic chapters in the entire Bible, and it is in it that we get a view of a *divine appointment*. In fact, we see not one but two *divine appointments*. Though there have been volumes written about this chapter, its depth, and its applications by great men and women of God, we will concentrate here on the judgment in verses 31-46. Matthew 25 is one of those rare chapters in Scripture where Jesus and Jesus alone does all the speaking and therefore we need not worry that His message has been tempered in any way. The overriding theme of the entire chapter is simply this: be ready and get ready - Jesus is coming back in all of His glory for judgment. The chapter begins with two parables that emphasize the theme. The first one (verses 1-13) is commonly referred to as the "parable of the ten virgins" while the second one (verses 14-30) is known as the "parable of the talents." Most of us are familiar with these two parables. The first emphasizes the need to be ready for our bridegroom Jesus, like the wise virgins in verse 4 who *took oil in their vessels with their lamps,* as opposed to the foolish virgins. The second parable underscores the fact that we will be accountable for the gifts (talents) God has given us.

Beginning in verse 31 and continuing to the end of the chapter, we have what is commonly known as the "Judgment of the Nations." To be very honest, different theologians believe the scene depicts significantly different things. Most all believe the judgment here occurs during Jesus' second coming to earth:

> *When the Son of man shall come in his glory, and all the holy angels with him, then shall he sit upon the throne of his glory.*
> *Matthew 25:31*

Some believe the *nations* represent only gentile nations. Still others believe that the judgment is reserved solely for those who have not received and treated the messengers of Jesus well. I cannot speak with authority about any of these or other varying opinions surrounding the time or other more obscure implications, but I do think this: too much conjecture about the details of future prophetic events can cause us to miss the reason Jesus is relating this to us in the first place! If we simply look at what Jesus is saying and doing here, I believe the truth of the passage speaks for itself.

What we do know is that in the 25th chapter of Matthew, verses 31-46, Jesus describes a day to come in the future that is at the same time comforting to Christians and terrifying for nonbelievers: Judgment Day.

> *When the Son of Man comes in His glory, and all the holy angels with Him, then He will sit on the throne of His glory. All the*

nations will be gathered before Him, and He will separate them one from another, as a shepherd divides his sheep from the goats. And He will set the sheep on His right hand, but the goats on the left. Then the King will say to those on His right hand, 'Come, you blessed of My Father, inherit the kingdom prepared for you from the foundation of the world: for I was hungry and you gave Me food; I was thirsty and you gave Me drink; I was a stranger and you took Me in; I was naked and you clothed Me; I was sick and you visited Me; I was in prison and you came to Me. Then the righteous will answer Him, saying, 'Lord, when did we see You hungry and feed You, or thirsty and give You drink? When did we see You a stranger and take You in, or naked and clothe You? Or when did we see You sick, or in prison, and come to You?' And the King will answer and say to them, 'Assuredly, I say to you, inasmuch as you did it to one of the least of these My brethren, you did it to Me.' Then He will also say to those on the left hand, 'Depart from Me, you cursed, into the everlasting fire prepared for the devil and his angels: for I was hungry and you gave Me no food; I was thirsty and you gave Me no drink; I was a stranger and you did not take Me in, naked and you did not clothe Me, sick and in prison and you did not visit Me.' Then they also will answer Him, saying, 'Lord, when did we see You hungry or thirsty or a stranger or naked or sick or in prison, and did not minister to You?' Then He will answer them, saying, 'Assuredly, I say to you, inasmuch as you did not do it to one of the least of these, you did not do it to Me.' And these will go away into everlasting punishment, but the righteous into eternal life.

Matthew 25:31-46

The identity of the characters in the scene is obvious: Jesus is the Son of Man; the sheep are believers, and the goats are nonbelievers. Not knowing exactly why, the sheep are immediately ushered into the Kingdom. To answer the unasked question of why, Jesus tells them about all the things they had done *to* Him. Taken aback, the sheep ask when they had seen Jesus in these situations, believing they certainly had not ministered to Him at these various times. Jesus' response, *"Inasmuch as ye have done it unto one of the least of these my brethren, ye have done it unto me"* is frequently quoted, but seldom understood. Likewise, the goats, or nonbelievers, are dispatched directly into everlasting fire; apparently for not doing the very things that Jesus has credited the sheep with doing. Also like the sheep, the bewildered goats try to explain that they had never seen Jesus in such need as He described. The response in verse 45 is both a corollary and contrast to His response in verse 40, *"Inasmuch as ye did it not to one of the least of these, ye did it not to me."* One would logically ask, "Did the sheep go to Heaven for the acts of service they performed and did the goats go to Hell for *not* performing those same acts as well?" Just how does this harmonize with all we understand about grace and faith?

This passage is commonly taken out of context and interpreted by people with little Biblical knowledge, even some Christians, that our works determine eternity for us: if good enough, we go to Heaven; if we're not good *enough*, we go to Hell. Perhaps this is why so many people, when asked whether they are going to Heaven, respond: "I hope so; I try to love everybody and do good things." Undoubtedly, this passage leads many people today, as it has in the past, to the wrong conclusion: that works can save us. They cannot and that is not what is taught here.

First, note that the sheep and goats were not proclaimed or pronounced to be sheep and goats as they entered the judgment - they were *already* sheep and goats even as they entered. This is an extremely important point. Jesus did not say, "Come into the Kingdom, because you've done ..." This common reasoning and belief that our works play some role in our salvation is completely contrary to the teaching of the entire Bible, best summarized by Paul in *Ephesians 2:8 - For by grace are ye saved through faith; and that not of yourselves: it is the gift of God.* No, Jesus welcomed them into the Kingdom because they were sheep (or Christians) before they came into the judgment! The sheep were simply doing what sheep do. Correspondingly, the goats (non-believers) were sent into *Everlasting Fire* not for their works, or lack thereof, but because they were already unredeemed goats when they came in. Like the sheep, the goats were simply doing what goats do. After understanding this passage in this way, we can only critically examine ourselves: are we in fact sheep and doing what sheep do, or merely acting like sheep? We must be sure we are the real thing.

Second, when we consider this passage with respect to the counsel of the entirety of Scripture, we can easily find further proof of the fact that our works will leave us wanting, if we are counting on them for salvation. This proof can be found in many other places in the Bible. The secular conclusion of the *Matthew 25:31-46* particularly stands in stark contrast to Jesus' words:

> *Not everyone who says to Me, 'Lord, Lord,' shall enter the kingdom of Heaven, but he who does the will of My Father in Heaven. Many will say to Me in that day, 'Lord, Lord, have we not prophesied in Your name, cast out demons in Your name, and done many wonders in Your name?' And then I will declare to them, 'I never knew you; depart from Me, you who practice lawlessness!"*
>
> *Matthew 7:21-23*

Jesus is clearly teaching here that our works, no matter how wonderful and noble they may seem to us, can never save us. Consistent with the passage in Matthew 25, Jesus' words here are plain and uncomplicated: to spend eternity in Heaven with Him, Jesus must *know* us, and we must *know* Him; we must have a personal relationship and nothing else matters.

So, we now see a *divine appointment* that we will all have one day: we are either sheep or goats and there will be no arguments or changing of Jesus' mind on that day. But, look closer because there is another real divine appointment mentioned here that we too frequently miss. The divine appointment to which I refer is stated clearly in verse 31 and then it is implied in verse 45, and that it is what has been missed. Let me explain. In this passage sometimes we are so concerned with what we must *do* or *be* to go to Heaven that we miss our divine appointment *here* and *now*. Look again at what Jesus lovingly says to His sheep, *Matthew*

25:45 - "Inasmuch as ye have done it unto one of the least of these my brethren, ye have done it unto me." Did you get it? Read it again. How about now? The divine appointment about which Jesus is speaking is simply this: when we reach out to others who are in real need (hungry, thirsty, lonely, naked, sick, and imprisoned), we minister not only to them, but to Jesus *Himself!*

"Who are the *least of these my brethren,*" we ask? Again there is theological debate here: some believe Jesus is talking about only Christians in need while others believe Jesus is referring to His fellow man in an earthly sense. I strongly agree with the latter, for nowhere in Scripture are we instructed to make certain that someone in need is a Christian before we minister to that person and, more importantly, how do we really know for sure? Further, when Jesus refers to the *least of these*, He is obviously doing so for our understanding – not from His perspective. From our limited perspective, the *least*, as He describes, are *less* in some way to us because they are in physical need. Jesus does not say when we do these things that we do them *like* or *as if* we're doing them to Him or that we do them symbolically to Him. No. He says we actually do them *unto* Him! Somehow in the interaction between us and them, Jesus is there - a *divine appointment*! In fact, many other translations simply say *"did it to me."* I don't understand this, but when we Christians reach out to others, Jesus is present and real: we meet Him in a *divine appointment*. If we are being Jesus' sheep and doing what Jesus' sheep do, we will encounter Jesus in these personal transactions. We do these things *not* to go to Heaven, but because that's what we do if we are truly Jesus' sheep. How many times have you heard Christians (or yourself, for I know I have) exclaim, "if only I could see or touch Jesus …?" Meeting and being with Jesus can be experienced now on this earth when we look into the eyes of the hungry, imprisoned, or homeless, and when they look into ours.

Though not specifically mentioned in this passage, the principle is certainly true and we are not stretching Scripture to include PURE people and their families as those in need. But, in a very real sense the PURE are no more *least* than any of us to Jesus. As most PURE parents and many, many others involved in the lives of PURE people can attest:

Jesus is indeed present when we minster to and are ministered to by PURE people! Jesus can be experienced in a deeply spiritual way in a place and in a time where we thought perhaps we were least likely to find Him. This is the point! What this means in the context of living our daily lives is simply this: If we can get outside of ourselves and reach out and befriend those PURE people around us, we will divinely encounter Jesus. *Divine appointments* have our name on them! Jesus is waiting to meet us there. The real question is will we seek out the uninvited (and most often unwanted), touch them in love, and meet Jesus in the process?

A Better Way?

These three little words are not only the main focus of this book, but also could be considered the most controversial aspects of it as well. For the casual observer glancing over the book cover, relating anything better with disability is too much of a stretch. Even for the struggling PURE parent, buried under the stress and frustration of caring for their PURE child, the very idea of *better*, when related to their daily world, might seem foreign. However, if we all, especially Christians, can stop for just a minute and look more closely at this reality we have in this world called disabilities, I believe God has something to say that is of life changing importance to all who will listen.

What is this *better way*? The remainder of this book will attempt to Biblically confirm, describe, and illustrate this simple fact:

God teaches us a better way to live as we learn through our relationships with PURE people. Through these relationships we are forever changed and, thereby, the church is transformed.

Simply through relationships with PURE people and in our response to what we have seen and experienced, God uses PURE people to change us. Through these relationships and also by simply being more spiritually aware, we begin reprioritizing our lives on what is really important to God. Since we *are* the church, the church is transformed. God can choose to do this transformation in many ways, and most probably is doing so even now. I'm just not aware of any *better way*. Zach taught me a better way and other PURE people have taught those whom they touched a *better way* as well.

So then, *Where* is *Least* the *Most*?

Read on. What we'll discover together is contrary to so much of what is being done, talked about, and proclaimed today as how we can be transformed and, in turn, transform the church in America. Just like He said in His Word, He is not using the powerful, wise, wealthy, and mighty in this transformation. He is using the powerless and weak – the *least*. He desires true transformation for His church; not superficial and shallow, but profound and literally life changing. Yes, He cares about the entire world, but He knows His church and His people must be changed first to be the change-agents required in such a sin-sick world.

> *If My people who are called by My name will humble themselves, and pray and seek My face, and turn from their wicked ways, then I will hear from Heaven, and will forgive their sin and heal their land.*
>
> *II Chronicles 7:14*

His transformation of His church will not be temporary or fleeting, but enduring and everlasting, for it will be built on Him. It will be done as He always does things, one heart at a time. This transformation will not be evaluated or judged by the conventional measures of success: size, wealth, and numbers. But rather it will be based on changed hearts and lives and authentic Christians impacting this world for Christ. He doesn't want larger buildings or more locations or branches of powerless church-like clubs. He doesn't want our trinkets we call sacrifice or an hour of church attendance on Sunday morning when we don't have anything better to do. He wants us - our hearts, our souls, our bodies, our minds, our strength, our all. This is what I believe God is doing through the most unlikely people and situations on this earth. Read on.

As I write this, Zach has been with Jesus more than ten years; much longer than the 4 ½ years he spent with us. Yet, he continues to impact the world in ways that we normal people never could and never will. Zach is not unique. The same thing can be said about many other PURE people. PURE people make a difference - a big difference in our world. Their impact endures long after they are gone, yet so many of us remain unaware of such special people on this earth.

A revealing question to ask yourself (I've asked myself this many times already) as you read now about this better way is, "Will people be saying this about me after I am gone?" Sure, people may think about us and probably miss us. But will people remember you and me and the life-changing impact we have had on their lives? Not sure? Read on. By becoming the *least*, we become *most* in God's eyes and that's really all that matters. PURE people can indeed show us a *better way*.

What Is PURE Ministry?

And the King will answer and say to them, 'Assuredly, I say to you, inasmuch as you did it to one of the least of these My brethren, you did it to Me.'

Matthew 25:40

A People in Need of Perspective

Today in America, we are truly a people in need of perspective. Once, we spoke God's name in reverence, worship, and awe. Now, His name is most often used to accentuate profanity and many times even in culturally accepted blasphemy. Once, God was creator of the universe, the merciful, gracious source of all that is good. Now, He is powerless, mocked, and can't even control the climate - we do! Once we were a people called by His name and who called on His name. Now, God is politically correct, His name is plural not specific, lest we offend someone. We can mention God's name in public for it means nothing. But, mention His Son's name, Jesus, and you're bigoted, narrow-minded, and mean-spirited.

On January 23, 1996, the Kansas State House had asked Joe Wright, pastor of Central Christian Church in Wichita, to be the guest chaplain and offer the opening prayer. His prayer, actually originally written by Bob Russell, pastor of Southeast Christian Church in Louisville, Kentucky, caused quite a controversy. One member of the House walked out and others criticized it. While Pastor Wright and his church reportedly received a huge, mostly positive response, there exists only conjecture as to the effect of the prayer on the legislature members. This prayer has been used since with similar responses.

> *Heavenly Father, we come before you today to ask Your forgiveness and to seek Your direction and guidance. We know Your Word says, "Woe to those who call evil good," but that's exactly what we have done. We have lost our spiritual equilibrium and inverted our values. We confess that:*
> *We have ridiculed the absolute truth of Your Word and called it pluralism.*
> *We have worshipped other gods and called it multi-culturalism.*
> *We have endorsed perversion and called it an alternative lifestyle.*

We have exploited the poor and called it the lottery.
We have neglected the needy and called it self-preservation.
We have rewarded laziness and called it welfare.
We have killed our unborn and called it a choice.
We have shot abortionists and called it justifiable.
We have neglected to discipline our children and called it building self-esteem.
We have abused power and called it political savvy.
We have coveted our neighbor's possessions and called it ambition.
We have polluted the airwaves with profanity and called it freedom of expression.
We have ridiculed the time-honored values of our forefathers and called it enlightenment.
Search us, O God, and know our hearts today; try us and see if there be some wicked way in us; cleanse us from every sin and set us free. Guide and bless these men and women who have been sent here by the people of Kansas, and who have been ordained by You, to govern this great state. Grant them Your wisdom to rule and may their decisions direct us to the center of Your will ... Amen.[1]

Such a powerful prayer. One would think all Christians in America, on reading this prayer, would immediately repent and ask God's forgiveness. Repentance? Our response: "Is that something we do to 'pay' for our sins or what?" Have you witnessed something that I haven't in America since that day in 1996: a national revival? I didn't think so. What does the slow, steady erosion of America and its values have to do with perspective, you might ask? My answer: everything. Further, what does perspective have to do with the disappearing, us, and the invisible, PURE people? My answer again: everything. Let's see why.

Have you ever stopped to think what allows or causes or makes (you choose the verb) certain people experience or view or accept similar circumstances quite differently? Some people can go through a serious time of trouble, testing, or human tragedy and seemingly be little affected by it all - in fact, they may even remain upbeat and joyful, while others go through a similar situation only to be destroyed. What is the difference? Simply being an optimist? Sheer toughness? Strong character? An ability to roll with the punches? Perhaps, but I think there is something much, much deeper.

It would be hard, if not impossible, for us to think of or even imagine a worse situation than to be imprisoned in a Nazi concentration camp during World War II. We have seen pictures and movies, but we really can't comprehend how horrible it must have been. With that thought in mind, consider this. In her inspirational book, *The Hiding Place*, Corrie Ten Boom takes us along on an unbelievable journey of faith, suffering, and ultimate victory. We are with her from growing up happy and secure in Amsterdam; to harboring Jews in her home in a special "hiding place" from the Gestapo and its Dutch counterpart; to being imprisoned along with her remarkable sister, Betsie, in the notorious Ravensbruck concentration camp in Germany; and finally to being freed when she was released at the end of 1944. Below, she recounts a very anxious encounter she had with one of her guards from Ravensbruck some years after the war:

> *"It was at a church in Munich that I saw him, the former S.S. man who had stood guard at the shower room door in the processing center at Ravensbruck. He was the first of our actual jailers that I had seen since that time. And suddenly it was all there-the roomful of mocking men, the heaps of clothing, Betsie's pain blanched face. He came up to me as the church was emptying, beaming and bowing. "How grateful I am for your message, Fraulein," he said. "To think that, as you say, 'He has washed my sins away!'" His hand was thrust out to shake mine. And I, who had preached so often to the people in Bloemendaal on the need to forgive, kept my hand at my side. Even as the angry, vengeful thoughts boiled through me, I saw the sin of them. Jesus Christ had died for this man; was I going to ask for more? Lord Jesus, I prayed, forgive me and help me to forgive him. I tried to smile; I struggled to raise my hand. I could not. I felt nothing, not the slightest spark of warmth or charity. And so again, I breathed a silent prayer.*

Jesus, I cannot forgive him. Give him Your forgiveness. As I took his hand, the most incredible thing happened. From my shoulder along my arm and through my hand a current seemed to pass from me to him, while into my heart sprang a love for this stranger that almost overwhelmed me. And so I discovered that it is not on our forgiveness, any more than on our goodness that the world's healing hinges, but on His. When He tells us to love our enemies, He gives, along with the command, the love itself." [2]

If you haven't read *The Hiding Place*, I recommend you read it. In the book, Corrie graphically describes the conditions in which she, her sister, Betsie, and the other women lived. Most of the women did not survive Ravensbruck and died horrible deaths at the hands of their cruel captors. Between 1939 and 1945, over 130,000 female prisoners passed through the Ravensbruck camp system with only 40,000 surviving. I can only begin to think how I would have responded if it had been me in the same situation. How about you? I know I wouldn't have the strength, courage, or love for those who were treating me so terribly. I just pray I wouldn't have crawled into a corner with the bugs and rats and literally cried myself to death. I, of course, cannot be totally confident in this, but I think Corrie Ten Boom would have been the same person whether she lived her life as she did being imprisoned in Ravensbruck or if she had lived in a mansion on the French Riviera. What I am trying to say is that Corrie's perspective was such that life's situations and circumstances, good or bad, only served to give her a platform on which she would not only share the love of Jesus Christ, but allow it to flow through her to those God brought near. Where did this perspective that allowed her to live such an inspirational life come from? Did she just have the inner strength to always have a great courage or a good attitude? I don't think so. In fact, based on Corrie's own words, I think her amazing life had very little to do with Corrie herself and is much more a result of the God she loved and the relationship they shared.

How did Corrie, who survived, and her equally sweet sister Betsie, who died, do it? If you read much about Corrie, you will quickly learn that she and her other siblings were taught early and often about the love of God. Their entire family was heavily involved at their church in the Netherlands. Not surprisingly, Corrie and Betsie worked with special needs children. They both would spend many afternoons helping and educating those who had mental and physical disabilities. They even had a special church service for them. As a young woman, Corrie was driven and drawn to hurting people. Even then, and as was evidenced in her entire life, Corrie's perspective or world view was not on the external, but rather the internal; not on the temporary, but the eternal; and, certainly not on herself or her desire for material or earthly things, but first and foremost, her worldview was focused firmly on her Heavenly Father. Just so we are on the same page, let's use a working definition of what *worldview* means. For the sake of discussion, worldview will simply mean:

> The way we think about the world and the belief system
> on which we think, interpret, and respond in it.

Another way to look at our worldview could be stated as the "sum total of all of our various perspectives we have about living." Both of these definitions are valid, but really nailing down what our worldview is or means is somewhat difficult and confusing. We normally tend to make most concepts harder than they need to be. However, rather than the typical, over simplistic optimistic or pessimistic choice, our worldview is indeed a bit more complicated. If we could imagine listing all of the perspectives or perceptions we have on and of everything, everyone, every system, every process, every concept, every ... Fill in the blank as you wish. We would then finally have our worldview on paper. Of course, this is literally impossible to do, and even if we could, it would never be complete. We would then have to list our perspective on making the list, and then our perspective on our perspective of our perspective on making the list and on and on.

Rather than looking at the minutiae of the infinitely many perceptions we have about our world, everything in it, and how it all works and affects us, a better question for us as Christians is what are the principles that should be the basis of our worldview? The nonbeliever is left to his own devices to make sense of the creation and the meaning of life, but the believer does have principles and values on which the lives we live do make sense. The nonbelievers are forever adjusting, adapting, and overhauling their perceptions, driven by their culture's prevailing attitudes. Therefore, they are never quite sure, confident, or at peace in a world created and controlled by the very God whom they refuse to admit exists, submit to, or let alone believe that He loves them. The believer, on the other hand, is wondrously blessed with not only principles and the knowledge, values, and wisdom incorporated in those principles, but also, more importantly, a personal relationship with the God of the universe, through His Son Jesus Christ, in the indwelling of the Holy Spirit! What a gift! You may have thought about all this when Jesus reached down, quickened, and saved you, but I know I certainly didn't realize then that this was included in salvation.

If this is true about what we as Christians possess in Christ, and it is, then a logical question is why do so many Christians act like non-Christians in living lives as James describes in Chapter 1, verse 6b, *like a wave of the sea, blown and tossed by the wind?* Further, shouldn't the Christian worldview provide for us the understanding and perspectives necessary for us to live as Christ intended as *more than conquerors? (Romans 8:37)* I certainly cannot explain why Christians live like non-Christians, but I do know that we don't have to! Because, yes, the Christian worldview does give us everything we need to live victoriously, confidently, and fearlessly in this world and, ultimately, with the Father in our Heavenly home.

The Power and Peril of Presumptions

How we form our perspectives is inherently based on some broad presumptions, that which we *know* to be true, about God, the world, others, and ourselves. For the purpose of clarity, I will use *presumption* rather than *assumption*. An *assumption* we make is not normally based on any substantial evidence. It is simply a hypothesis or premise yet to be proven. A *presumption,* however, implies that there is some basis of truth or evidence for the belief.

From these presumptions flow our thinking process, and ultimately our perspectives. If we start with incorrect or invalid presumptions, our thinking is flawed, and our perspectives are unreliable and inconsistent. For example, though we don't understand why or exactly how (rudimentary astronomy doesn't really *explain* it as much as *describe* it), we believe the sun *will* come up tomorrow. If we didn't believe this, the world would immediately be thrust into mass chaos – what are we going to do without the sun? The basic presumption is that because the sun has always risen, it will rise tomorrow.

The sun example is perhaps too simplistic, but just as we believe the earth is stable beneath us (with special acknowledgement to my California friends), rain will fall, and stars will continue to shine in the Heavens, these beliefs give us a security and peace about the world in which we live. But, what about more personal presumptions? We believe our spouses will be faithful, thus we trust them. We believe a chair will hold our weight, so we sit without testing it. We believe our parents love us; thus we are secure.

Many of the presumptions we make are verified by our experience and reinforced daily as we live. Others are simply accepted as true. A wonderfully funny man and talk show host in Georgia, Ludlow Porch, who died recently, illustrated frequently the fragile and delicate balance on which our presumptions rest. Ludlow hosted a three hour radio program, always interacting with his callers. Ludlow was a very kind man and was always cordial and nice to all of his callers. Often he would present a funny, plausible, but outrageous premise and then wait for the spirited response from his listeners. It always intrigued me that though his faithful listeners would know he would do these kinds of things, many seemed to fall for it every time. Ludlow would begin a show with a simple statement such as, "I have a confession today: I am bipedal." He would go on to say, "I probably caught it from my mother and father because they were bipedal too." Just in case I caught you off guard with the word *bipedal,* it simply means "having two feet," but don't feel bad, because many of Ludlow's listeners did not know what bipedal meant either! The conversation was hilarious. Presuming on what they thought bipedal meant (generally something horrible or shameful), many callers didn't catch on, but were too proud to admit it. Though most listeners knew what was going on, they would play along and agitate the discussion even more. But perhaps Ludlow's most memorable show began with, "Montana doesn't exist - there is no such state." Well, a war of words began. As people would call, Ludlow would good-naturedly challenge them. Another caller countered, "But it is on my map and I studied it in high school!"

Then Ludlow would respond, "But, have you ever *been* there or known people from there?" Another would say, "We have 50 states and Montana is one of them!"

Ludlow, "No, that area is really part of Canada; the mapmakers made a mistake." The back-and-forth went on and on with some people even getting angry with Ludlow's confidence in his "fact."

We need not be too quick in ridiculing Ludlow's fans for we probably do the same thing every day with presumptions we make about things based on something we *know* to be true, but really are not. For example, one need only look at the history of medical advances over time to see this perfectly illustrated: the sure cure for virtually any ailment in medieval times was simply bleeding the patient. Thankfully, we've learned this presumption was wrong. The importance of having the right presumptions on which to base our thinking processes and to form our perspectives cannot be overemphasized.

The Renewal of Our Minds

What then do we do with our presumptions? We base our thinking on them whether we realize it or not. The Bible tells us we are what we think, *For as he thinks in his heart, so is he. (Proverbs 23:7)* Think about this: the words *know, mind,* and *think* are used 1485 times in the Bible. *Know* is used 496 times in the Gospels and 31 in the book of I John alone. Though the word *heart* also may mean emotions, in Scripture it can imply the mind as well. The International Bible Encyclopedia says this about the word *heart* in Scripture:

> *Though it is considered to be the seat of the emotions and passions and appetites, it also embraced likewise the intellectual and moral faculties. As the central organ in the body, forming a focus for its vital action, it has come to stand for the center of its moral, spiritual, intellectual life. In particular the heart is the place in which the process of self-consciousness is carried out, in which the soul is at home with itself, and is conscious of all its doing and suffering as its own (Hence, it is that men of "courage" are called "men of the heart;" that the Lord is said to speak "in his heart;" that men "know in their own heart;" that "no one considereth in his heart." In the King James Version, "Heart" in this connection is sometimes rendered "mind."* [3]

In this context, the word *heart* (implying our thinking or center of our being) is used over 833 times!

By contrast, the words *feel* or *feeling* occur only nine times. Simply by the number of uses of the words alone, it is obvious that we are to be much more *thinking* oriented than *feeling* oriented. In *Isaiah 1:18* God did not say, *"Come now, and let us "feel" or "experience" together."* No, He said, *"Come now, and let us reason together, says the LORD: though your sins are like scarlet, they shall be as white as snow; though they are red like crimson, they shall be as wool."* God made us to use our minds - to reason - to think.

In Romans, the Apostle Paul states:

> *And do not be conformed to this world, but be transformed by the renewing of your mind, that you may prove what is that good and acceptable and perfect will of God.*
>
> *Romans 12:2*

Paul is instructing us here to say we are not to be *of* and *conformed to* this world around us, but we are to be *transformed by the renewing of our minds* - we must *think* differently. Though we obviously cannot do this with perfection, the *renewing of your mind* here means that we are to be transformed into thinking like our Heavenly Father. Paul continues to tell us how we are to do this. He tells us not to be conformed to this world or, in other words, not to let the world determine how we should live, or shape us to and by its values. The tense of the verb conformed implies that it is *we* that are being conformed. We are active participants by our choices, but it is that world that we must not allow to *change* us.

Contrary to being *conformed* by outside influences, he tells us to be *transformed by the renewing of our minds*, or in other words, *thinking differently*. We are conformed by outside pressures, but we are transformed from within, *by the renewing of your mind!* Our thinking, this renewing of our minds, transforms us so we *can prove what is that good and acceptable and perfect will of God*. Our actions will follow only when our thinking changes. If we have made the wrong presumptions and our thinking is wrong, wrong actions will naturally follow.

It is safe to say that, based on this passage, godly thinking will always lead to thanking God, and thanking God will then lead to a different perspective on how we live. It is anathema in most churches to ever use the word "obligate" or "obligation" when referring to our Christian service. Think I'm being over dramatic? Test me. In your next church leadership meeting, say something like "I think all of us here at First _____ Church of Podunk should feel obligated to take a turn working in the baby nursery." In the best case, you'll most likely be called narrow-minded, legalistic, probably unspiritual and even be quoted some verses having to do with freedom from the law, grace, and the fact that as Christians, "we don't *have to do* anything." In the worst case, you may be asked to resign from your leadership position, or worse, leave the church! Obligated? Why, who ever heard of something so foolish? We at First _____ of Podunk *volunteer* to do *only* things we *want* to do!

We've been very careful to avoid using these *obligate* terms in our churches. I think too carefully – and wrong. Let me explain it this way. Our traditional definition of obligation is invalid and illogical with respect to our serving the Lord and His church. The common definition (and our secular understanding) of *obligate* or *obligation* basically involves one being "bound legally or morally" to *do* something. Thinking through how these words have been used in our culture today, it is easy to understand how we might take exception to someone telling us we "had" to do this or that in the name of Christ.

Consider this. When we normally use the obligate words, we are referring to something we are bound to do, not because of our *desire* to do *it*, but rather out of our *fear of the consequences if we don't*. For example, we feel obligated to pay our taxes, obey the speed limit, cut our grass, change the oil in our cars, or vote because we *fear* what will happen if we don't! Most of us don't *want* to pay taxes; go 35 MPH in a 35 MPH zone when we could easily and safely do 50 MPH; work and sweat to cut grass only to have to do it again next week; get all dirty changing our car's oil; or take the time to vote (one vote doesn't really matter, anyway). We don't want to do these things, but we do them because we fear what will happen if we don't. We don't want the IRS to visit us; the blue light to appear in our rearview mirror; get written up by the home owners' association; have our car suffer a major catastrophe; or the wrong candidate elected. It is fear that we associate with obligation as we commonly understand it. When it comes to serving our Lord, however, we must talk about another type of *obligation*.

Jesus frequently uses marriage to explain or, at least, describe His relationship with us, His church. *The Parable of the Wise and Foolish Virgins* in Matthew 25, as well as numerous references in Mark, Luke, John and the Revelation, speak about the bridegroom (Jesus) and the bride (the church). Paul in the fifth chapter of Ephesians is even more descriptive:

> *Wives, submit to your own husbands, as to the Lord. For the husband is head of the wife, as also Christ is head of the church; and He is the Savior of the body. Therefore, just as the church is subject to Christ, so let the wives be to their own husbands in everything. Husbands, love your wives, just as Christ also loved the church and gave Himself for her, that He might sanctify and cleanse her with the washing of water by the word, that He might present her to Himself a glorious church, not having spot*

or wrinkle or any such thing, but that she should be holy and without blemish.

Ephesians 5:22-27

It is with this marriage analogy in mind and within the actual context of marriage that I think we can discover the difference between the common meaning of *obligation* and perhaps the one we should be using when we talk about our *obligation to Jesus.* The illustration I will now use could also be extended to include most close family relationships. However, I feel marriage is the most appropriate because it is the only family relationship we enter into willingly. All other family relationships exist simply as a result of the family into which we are born.

I love my wife. I frequently travelled both nationally and internationally in my earlier business life, so I know a little about temporary separation caused by necessary travel. After only a few trips, I learned to dread it. I remember even becoming ill just thinking that I had to go to Sydney, Australia, for two weeks. Now, I literally can't bear it when Lee and I are physically separated for even a day. With my daughter, Anna Lee, and her family recently moving to another city, Lee spent a week there helping them unpack and playing with our grandson, River. I took her down on a Sunday, left to come back home to work, and would pick her up that Friday. Sounds like a pretty common occurrence? I was a wreck for the whole week. I *need* my wife. I need to *talk* to her. I need to *see* her. I need to *be with* her. Not occasionally, but every day.

I say all this simply to make a point. I care for my wife. I provide for my wife. I protect my wife. I do things for her that I know she likes. I try not to do things that I know she doesn't like. Here is the point I am trying to make. I do things for Lee *not* because I fear what will happen if I *don't do* them. I do things for Lee because I *love* her and *want* to do them! That makes all the difference.

In this illustration, I obviously am not Jesus, nor is Lee the church, but the clear meaning is there. Do you see the difference between our worldly understanding of obligation based on fear of consequences and what our obligation based on love and gratitude should be to Jesus? I'll go ahead and say it: if we have surrendered our lives to the Lord Jesus Christ, we are *obligated* to serve Him. We do this by serving others. Because He first loved us, gave His very life for us, and has paid the price for our eternal home with Him in Heaven, how could we not be obligated to spend the rest of our lives serving Him? I maintain we can't. If we belong to Him, we should be obligated to Jesus not because of fear of what will happen if we don't serve Him, but simply because we love Him so and are so thankful for what He has done for us! If we can think like this, our entire world is turned upside down. Drudgery is changed into joyful opportunity. Fear of the unfamiliar situation is replaced with expectation of how God will bless in and through it. Self reliance is replaced and rewarded with dependence on Him. This easily understood, unambiguous, and most profound truth should change our thinking and, I believe, is a major component of this renewing of our minds to which Paul is referring.

When we begin to think differently, our confidence is transferred from resting in ourselves to being firmly planted in our God. If we can go through daily life and keep our minds fixed on these truths, our attitudes and actions are also transformed. No, everything that happens to us may not be fun, pleasurable, or uplifting, but knowing they come through the hand of God is all we need to know. Our ability to think differently will ultimately be based on one single factor: our faith. Do we really believe God?

The Foundation of the Christian Worldview: The Word

The Bible, the very Word of God, is obviously the foundation on which we as Christians must base our worldview. In it is contained everything we need in order to live for Christ. Its principles are fathomless in their richness, but are understandable to us His children. Our following the Word of God creates these things in us and in our lives: order out of chaos; joy out of despair; security out of risk; understanding out of confusion; peace out of anxiety and worry;

and love out of hate and apathy. It gives us reason to live as well as reason to die. It brings clarity to a world of murkiness, hope for the hopeless, mercy for the undeserving and the merciless, and grace for the unworthy.

All the words ever written or that will be written cannot do justice to the truth of the Word of God. But how can we boil it all down to something we can grasp and hold both in times of great happiness as well as times when all seems lost? All of us have our favorite verses which give us direction, hope, and serve as anchors and plump-bobs in our lives. God speaks to us differently at different times and in different seasons of our lives. However, He always affirms, confirms, and never contradicts His word and His truth.

Though we are finite in our ability to think, reason, and understand, God has given to us sufficient abilities to know what we really need to know about Him to live our lives for Him. That is certainly not to say that we know *everything* about God, His character, His attributes, His purposes … - well, you get the idea. One day we will fully understand because God tells us that we will in His Word: *For now we see through a glass, darkly; but then face to face: now I know in part; but then shall I know even as also I am known. (I Corinthians 13:12)*

Any attempt by anyone, particularly me, to select and identify truths and principles from the Bible and say categorically that these are *the* foundational truths will always be insufficient and leave us wanting. Where do we start? To be completely thorough, we would be forced to somehow summarize the entire Bible and we would still miss important truths. Since we, in this book, are talking about how our worldview ultimately affects how we see and relate to others, particularly PURE people, let me make some assumptions and then try to do the impossible: pick three principles as foundational to the Christian worldview. Of course we won't all agree that these three are foundational - you might have your top three, someone else three others, etc. but since the Christian worldview is, by definition a never-ending, work in progress, I believe my three are a good place to start for the Christian.

Before we continue further and for the sake of time and space, I'm going do something that I know is very risky at best, and, more probably, flat out wrong: I am going to assume you, the readers, are born-again believers. If you aren't a believer in Jesus, what I have said up to this point probably hasn't made much sense to you. What I will be talking about as we continue will probably mean even less, but it is what it is. And just what type of Christian do I assume you to be? A *real* one, a Christian who believes the following: God is the creator and sustainer of all *(John 1:1-3, Job 38-41, Psalm 104);* in the Trinity *(Genesis1:26, I John 5:7);* that Jesus, the Son of God, came to this earth as a man (though still God), lived a perfect life, died on the cross for payment for our sins, and was resurrected from the dead and lives today (Matthew, Mark, Luke, and John); that Jesus in living life on this earth as recorded in the Bible is our perfect example of how we should live (the New Testament); God indwells us in the person of the Holy Spirit through His power and presence, provides all that we need to live according to His purposes *(John 14:18-26, Romans 8:25-26)*; and that Jesus will return one day just as it is recorded in the Revelation. Obviously, I have left out so many basics that a theologian might question my sanity, not to mention my lack of knowledge. However, if we read between the lines of these assumptions and also believe the additional truth necessary to believe the ones I have identified, a broader doctrinal base is built. For example, to believe that God is the creator and sustainer of everything, we must also believe that God has always existed, exists today, and will forever (Exodus 3:14). Or, for us to believe that the God of the universe would sacrifice His only Son to suffer a cruel death on the cross for our sin, forces us to believe that God loves us in a way that we cannot fully comprehend. Get the idea: believing in one truth will require and compel us to believe other biblical truths, and in others ad infinitum.

In man's typical fashion, we might think a Christian worldview is nothing more than a list of do's and don'ts that we must keep. Just as we are wrong to think of our salvation in such terms, we are wrong to think that we must live this way as well. Trying to work our way into a proper perspective is as useless as trying to work our way to Heaven. No, for the Christian worldview to be valid it *cannot* in any way be anything that focuses or depends on me - it *must* be based solely on God and God alone. As for everything else, we are like the proverbial saying, *"We are beggars telling other beggars where to find bread."* We are also beggars of God to understand how we should view and respond to this life He has given us.

More importantly, I'm going to make one other assumption about those of you still reading: you are either a *practicing* Christian or one who wants to be, as opposed to one whose life is not significantly changed by the indwelling Holy Spirit. Are you living totally committed to and growing daily in Christ or is He just someone you have added as another part of your persona *or who you think you are*? The answer to that question is crucial. As Francis Chan, noted author and pastor, explains in his wonderful book, *Crazy Love: Overwhelmed by a Relentless God*:

> *Let's face it. We're willing to make changes in our lives only if we think it affects our salvation. This is why I have so many people ask me questions like, Can I divorce my wife and still go to Heaven? Do I have to be baptized to be saved? Am I a Christian even though I'm having sex with my girlfriend? If I commit suicide, can I still go to Heaven? If I'm ashamed to talk about Christ, is He really going to deny knowing me?*
>
> *To me, these questions are tragic because they reveal much about the state of our hearts. They demonstrate that our concern is more about going to Heaven than loving the King. Jesus said, "If you love me, you will obey what I command" (John 14:15). And our question quickly becomes even more unthinkable: Can I go to Heaven without truly and faithfully loving Jesus?*
>
> *I don't see anywhere in Scripture how the answer to that question could be yes.*
>
> *James 2:19 says, "You believe there is one God. Good! Even the demons believe that – and shudder." God doesn't just want us to have good theology; He wants us to know and love Him. I John 2:3-4 tells us, "We know that we have come to know Him if we obey His commands. The man who says, 'I know Him,' but does not do what He commands is a liar, and the truth is not in him."*

Call me crazy, but I think those verses mean that the person who claims to know God but doesn't obey His commands is a liar and that the truth isn't in him.

In Matthew 16:24-25, Jesus says, "If anyone would come after me, He must deny himself and take up his cross and follow me. For whoever wants to save his life will lose it, but whoever loses his life for me will find it." And in Luke 14:33 He says, "Any of you who does not give up everything he has cannot be my disciple."

Some people claim that we can be Christians without necessarily becoming disciples. I wonder, then, why the last thing Jesus told us was to go into the world, making disciples of all nations, teaching them to obey all that He commanded? You'll notice that He didn't add, "But hey, if that's too much to ask, tell them to just become Christians – you know, the people who get to go to Heaven without having to commit to anything."[4]

So, before we go any further, I implore you: stop now and join me as I pray and ask the Lord to show me how I can truly be His disciple and not just a Christian in name only. As we will see later, God can use PURE people to reveal our true hearts and to prove that we are in fact being led by the Holy Spirit, but only if we let Him. You may not be living as His disciple today, but if you ask Him to make you one, He will. However, the process of becoming a disciple may unfold in ways that you least expect it to happen. Being His disciple will cost us everything, but more importantly, it will give us Jesus, who made everything. Whether we really believe this or just intellectually accept it, defines our discipleship as *real* or only a figment of our imagination.

As we explore now these three principles which I believe are the basis for a Christian worldview, consider how fully embracing them will change how we look, perceive, and understand everything in our world – especially PURE people.

Principle 1: God Is Sovereign, the Perfect Creator, and All-powerful. He Is in Total Control of All Things.

The Word of God speaks directly, clearly, and often about the sovereignty of God. We'll never understand the sovereignty of God - we can only *accept* it as truth. But, when you stop to think about it, do we really *understand* any doctrine fully? Can you explain the virgin birth? How about the miracles Jesus performed? Got a good handle on the Resurrection? Try to *understand* and connect the dots that are sovereignty, predestination, and man's free will (all doctrines clearly taught in Scripture) and you'll find yourself not only confused, but you'll run out of paper, pencils, and space. This is where faith comes in and why it is so important. We sometimes use the word *understand* when we really mean *know* and we can only really *know* by faith. What is illogical, impossible, unreasonable, irrational, unfair, and even contradictory to us as finite human beings is perfectly logical, possible, reasonable, rational, fair, and in complete harmony with our perfect, loving Father God.

Without a doubt, it is in those *difficult* times, the times when nothing makes sense and when we are hurting that we wrestle most with the truth of the sovereignty of God. "Why did God *let* her die?" "You want a divorce, now, after 30 years of marriage?" "You're firing me, but I have a family to support?" "Will chemo and radiation give me more time?" These are but a few of the questions we find ourselves asking in these times of trouble. Without a firm acceptance of the sovereignty of God, these times can stretch and sometimes even shatter our perception of what a loving God should be. Though we can't understand these life events, we must never allow ourselves to doubt God or that He is in total control. Falling into this trap of faulty thinking can only be avoided by faith in God and that He always knows and does only the *best*.

PURE parents certainly are not strangers to difficult times. They encounter one of these difficult times when they are told that their child has special needs. Even PURE parents who are Christians sometimes find themselves questioning God. Unable to comprehend a god who would *make* their child less than perfect, the PURE parents desperately want a *reason* to explain it all. *Why* would God do this? The most plausible *reason* that they, the PURE parents, can assume and rationalize is *themselves: they have done something wrong and God is punishing them for it.* In fact, it is common for virtually *all* PURE parents to feel *guilty.* Though completely and utterly unfounded (except in the rarest of accidents and even then the guilt could be misplaced), PURE parents believe they caused their child's disability by something they did or did not do in their past. Not only is this thinking Scripturally wrong, for God is merciful and forgiving and has paid the price for our sins – but, it further underscores our incorrect view of disability and, ultimately, of God Himself. Of course, even with the mercy of God, He sometimes allows us to suffer consequences for our sins. Being the parent of a PURE person is not, nor could it ever be, punishment for our sins, no matter how many or how dark they may be. PURE people are God's creation just like you and me and there is no Biblical account of God ever *punishing* people by *blessing* them with children with disabilities. It is totally illogical to accuse God of punishing us with gift of one of His most precious creations: a PURE person! Not only is our perception wrong about a PURE person in that they somehow are punishment for something another person did in their life, but also our perception of God is skewed as well. Regardless of logic, it is indeed rare to find a PURE parent not suffering from some amount of outright or obscure feelings of guilt.

Though impossible for us to understand, the sovereignty of God cannot be some theological *concept* to which we blithely acknowledge. It must be the *foundational truth* by which we think of and know God Himself. He is not a concept. He is the God in control of all and, just as important, the God who loves us like no other.

Let's look at some of the passages that speak about God and His sovereignty:

- *And God said to Moses, "I AM WHO I AM." And He said, "Thus you shall say to the children of Israel, 'I AM has sent me to you.' (Exodus 3:14)*

I AM is such a perfect description of God! Since *He is*, time has no boundaries or limits – the implication is He was, He is, and He will be.

- *And you shall remember the* Lord *your God, for it is He who gives you power to get wealth, that He may establish His covenant which He swore to your fathers, as it is this day. (Deuteronomy 8:18)*

  God not only gives us life but He also gives us everything else, including *power* and *wealth*. Our influence, our positions, and roles in various parts of our lives come from Him. Our minds to think, our hands to work, our mouths to speak, our jobs: all come from God's Hand.

- *Indeed Heaven and the highest Heavens belong to the* Lord *your God, also the earth with all that is in it. (Deuteronomy 10:14)*

  This pretty much covers it *all*! It is all His – He made it and He owns it.

- *Before the mountains were brought forth, Or ever You had formed the earth and the world, Even from everlasting to everlasting, You are God. (Psalm 90:2)*

  God has existed *before* time began. He existed before He created the earth. He is everlasting!

- *Of old You laid the foundation of the earth, And the Heavens are the work of Your hands. They will perish, but You will endure; Yes, they will all grow old like a garment; Like a cloak You will change them, And they will be changed. But You are the same, And Your years will have no end. (Psalm 102:25-27)*

  Everything else besides God is decaying, because that's the way He designed it. But He shall have no end.

- *he king's heart is in the hand of the LORD, as the rivers of water: he turneth it whithersoever he will. (Proverbs 21:1) (KJV)*

  God is in control – even of powerful leaders, whether they know it or not.

- *"Am I a God near at hand," says the LORD, "And not a God afar off? Can anyone hide himself in secret places, So I shall not see him?" says the LORD; "Do I not fill Heaven and earth?" says the LORD. (Jeremiah 23:23-24)*

  God speaks here of His personal closeness to each of us. Since distance is a meaningless concept with God, He can be everywhere at all times -– omnipresent. Since God is everywhere all the time, why do we ever try to hide from Him?

- *For I am the LORD, I do not change; Therefore you are not consumed, O sons of Jacob. (Malachi 3:6)*

  Our God is not only ageless, but *never* changes. He is forever, perfectly loving, just, merciful, full of grace, forgiving, …

- *In the beginning was the Word, and the Word was with God, and the Word was God. He was in the beginning with God. All things were made through Him, and without Him nothing was made that was made. (John 1:1-3)*

  God created everything – period!

- *Therefore He has mercy on whom He wills, and whom He wills He hardens. (Romans 9:18)*

  Ultimately, God is in control of our hearts, and His *will* is always accomplished.

- *God, who made the world and everything in it, since He is Lord of Heaven and earth, does not dwell in temples made with hands. Nor is He worshipped with men's hands, as though He needed anything, since He gives to all life, breath, and all things. (Acts 17:24-25)*

> God is master of all – everything is under His control. God needs nothing from us, His creation. It is God who creates all life, gives us and all living creatures their very breath, necessary for life. Might I add that He also causes our hearts to beat, our livers to work, our nervous systems to function, and *nothing* lives unless God gives and maintains life?

- *But, beloved, do not forget this one thing, that with the Lord one day is as a thousand years, and a thousand years as one day. (II Peter 3:8)*

> As with all other physical measures and limits, time means nothing to our God.

- *"I am the Alpha and the Omega, the Beginning and the End," says the Lord, "who is and who was and who is to come, the Almighty." (Revelation 1:8)*

> Even at the end of His Written Word, we are reminded of the everlasting God.

When we say we believe the statement "God is sovereign, the perfect creator, and all powerful. He is in total control of all things," we've said a lot! When we read the Scriptures above that describe this awesome God, we *should* be able to live boldly, confidently, securely, and without fear. We need not fear anything or anyone and even death cannot touch us until God permits it. Where we tend to get into trouble is when we cannot conceive of a loving God allowing things to happen that do not *appear* to be consistent with our perception of His character. Because we do not know what God knows, we find ourselves questioning Him and His reasoning. As you no doubt have already learned, as have I, this is a worthless and fruitless activity. It is at times like these that we must depend even more on the second fundamental.

Principle 2: God loves us more than we can understand or comprehend and desires only His best for us. He is forever loving, merciful, and just.

God is firmly, forever, and lovingly in control of us and everything around us. The Word of God not only tells us this, but that He loves us in such a way and with such depth and expression that we will never be able to fully understand or comprehend that love. This means, that even when we find ourselves in the midst of trouble and heartache, it doesn't mean God doesn't love us or somehow loves us less. Many books have been written about suffering and its various assumed causes: but based on the Bible, we will never see suffering caused by the *absence* of God's love. Thinking of God in any way other than *perfectly* loving can lead us down a path that we do not want to go. Doubting God's love will cause us to doubt His ways and ultimately His sovereignty.

What kind of God, with all power and knowledge, would send His Son to earth to ultimately die for the sins of a people, many of whom reject His gift? Couldn't He have reconciled sinful man to Himself in another way? Obviously, God can do whatever He wishes, but since He always does only what is best, we must assume Jesus' coming, dying, and being resurrected was the *best* way. And so it is with us as we live our daily lives. God does love us more than we can comprehend. When we are trusting and seeking Him consistently, whatever comes our way is also best for us as defined by God as stated in *Romans 8:28 - And we know that all things work together for good to those who love God, to those who are the called according to His purpose.*

There are literally thousands of verses that tell us about the character of God and His involvement in our lives. Let's look at a few.

- *And the LORD passed by before him, and proclaimed, The LORD, The LORD God, merciful and gracious, longsuffering, and abundant in goodness and truth (Exodus 34:6) (KJV)*

  These are some of the never-changing attributes of God: merciful and gracious, longsuffering, and abundant in goodness and truth.

- *For my thoughts are not your thoughts, neither are your ways my ways, saith the LORD. For as the Heavens are higher than the earth, so are my ways higher than your ways, and my thoughts than your thoughts. (Isaiah 55:8-9) (KJV)*

  No matter how hard we try, we cannot think or reason like our Heavenly Father.

- *For the LORD is good; His mercy is everlasting, And His truth endures to all generations. (Psalm 100:5)*

  Not only are the attributes of God's character amazing, they are everlasting and forever.

- *The LORD is merciful and gracious, Slow to anger, and abounding in mercy. (Psalm 103:8)*

  Among God's attributes, perhaps none is more important and significant to us, a *stiff necked people*, than His patience.

- *Trust in the LORD with all your heart, And lean not on your own understanding; In all your ways acknowledge Him, And He shall direct your paths. (Proverbs 3:5-6)*

  This may very well be the most understandable and unmistakable tenet in the Word about God leading us on a minute-by-minute basis. Note that His leadership is conditional: we must first *trust* and then He *directs*.

- *A man's heart plans his way, But the L*ORD *directs his steps. (Proverbs 16:9)*

  We make our plans and might *think* we are in control, but it is God who directs it all.

- *For I know the thoughts that I think toward you, says the L*ORD*, thoughts of peace and not of evil, to give you a future and a hope. (Jeremiah 29:11)*

  This is *the* quintessential verse that confirms for us God's love and concern for the details of our lives – He has it all planned.

- *But God demonstrates His own love toward us, in that while we were still sinners, Christ died for us. (Romans 5:8)*

  Despite our sin and even when we sin, God still loves us!

- *However, for this reason I obtained mercy, that in me first Jesus Christ might show all longsuffering, as a pattern to those who are going to believe on Him for everlasting life. (I Timothy 1:16)*

  According to the pattern set by Jesus, and just as God is longsuffering as He cares for us, we too are to be longsuffering with others.

- *But may the God of all grace, who called us to His eternal glory by Christ Jesus, after you have suffered a while, perfect, establish, strengthen, and settle you. (I Peter 5:10)*

  The prospect of our suffering is sure, but God uses it to *perfect* or complete us, to make us more stable, strengthen us, and give us His peace.

- *And we have known and believed the love that God has for us. God is love, and he who abides in love abides in God, and God in him. (I John 4:16)*

The significance to us of God being love and of His love indwelling us cannot be over emphasized.

When we, by faith, accept the reality of God's unfailing love coupled with His Sovereignty, we can then rest in the knowledge that *all* things that happen to and with us have been filtered through *His* hand. This simply means that we can view everything in a completely new way: "I'm not sure why _____ is happening, but God does and that's fine with me!" *Knowing* that God loves me and is only considering what is best for me is sufficient. I can enjoy the many pleasures and blessings of life that He gives, find purpose in the monotonous and the mundane, and suffer with peace and joy as He is ever present with me through it all. Being able to, in reality, look at all phases, facets, and people in our lives not as haphazard and without reason, but rather as given to us by a God who loves us supremely and wants only to be loved for His goodness to us is indeed revolutionary. Don't ask me how sin, bad personal choices, mass tragedies, and other inexplicable things that exist in our world affect this. I can't explain nor can anyone else. All I know is somehow God is in total control and His purposes are being fulfilled *despite* what we view as irreconcilable events and sin. In His perfect will and for His purposes, He will do anything and everything to grow us as His children, bring us closer to Himself, and cause us to depend more on Him. As with Paul, we can live our lives confidently and free from fear as he proclaims in his letter to the Romans:

What then shall we say to these things? If God is for us, who can be against us? He who did not spare His own Son, but delivered Him up for us all, how shall He not with Him also freely give us all things? Who shall bring a charge against God's elect? It is God who justifies. Who is he who condemns? It is Christ who died, and furthermore is also risen, who is even at the right hand of God, who also makes intercession for us. Who shall separate us from the love of Christ? Shall tribulation, or distress, or persecution, or famine, or nakedness, or peril, or sword? As it is written:"For Your sake we are killed all day long; We are accounted as sheep for the slaughter." Yet in all these things we are more than conquerors through Him who loved us. For I am persuaded that neither death nor life, nor angels nor principalities nor powers, nor things present nor things to come, nor height nor depth, nor any other created thing, shall be able to separate us from the love of God which is in Christ Jesus our Lord.

Romans 8:31-39

Principle 3: God Desires Relationship with Us and Will Do Whatever *He* Desires to Bring Us Closer to Him.

Lest we forget where we are going with this discussion on perspective and how it affects us and how we look at PURE people, we come now to one final fundamental principle. I hope that this exercise can culminate with this all important understanding for it applies to all of us, all the time, and in all things.

If our purpose as Christians on earth is to glorify God, then God's purpose is to have relationship with us individually through Jesus. And, He will do whatever He desires to make that happen. God's *desire* doesn't necessarily mean that it *will* happen. God alone knows what each of us needs to be drawn to Him. Somehow in the sovereignty of God He still allows us free will – we can choose to have that relationship or not; the choice is ours. In some way, this gives us some understanding of why different people can go through similar circumstances and view them totally different: the choice is left to us and that choice is based on how we view the circumstances.

For the unsuspecting parents who suddenly become PURE parents, the joyful experience of having a baby and the life they had expected is drastically changed forever. Their life engulfed in day-by-day survival soon becomes reality. Visions of taking their new baby home to live a life *hoped for* will never happen as they planned. Totally unexpected, a single event has changed it all. Happiness and hope have been replaced with sadness and despair. Eight little words, "There may be something wrong with your baby," have changed everything forever. Many parents, still experiencing the euphoria that comes with a new birth, are literally devastated with these words and what they, the parents, perceive that they mean. Now, not knowing how to care for their new baby, they too must deal with their own broken hearts, their shattered dreams, and anxiety about the future.

God's grace and mercy are truly unfathomable, and I speak often of this fact in that God does not reveal the future to us. Sometimes it would be too glorious for us to believe and sometimes too hard for us to endure. What He promises is His presence in each step along our way. Every parent who receives these words is obviously different and accepts the news differently. Each PURE parent handles the situation in his or her own way. Even in the midst of this time of great apprehension, worry, and sadness, well-meaning Christians will try to comfort the new parents with: (a) "This is God's will" or (b) "God has chosen you to be special parents" or c) "Maybe *it* won't live long and be a burden to you." With Christian *friends* like these, who needs enemies? The truth is: (a) and (b) are true, though the sentiments along with b) are misguided, and c) is not worthy of response.

The truth at that moment is that most PURE parents in this situation are not ready to either comprehend or accept those truths. They are hurting and confused and need our love, support, and presence – not our feeble attempt to "make it all right." Their perspective is damaged - for some temporarily and for others permanently. To try to explain *why* God has given them a PURE child is not our job, for we are woefully ill-prepared to do so. Our job as Christian family or friends is to comfort, encourage (most times with our presence and not our words), and to watch as God works.

Many questions arise for the parents: Did I/we do something that caused this? Is God punishing me/us? How will we care for our child? What will he/she be able to do – sit up, talk, walk …? How will our family change? How will we pay for all the doctor, hospital, and therapy costs? What does the future hold? The bigger question, however, is the same for these parents as it is for us as we live our lives each day:

Will we choose to accept *this* as from God because He loves us and wants us to be closer to Him?

The answer to this question ultimately reveals our worldview. If we want to rebel against God for giving us something which we feel we don't deserve, want, or for which we feel unprepared, we can - the choice is ours. If, even in times when we don't understand *it* or want *it*, we still choose to embrace all that comes our way, God will bless us. Again, the choice is ours and that choice makes all the difference. It is just as important for the parents who have been told they have a PURE child as it is for us in the course of our lives when we face life's circumstances such as a spot being found on the lung of the x-ray of our spouse, our daughter marrying the man of her dreams, enjoying a sunset, holding a grandchild (PURE or normal), breathing, discovering a flat tire, or experiencing everything else in life. No matter how large or how minor or insignificant, it all comes from Him because He is God! And, it all comes from Him, because He loves us and through it all is trying to draw us ever closer. We can choose to see it differently, but life will not be what He wants for us – and besides, we'll be forever miserable waiting for the next shoe to drop.

Our perspective, our worldview, makes the difference. God speaks about His love and His desires for us in His Word. Below, are but a few of those truths on which we can rest and be sure of His intent:

- *I will walk among you and be your God, and you shall be My people (Leviticus:26:12)*

   God is personal and present.

- *The LORD did not set His love on you nor choose you because you were more in number than any other people, for you were the least of all peoples; but because the LORD loves you. (Deuteronomy 7:7-8)*

   God chooses to love us for reasons He alone knows.

- *For I know the plans I have for you,' says the LORD. 'They are plans for good and not for disaster, to give you a future and a hope. (Jeremiah 29:11)*

    God has plans for us and they are always good!

- *I love those who love me, And those who seek me diligently will find me. (Proverbs 8:17)*

    Our response is to love Him, to seek Him who first loved us.

- *The LORD your God in your midst, The Mighty One, will save; He will rejoice over you with gladness, He will quiet you with His love, He will rejoice over you with singing. (Zephaniah 3:17)*

    Our Heavenly Father loves being with us and comforts us with His love.

- *Greater love has no one than this, than to lay down one's life for his friends. You are My friends if you do whatever I command you. No longer do I call you servants, for a servant does not know what his master is doing; but I have called you friends, for all things that I heard from My Father I have made known to you. You did not choose Me, but I chose you and appointed you that you should go and bear fruit, and that your fruit should remain, that whatever you ask the Father in My name He may give you. These things I command you, that you love one another. (John 15:13-17) (KJV)*

    Our only response to love like this is obedience to His Word and to love others.

- *Not that we are sufficient of ourselves to think of anything as being from ourselves, but our sufficiency is from God. (II Corinthians 3:5)*

    We need God and His presence more than we realize.

- *Behold what manner of love the Father has bestowed on us, that we should be called children of God! Therefore the world does not know us, because it did not know Him. Beloved, now we are children of God; and it has not yet been revealed what we shall be, but we know that when He is revealed, we shall be like Him, for we shall see Him as He is. And everyone who has this hope in Him purifies himself, just as He is pure. (I John 3:1-3)*

> What manner of love is this that we can become children of the God of the Universe and that in some way He is purifying us to be like Him?

• *He who does not love does not know God, for God is love. In this the love of God was manifested toward us, that God has sent His only begotten Son into the world, that we might live through Him. (I John 4:8-9)*

> Jesus, God's son, came to this world not only as the perfect manifestation and evidence of God's love, but to give us life itself.

Now, back to those parents whose lives seem devastated when they received the news of their PURE child. If you wait a while and ask them about it all, you'll normally get a startlingly dramatic and different response. After some time has passed and though life is hard, they start to get *it*. Though some PURE parents never seem to quite come to grips with the situation, most will tell you later that their PURE son or daughter is probably the greatest thing that ever happened to them! How can that be? This is something really astonishing: what seemed a tragedy and catastrophe and the end of life as they knew it, is now a blessing and gift! What they thought they didn't *deserve* because of their perceived goodness, they now feel they *don't merit* or are *unworthy* of such a precious gift. Most importantly, a life prospect of only pain and hurt has been replaced with joy and thanksgiving. We'll talk much more about this later in the last chapter.

These remarkable people aren't just super optimistic. No, simple optimism won't quite cut it or see us through the dark times. As Christians, we have the power to be more than just optimistic. Though we don't know what is going to happen, we do know *Who* will be with us as it does. Our Heavenly Father is always actively drawing us closer. The choice to be drawn is ours.

The Problem With Our Perspective

Are you a "the glass is half full" kind of person or are you a "the glass is half empty" kind of person? Maybe you're very analytical and systematic and you might respond, "An optimist will tell you the glass is half-full; the pessimist, half-empty; and the engineer will tell you the glass is twice the size it needs to be!" Or maybe you're like this man caught in a terrible flood. It had been raining for days and days in the land. The waters rose so high that the man was forced to climb onto the roof of his house. As the waters rose higher and higher, a neighbor in a rowboat appeared, and told him to get in. "No," replied the man on the roof. "I have faith in the Lord; the Lord will save me." So the man in the rowboat went away. The man on the roof prayed for God to save him. The waters rose higher and higher, and suddenly a speedboat appeared.

"Climb in!" shouted a man in the boat.

"No," replied the man on the roof. "I have faith in the Lord; the Lord will save me." So the man in the speedboat went away. The man on the roof continued to pray for God to save him. The waters continued to rise. A helicopter appeared and over the loudspeaker, the pilot announced he would lower a rope to the man on the roof.

"No," replied the man on the roof. "I have faith in the Lord; the Lord will save me." So the helicopter went away. The man on the roof prayed for God to save him. The waters rose higher and higher, and eventually they rose so high that the man on the roof was washed away, and alas, the poor man drowned. Upon arriving in Heaven, the man marched straight over to God.

"Heavenly Father," he said, "I had faith in you, I prayed to you to save me, and yet you did nothing. Why?" God gave him a puzzled look, and replied "I sent you two boats and a helicopter; what more did you expect?"

A funny story for sure, but it serves to illustrate a very important point as we begin to examine Christians and ministry, especially to PURE people around us. The point is that our worldview determines how we react to the world around us. I am not just talking about attitude, but our attitude is obviously involved. Attitude is really the way we feel when we're confronted with or are experiencing something. The operative word is *feel*. Since our feelings are constantly changing, so many times our attitudes change as well.

In a very real way, we Christians are many times just like this man on the roof in how we think about and relate to PURE people. Let me explain. Unless we have had personal experience with a PURE person and/or PURE family, most likely our perspective of the life of a PURE person is one of extreme, based on some very inaccurate and limited assumptions. If we are honest with ourselves about how we actually perceive PURE people, we will begin to understand that perception is based on unfounded assumptions. Further, that incorrect perception is actually reflected in our speech and choice of words. We make a startling discovery: we've been wrong! In fact, the simple fact is that our total perception of PURE people is normally based on our own personal experiences with one, or only a few, PURE people.

For example, if we have had no real personal experience (i.e. someone in our family, extended family or close friend), our perception of PURE people is very often based on limited observation and experience in various settings with little or no personal interaction. Therefore, we make inaccurate and erroneous *assumptions*. If on the other hand, we have had personal experience with a PURE person in our close family or friends; we tend to think of *all* PURE people in terms of the PURE person we knew and/or know well. Again, we make inaccurate and erroneous *presumptions*! In other words, if the PURE person with whom we are familiar had Down syndrome and functioned fairly well and the PURE family also functioned fairly normally, we tend to think of *all* PURE people and families in this very erroneous way—

> *"Being a PURE person or in a PURE family is not really such a big deal - they seem to do okay and are pretty much like us, 'normal' people."*

At the other end of this spectrum of incorrect perceptions of PURE people and their families is the situation in which our own personal experience is perhaps with a distant family member with multiple and severe disabilities. In this case our understanding of people with disabilities is often one of fear of *any* PURE person. Our view of PURE people and PURE families at this extreme can best be summarized with the following statement –

> *"Everybody and anybody with disabilities are way too much for me – I'm too uncomfortable to be around them and, besides, I really can't do anything for them!"*

Both of these extreme, but often very common, views of PURE people and their families are not only incorrect, but many times actually keep us from reaching out to these special people. If we think they are "okay, and pretty much like us," we'll most often tend not to get involved because we think they don't need us. In other words, since they are doing so *well*, they certainly don't need our friendship! On the other extreme, our fear and belief that we cannot really do anything for the PURE person and family will frequently keep us at a safe distance. Both of these erroneous perceptions of the PURE situation not only inhibit our involvement, but, in many cases, also serve as the justification of why we don't reach out: if they are okay, they don't need us or if the situation is hopeless, we can't do anything anyway. What we must realize is that the world of disabilities is much, much broader than our own individual and limited experience reveals. This world of disabilities is an unlimited spectrum and a wonderful evidence of God's creative hand. All PURE people are not *okay*, nor are they all *hopeless*. God is infinitely creative, is He not, in how He makes each of us; why would He be any less creative with PURE people? Just like us, each and every PURE person is totally and completely unique and, just like us, each and every PURE person is neither totally *okay* nor *hopeless* as we commonly believe.

Erroneous assumptions and presumptions invariably lead us to problems with our perspectives. This is a principle that is not only true for all perspectives or views, but is particularly true about our perspective of PURE people. If we are basing our perspective on false presumptions, our perception is, by definition, false or invalid.

Want proof of the common perspective we have of PURE people? Interestingly, our very terminology reveals and exposes our perspective. Look up "terminology" in the dictionary and you'll find:

The system of terms belonging or peculiar to a science, art, or specialized subject; The body of specialized words relating to a particular subject.

Generally speaking, our terminology is simply the words we use to talk about something – anything. Most sciences, disciplines, or specialized groups have their own terminology. Many times it is a necessity for people dealing with certain issues (e.g. medicine, computers, science) to use words that they understand, but that we *uninformed* don't necessarily comprehend. The terminology is used by those in a certain field to simply communicate. Its purpose is not to demean, to separate, or put down.

However, if we look at some of the terms used by our culture and, particularly in our churches, with regard to PURE people, a totally different picture emerges. Words can be used to divide. I'll not even address the hurtful words like *retarded, slow,* and other derogatory terms, though they are used by many people even today. But let's look at some of the common and acceptable terms we use every day that are all too revealing and give evidence of a less than PURE perspective.

Special Needs – Sounds perfectly innocent, doesn't it? But how would you like to constantly and solely be referred to and identified as having *special* needs? You're not Mr. or Mrs., you're not boy or girl, you're not a teenager or adult, you don't have blonde or brown hair, and you're not *anything* else but *special needs.* What's so special about someone's needs versus another person's needs? What makes a PURE person's needs so special that we only know them as a *special needs* person? I joke many times with audiences and explain that our seeing PURE people as only special needs is exactly like me or you being known forever and only as bald, short, tall, or left-handed. Try going into a new church, approaching the visitor table, and asking, "As you can see, though I am married, 64 years old, and have grandchildren, I am bald. Do you have any classes for bald people or for families with bald people?" Ridiculous? Not if you're a PURE person – this is life for you and your family.

Disability – Ditto for *special needs*, except here the person is also identified being *less* than *able* – whatever that means and even worse than having special needs! Our common response is "We are all disabled in some way." Though this is a true statement, we all do have one or more types of minor imperfections, big ears, small hands or large nose, our words sound very shallow to a true PURE person with a real disability. We may have made the statement to somehow identify with our PURE friend, but it really just doesn't work. Our minor physical imperfection just can't compare with cerebral palsy or birth defects, for example.

Developmentally Delayed – Yes, we understand that one's development in certain living areas may be delayed when compared to the normal person, but do we really need to identify people solely and forever by this apparent fact? Further, the term is mostly incorrect. Though many PURE people's development in various areas is delayed, many times the development in these areas is not just temporarily delayed in that it will eventually be normal, but it is most times *permanently* delayed in that it may never reach the typical norm. Does this mean that PURE people are to be forever looked down upon simply because in certain areas of their lives they may never be considered normal? If so, we're all in trouble because *not one of us* is normal!

Specific Diagnosis (Autistic, Down syndrome, schizophrenic, etc …) – It is hard to believe we can be so cruel and insensitive in our modern society, but many times we are not content in identifying PURE people with broad, negative terms like those above. No, we go further and actually call the person by their diagnosis. "There is that little autistic boy," and "She's the mother of the Down syndrome girl in our neighborhood" are typical, common, and accepted as perfectly normal descriptions of PURE people. We'll say these kinds of things in front of PURE people and not believe that it is wrong or offensive. Our thinking is that they don't understand that they are being called something offensive and hurtful, but they do and our faulty thinking is hurtful in itself. Once again, let's put ourselves in their shoes: how would you like to be labeled as "The man with the bad case of psoriasis" or "The guy with flat feet?" Silly, unrealistic? If you're a PURE person or family, it isn't.

Inclusion – Perhaps no more ridiculous term is used in talking about PURE people than the scholarly, innocuous term *inclusion*. Inclusion, as we will see later, is certainly valid in terms of a PURE ministry model for classroom settings, but it has come to mean so much more to most people. The great debate in churches even considering ministry to PURE people, especially PURE children, is the entire concept of inclusion, which is the mainstreaming of PURE children with typical children in the classroom. Unfortunately, this thinking has *not* been applied or extended over into all areas of ministry in our churches as it relates to PURE people and their families. The PURE children may well be theoretically included in the classroom, but for all practical purposes, remain totally excluded and isolated in every other way in the life of the church. Yet, we continue to have this rhetorical debate: should we *include* the PURE person in our normal classrooms? When, in actuality, we do very little to *include* them in the life of our church, our fellowship! Can you imagine what would happen if we had this debate about other demographic groups or ministry in our churches? "Since these toddlers aren't really contributing much to our church and they take up so many resources and time, should we really include them?" or "Our senior saints are such trouble, always having to make special provisions for them – in our next deacon/elder meeting we need to take up whether we should include them in our fellowship as we become a more dynamic church." You haven't heard these type comments in your church lately? No, and you most probably won't either. Yet, even those among us involved in PURE ministry in our churches, self-satisfied and pleased with ourselves that we are really doing ministry, continue to focus on classroom models while ignoring the elephant in the room: PURE people and *their families* remaining largely isolated and alienated in our fellowships. Yes, the term *inclusion* has taken on much more hidden meaning than we will admit. As long as we allow its perceived implication to prevent us from dealing with true inclusion of PURE people and their families in our churches *in every and all ways*, we only delude ourselves, and our worldview is certainly not Christian according to Jesus.

Yes, our words give us away. In many cases our terminology has made the typical Christian impotent and has given us an excuse to do what is sinful: simply ignore people who may make us uncomfortable. Though I cannot speak to the church of all of the centuries in its ministry to PURE people, I think it is safe to say that the modern church has been complacent and has felt justified in not reaching out to PURE people and their families. Our history in this regard has been one of isolation, but the broader goal of all Christian endeavours must be to bring people to Christ *and*, as a vital part of their sanctification, into fellowship with other believers in the local church. Who has ever heard of telling the body of Christ to *include* others into their fellowship? Only the PURE and their families have this dubious distinction. We don't need to know the health, emotional or physical, of anyone else who comes to our church -- why PURE people? We are called simply to love all those God brings our way. With the correct worldview, all we need to know is that God has brought them and that's all we need to know! We don't need to know the diagnosis and we are to think of them as friends, not developmentally delayed, not autistic or Down's or whatever. They are just people who need Christ like we do. Moreover, they need us and our friendship, and we need them in our fellowship.

The Birth of PURE Ministry

It was the fall of 2007 and I remember driving out of Eagle Eyrie, a beautiful Baptist camp just north of Lynchburg, Virginia. Lee, my wife, and I had just spent one of the most wonderful weekends we had ever experienced in this beautiful place. You know the kind of retreat weekend I'm talking about: inspirational speakers, great food, good fellowship, Scriptural teaching on loving each other more and making our marriages and families better, and time to practice what we had learned with long walks and quiet times? Well, it wasn't quite *that* kind of retreat; it was much, much better.

You'll probably have some difficulty wrapping your mind around this, but imagine more than 400 adults gathered there; with the majority of them developmentally disabled and the other folks their caregivers, parents, and volunteers. They come from churches, groups, private homes, and group homes from Virginia, Maryland, North Carolina, and other surrounding states. They have been coming now for 38 years for a beautiful autumn weekend in the Virginia mountains. The annual Eagle Eyrie Retreat has become an event Lee and I will not miss. Everything in our fall is planned around our attending. As I look back over the years, I realize that this unique event has become a type of real world "laboratory" for me. It is a place where people like me can interact with and observe a large population of PURE people where *they* are a majority and normal people are a definite minority. That one weekend in October each year, Eagle Eyrie is transformed into a world that is virtually devoid of the prejudice, discrimination, and intolerance PURE people must endure all the other days of the year. More importantly, in the absence of this negative environment, it becomes a world in which we can clearly see and experience the beauty, sweetness, kindness, talents, and so many more wonderful character traits that PURE people seem to so effortlessly demonstrate. If this sounds moving and/or inspirational to you, you probably don't need to read anymore, for you probably have "gotten" it. We'll pick you back up at the next chapter. For the rest of us, read on. Let me paint the picture of the Virginia Baptist Retreat for Youth and Adults with Special Needs for the rest of us, because I don't want you to miss this. Eagle Eyrie is owned and operated by the Virginia Baptist Mission Board and is gorgeous. Rod Miller, the Director of Eagle Eyrie, and his wonderful staff are true servants and treat everyone with impeccable service and kindness. The retreat leaders meet at lunch on Friday and then the first praise gathering gets the retreat officially started later that afternoon. The remainder of Friday afternoon and evening, all day Saturday (with a big dance on Saturday night!), and through worship time and lunch on Sunday, we are all gathered literally on top of and on the side of a gorgeous mountain looking down into Lynchburg. Sound like fun to you? This is truly a unique place and time.

Let me backtrack and explain how I got involved in this retreat. It was through a series of God-ordained events. After speaking at a conference in Richmond, Virginia, in 2005, I subsequently got involved in ministry with a number of churches in Virginia, and became good friends with many wonderful people in the state. At Spring Hill Baptist Church, just outside of Charlottesville, I met a number of people who were to play a very important role in the evolution that was and is PURE ministry.

It was at that initial conference in Richmond that I first met two delightful people, Gene and Jeannie Arnold. Though none of us realized it at the time, they were to be very influential in the formation of PURE Ministry. With Gene and I both being dads, granddads, and Georgia Tech engineering grads, we realized that we had much in common. Though separated by hundreds of miles, we grew close and became special friends. Lee and I are still close friends with Jeannie, a wonderful, godly PURE mom, and their awesome grown children, Kenny, Ben, Joe, and Patty. When Gene retired, he began working with and promoting *PURE Ministries* until he was suddenly stricken with a rare, quick, debilitating, and fatal disease that took him home to Heaven in just a matter of weeks. Though Gene was very well known professionally and was head of Special Olympics in Northern Virginia, it was his tender spirit, godly character, and wonderful example of what a PURE dad should and could be, that continues to inspire and encourage me in unspeakable ways even today. During those short last days when I visited, we often talked and wondered why the Lord had waited almost sixty years for us to even meet each other while on this earth. We concluded the Lord was saving our friendship for Heaven where we would have sufficient time to talk and laugh!

Also at Spring Hill I met Mark and Mary Buckner who had been PURE parents of a daughter, Becky, now in Heaven. Mary has been the official head honcho of the Virginia retreat for many years and does a great job each and every year in pulling everything together. She asked me if I would like to come speak to the parents and caregivers for that upcoming retreat weekend and, always ready and eager, I said, "Sure." Little did I realize then, with this simple invitation, the impact that this special event would have and continue to have on me. I haven't missed a retreat since then. It is still my honor and privilege to speak to the parents and caregivers during the weekend and I don't intend to ever miss another one as long as the Lord allows.

As you have had to do previously in this book, you'll just have to trust me again on this, because if you haven't been there, you just can't grasp fully what happens when you have a large number of PURE people in one place at one time. Also, when people begin to talk emotionally about someone or something, they tend to exaggerate and embellish. In the following paragraphs you will undoubtedly think that I am doing the same, but I can assure you I'm not. I do not possess the words skills or vocabulary, nor do I believe anyone else does for that matter, to sufficiently describe what occurs at this retreat at Eagle Eyrie. Further, as I describe my PURE friends and their impact and effect they have, you might well accuse me again of embellishing. I'm not. Finally, as you read these words, you might think that I am in some way even marginalizing or minimizing the real difficulties and struggles of being a PURE person. Again, I'm not. I simply have learned that the blessing of being in such a group literally changes one's perspective about it all. More about this in the last chapter.

It must be noted that this retreat is unique. We are aware of no other Christian retreat for PURE adults of this size in any state or region. PURE people (*students*) there vary in age from their 20's to late 70's to even 80's – all cognitively/intellectually disabled to some degree and many also physically disabled in some ways. The *students* attend classes similar to Vacation Bible School and have a great time seeing old friends and fellowshipping together. The cafeteria is a joyous place with much laughter and more authentic Christian fellowship than most of us ever get to witness, much less be participants. Talking about being around true servants? We rarely have to take our own tray back – one of our kind PURE friends is always politely asking us if they can do it! Sound like your last church retreat? I didn't think so.

Praise and worship take on an entirely new and wonderful meaning when you sit in a large auditorium with these sweet people who so freely express themselves. Barry Green, Minister of Music at Bonsack Baptist Church in Roanoke, VA, one of the very best and kindest praise and worship leaders in America, leads us through wonderful worship, praise, and fun songs that everyone enjoys. Everyone who is able sings and participates with joy and abandonment that must be witnessed to be believed. There is seemingly no evidence or concept at all of being self-conscious whatsoever. This is simply amazing to see.

A couple of experiences I've had there may help you begin to understand that this is not your average gathering. I have attempted before to describe an interaction in a group of PURE people when we normal people are in the minority rather than the majority. Let me try to do it this way, for it happened to me that first weekend. Imagine if you will, two PURE people talking and conversing. I am friends with one of the PURE people. As I approached them, perhaps a little apprehensive, I greet my PURE friend. I extend my hand as *real* men are to shake hands, only to find myself the recipient of a big hug! My friend then introduces me to his PURE friend. Again, I extend my hand (yes, I catch on slowly) only to find myself in a second hug from my now new friend. I mutter some small talk and then my two friends continue their animated conversation. It is was at that moment that I came to a staggering and astonishing realization: *they don't see me any different from themselves.* They don't change and put on airs for my benefit. They don't see me as normal and themselves PURE; I'm just another friend! But wait a minute, I'm *normal* (read, in our pride: smarter, more educated, more aware, better spoken, and better dressed). By definition, don't I *merit* and *deserve* some extra respect and deference here? The uncomfortable, yet resounding answer - No!

Think about it and put yourself in my situation and be honest. Wouldn't *you* expect a little extra attention? After all, you are normal. In all honesty and, though we are embarrassed to admit it, we do think we should be respected just a little more. The truly amazing thing about my incident was the two PURE guys: they didn't treat me any differently – good or bad – because of the way I looked, spoke, or acted. I was just another person! This is amazing because no matter how hard I try, I can't do this, yet they do it seemingly without effort! When I approach my friends, I have preconceived notions and expectations; I'm inhibited and I'm a little guarded and concerned that I don't misspeak. However, with the typical PURE person, like these two young men, they are just themselves and not worried about how *they* are perceived by me at all! In fact, most PURE people are completely and totally transparent; if they like you, they hug you; if they feel like crying, they cry. What you see is what you get and it is refreshing beyond belief to be in such an environment.

It is in this environment of openness and transparency that we begin to get a glimpse of authentic love and sacrifice. That evening after supper we were all walking up the long hill to the auditorium for the nightly praise, worship, and fun time. A few yards ahead I saw a young lady struggling to walk up the steep incline. The debate in my mind began. Should I just walk on up to her and help her? What would she think about me just grabbing her arm? Maybe she *didn't want* any help – then what? What would the other people watching think? While I pondered, an older PURE man walked right past me, gently took the young lady's arm and helped her up the hill. Oh yeah, did I mention that he struggled to walk even more than the young lady he was helping? I just stood there with my thoughts and good intensions around my ankles.

The highlight of the entire weekend for most of us is the annual Saturday afternoon talent show. These folks practice their *talents* all year. Different group homes, other community groups, and individual PURE people put on skits, sing, and dance for three hours and nobody wants it to end. *Talent* can be pantomiming a favorite song, quoting a poem, singing, telling jokes, or literally *anything* someone wants to do. I truly believe that if enough Christians could somehow cram themselves into this auditorium and simply observe what happens during this afternoon that the church, as we know it in America, could instantly be revived! If we ordinary Christians could witness the kindness, compassion, encouragement, concern, guilelessness, inspiration, love expressed, and true joy on display, our lives would change. I speak from experience, for mine certainly did.

Remember that these are developmentally disabled adults. Many have difficulty speaking. Many have trouble walking. Many have issues limiting their awareness and ability to respond. How then can we explain such unbridled happiness as each person or group walks, totters, rolls in their wheelchair, or is carried onto the stage to perform? You haven't heard anything until you've heard a 60 year old man pantomime a Johnny Cash hit! Though he may be about two beats behind the recording and miss ¾ of the words, it really doesn't matter. He envisions himself really singing the song just like Johnny Cash and all of us watching and listening do, too. When the song is over, the crowd goes wild, and I do mean wild. Everyone claps and cheers wildly and standing ovations are common. The next act is a group home doing a medley of Broadway songs, though a New York critic may have difficulty recognizing any of them. Again, the crowd goes wild! Next is a middle-age woman who wants to recite her favorite Scripture passage, or, as she, non-embarrassed and honestly says with a chuckle before she begins, "or as much as I can remember!" Laughter *with* her (not *at* her) and then totally quiet as she talks about her Jesus. When she finishes, everyone is on their feet; the love in the room is palpable.

One of my personal favorite acts each year is Kris O'Neill and his wonderful parents, Bob and Luanne, who have become my good friends. I have told them before, that if more parents were like them, we would have a much better world. Kris is a precious person, very quiet, and totally dependent on his mom and dad for everything. He can walk, says very little, unless the conversation is about pro football, and lives at home with them. They are dedicated to loving and caring for him. Though they don't have to, at each talent show they take Kris on stage and do some kind of performance *with* him. Though quiet and unassuming people themselves, they don't want their son to miss anything in life. They don't brag about this; they just live it. They are willing to get in front of 400 people and sing, dance, or whatever with Kris so that he has the experience. It brings me to tears each time I see them up there. Seldom have I seen such selflessness and sacrifice on display.

Finally, the talent show ends. Many of us wipe our eyes – laughter and devotion witnessed will do that to you – and head down to the cafeteria for supper. As I think back now of my thoughts from the end of that first talent show, I remember asking myself, "What in the world have I just witnessed?" Trying to explain it to myself, I had no other similar experiences with which to compare it. As I thought through it, two shocking realities became apparent:

- Such an event could never be held in a normal environment - especially in a regular church with regular folks. From a worldly perspective, these people, though sincere, were certainly not *talented* from a worldly perspective.
- If such an event, even with our peers, were ever attempted in one of our churches and *real* talent expected, the people watching would at first be courteous and polite. Giggles would follow. Loud jeers, jokes, and catcalls would soon follow, and the *talent* would literally be laughed off the stage!

So why am I calling this talent show one of the best experiences of my life? It is simply because it is in this place, where so many people that the world has labeled worthless and of no value, that I see the personification of all those attributes that I desire as a Christian. They don't have to think about being open, loving, caring, and gracious – they just are and I want to be like them! For example, I have one delightful PURE friend, Bryant

DeLoatche, who takes the time every Saturday afternoon to send me his weekly movie review. We have developed a close group of parents and caregivers over the years and it's always so good to be with them. I joke and kid with Joe, Patty, and many others – I'm never more free nor do I feel more accepted than with these sweet people. Amazing, isn't it? I do now realize it's not the place or setting, though it is very beautiful: it's the people and the relationships I have with them.

The culmination of all these thoughts and activities occurred on that first Sunday afternoon as we left Eagle Eyrie, as I mentioned when I started this story. As we drove out, I looked at Lee and said, "Something is wrong here. If those people are disabled, then that's what I want to be." We continued to talk about the people we had met: their transparency, their innocence, and their lack of guile. As God frequently does, He gave my wife the crowning conclusion to our description of these wonderful people. Lee simply said, "There is a *purity* about them that I just can't explain." That was it: *pure*. That's what these people were. Not necessarily pure *from sin*, but certainly more pure than we are.

From that moment and over the next several months, God began planting in my mind and heart the word PURE and how it could be applied to special needs ministry. Gradually over the next few months, God revealed to me the whole concept of PURE and refined it more and more each day. Out of this process and from God's leading came PURE ministry and The PURE Ministry Project.

The PURE Ministry Project

When *PURE Ministries* first introduced "The PURE Ministry Project" as our main ministry focus, we began using the following tag line in an attempt to capsulate and to describe it:

A wakeup call for Christians - Transforming the way we think
A Christian Awakening, a Nationwide Project to Increase Awareness of and
Ministry to People with Disabilities and their Families in our Churches

We at *PURE Ministries* see the main purpose of The PURE Ministry Project as being a wake-up call for the church. "A Christian awakening" implies our becoming aware of something which we have not been formally been aware. This awakening will not happen if we continue to view PURE people as most of us do today - our perspective must change. Further, most likely our perspective will not change until our thinking changes. As God moves and we begin thinking differently, the words we have used in the past will be lacking and our words will change. Thus, the PURE Ministry Project was born.

Rather than a grand and glorious public relations movement, The PURE Ministry Project is aimed at you and me, average Christians sitting in a church pew, and our pastors. The PURE Ministry Project is a plan to emphasize and focus on a people and a ministry that has traditionally been virtually non-existent in our consciousness and, therefore, in our churches. Yet, it is this very ministry in which we see Jesus most often concerned and involved while on this earth. That ministry is described by Jesus in the following Scripture:

> *Then Jesus said to his host, "When you give a luncheon or dinner, do not invite your friends, your brothers or relatives, or your rich neighbors; if you do, they may invite you back and so you will be repaid. But when you give a banquet, invite the poor, the crippled, the lame, the blind, and you will be blessed. Although they cannot repay you, you will be repaid at the resurrection of the righteous."*
> *Luke 14: 12-14 (NIV)*

This passage is foundational to all we do at *PURE Ministries* and, just to forewarn you, I will be referring to it many times throughout. Here, Jesus is using contrasts as He so often does as He teaches. He uses the metaphor of the *dinner* (or *feast* in the KJV) in the home, which in the Jewish tradition is an overt act of worthiness, of friendship, and of acceptance. What He is saying to us Christians today, however, is not disguised but shockingly clear: we are to be about this very thing today – ministering to the disabled and their families. The PURE

Ministry Project is a practical plan to do just that: enable churches to better minister to the disabled in their communities, *just like Jesus did.*

The PURE Ministry Project not only accurately describes the people who are the recipients of the ministry, but also we who minister. The PURE Ministry Project underscores the other crucial principle Jesus speaks about in the passage in Luke. When we reach out to PURE people and their families, we must do so with PURE hearts and motives. We must minister not for anything in return, but simply because Jesus has commanded us.

The one place in our culture where people with disabilities and their families should find love, acceptance, and comfort is the church. Sadly, that's not reality today. The questions are, "In light of the example of Jesus, will we, as average Christians, embrace this PURE ministry? Will we commit humbly to this mission at God's urging? Will we lead people in this ministry that, if we simply look at Jesus' life, is probably the closest to His heart?"

To state it very succinctly, The PURE Ministry Project is a nation-wide effort to:

- Make pastors and ordinary Christians more aware of disabled people and their families in their communities.
- Encourage ministry that will reach out to these wonderful people and draw them into the fellowship of the church.
- Equip and train all Christians, pastors and others, to better minister to PURE people and their families.

This effort is being accomplished by:

- Hosting regional "PURE Celebrations" which are inspirational, regional events with nationally known speakers, Christian musical artists, with the sole purpose of introducing average Christians to the PURE world through an evening of great praise and worship, with PURE folks and families included as our guests!

- Conducting in-church training seminars to help individual churches implement PURE ministry.
- Developing ministry partnerships with various denominations and other Christian-based ministries.
- Spreading and teaching PURE ministry principles and issues in seminaries.
- Developing and offering educational resources on PURE Ministry issues.
- Introducing creative and outside the "Sunday school class on Sunday morning" box ministry ideas to churches.
- And, finally, initiating and growing a national network (the PURE Ministry Network) of local churches actively involved in PURE ministry in their local communities.

As part of The PURE Ministry Project, we have introduced the word PURE to better describe people with special needs. However, we are not so naïve to think by just changing words that we can change hearts. Nor are we similar to a local government who, faced with a street in the city with a high crime rate, will simply change the *name* of the street as a solution to the problem. However, we do believe that if Christians can start to use the word PURE in describing and talking about their friends, who once were called special needs or disabled, slowly but surely PURE will become commonplace.

As we first described in the Preface, PURE is not only a more positive descriptive term, it is also more scriptural. PURE is an acronym and each letter is meaningful:

P erfectly created by a loving sovereign God, designed for His purpose

U nique in his or her own gifts, blessings, talents, desires, and contributions

R eceptive and responsive to our communication, touch, and acts of love

E ternal, because there are no Disabled Souls in God's eyes

Let's examine in detail for a minute this word PURE and what it really means. First, in a way, we are all PURE by this definition. However, we reserve the word PURE exclusively for people and families affected by disabilities. We normal people certainly don't need another term to describe us. As PURE becomes more accepted and is used more widely, there is bound to be criticism. "Are you saying that all PURE people are PURE from sin?" is a common question/criticism. The short answer is "No," but, I am quick to add, many PURE people are. PURE people, regardless of age, who are intellectually and cognitively incapable of discerning right from wrong, are no different positionally than infants and small children or even aborted infants. Like infants and small children, and though these PURE people have sin *natures* like all men, they cannot sin any more than a one-year-old can sin – they cannot sin because they do not *know* it is sin. We go to Hell not because of our sin *nature*, but because of sins *committed*. At the Great White Throne Judgement as recorded in Revelation 20, verse 12 states *"And I saw the dead, small and great, standing before God, and books were opened. And another book was opened, which is the Book of Life. And the dead were judged according to their works, by the things which were written in the books."*

We'll not get into a theological debate over this issue, but I believe Scripture teaches us that the nature of God is *good*. To quote the great Bible teacher and pastor, Dr. John MacArthur, in his book, *"Safe in the Arms of God,"* in which he discusses this topic in great detail, when babies (or young children or some PURE people) die, they have "instant Heaven"[5]. As Dr. MacArthur exclaimed to a young mother whose baby has just died, "Your baby is in Heaven. He is safe in the arms of God." Further proof of this can be found as King David exclaims after his and Bathsheba's child dies in *II Samuel 12:22-23, And he said, "While the child was alive, I fasted and wept; for I said, 'Who can tell whether the LORD will be gracious to me, that the child may live?' But now he is dead; why should I fast? Can I bring him back again? I shall go to him, but he shall not return to me."* Clearly, this passage teaches that David believed that he would be reunited with his child in Heaven -– David knew the baby could not *come back* to this life, but he also believed that he *would go* to him in Heaven.

Other criticism of the use of the term PURE in describing people with disabilities can be summarized in this statement. "Special needs, disabled, and handicapped are simply *symbolic* terms – no harm or hurt is intended and, besides, they are commonly accepted in our culture." My response is simply that if these terms are only symbolic, they are symbolically negative, disparaging, and inherently, whether we intend to or not, carry hurt with them. Is it too much to ask of us Christians to at least use a positive, edifying term, like PURE, in describing these precious people? No, I don't think it is. Again, how would we like to be solely and constantly identified by some personal or physical trait or characteristic and be told, "Don't take it personally – it's just *symbolic?*" We can do better than that.

What are we trying to say and convey when we refer to a person as PURE? Let's look at the acronym for PURE in more detail.

P - Perfectly Created by a Loving Sovereign God, Designed for His Purpose

The very idea that a loving sovereign God would create a person with disabilities can cause many of us to question just what kind of God we serve. To further call this obviously imperfect person *perfectly created* causes many of us even more angst. Not only is our definition of the very nature of God challenged, but also our understanding of how we label His creation is called into question. Based on Scripture, we know God is the creator of all things - *For by Him all things were created that are in Heaven and that are on earth, visible and invisible, whether thrones or dominions or principalities or powers. All things were created through Him and for Him. (Colossians 1:16)* However, when confronted with the reality of the existence of, for example, a severely disabled PURE person, our generally accepted grasp of our view of God and what is *perfectly created* could not be further apart. In fact, we might reason that God was not somehow *directly* involved when such a person was created – surely God couldn't and wouldn't create a person destined for such suffering. But, obviously, He has and He did! What are we to make of this? Though we certainly don't understand, we must accept God's sovereignty. If we do accept the inescapable truth that God does what He desires for His purposes and for our good. However, if all God does is perfect, right, and just, we have a dilemma: one of us, either us or God, doesn't *get* it! Guess who doesn't *get* it? In *John 9:1-3*, we find a real life account of Jesus addressing this very topic. As He passes a blind man, He is asked by His disciples whether the man is blind as a result of his or his parents' sin. We can only assume this outspoken disciple is none other than Peter, who was known for frequently putting his foot in his mouth. Jesus literally turns the world, and our understanding of disability, upside down, when He responds (and I paraphrase verse 3), "No, sin isn't the reason for his blindness – I created and designed this man *perfectly* the way I desired for My purposes, that My power might be evident in him." We are left with this undeniable conclusion: God does *only* what is right and He does everything with perfection. Therefore, like you and me, PURE people are perfectly created by this loving, sovereign God for His purposes. Think about that the next time you are in the presence of a PURE person and let it sink in to your consciousness. The PURE person is not a mistake, but like you, perfectly created.

U - Unique in His or Her Own Gifts, Blessings, Talents, Desires, and Contributions

Contrary to the common misconception about PURE people, one person with Down syndrome is not like every other person with Down syndrome. Nor is a given person with autism like every other person with autism. I realize we know this at one level and yet at some other level, we somehow want to group people together who have the same diagnoses. Again, we normally don't do this with any other group and aren't even aware that we do it with PURE people. Just like us, PURE people are not only perfectly created; they are also totally and completely in every way, *unique*. The PURE person may be in a wheelchair, but we can be assured that person is unlike any other person, whether they are in a wheelchair or not. Again, we are not trying to be condescending or patronizing in trying to emphasize this point, but far too many of us unconsciously and because we don't have many relationships with

PURE people, tend to think this way. Once we become friends with a variety of PURE people and if we have had the common mistaken idea about the sameness of PURE people, our perception of their uniqueness will quickly and delightfully be confirmed. Further, we begin to realize that *all* PURE people can contribute in some way. In fact, many PURE people can contribute many times in ways that we cannot. PURE people have much to offer and contribute, especially to the church, if they are afforded the opportunity.

R - Receptive and Responsive to Our Communication, Touch, and Acts of Love

Another common misconception about PURE people is that, since they may not respond in a typical or normal way to us, we infer that they are not particularly receptive or responsive to our attempts to communicate. In a later chapter, we will deal with some good communication techniques, but suffice it to say, PURE people are not only receptive to our attempts to converse, but are eager and desirous of them; they just might not respond the way we *think* they should or in a way that we *think* is appropriate. Once again, our perceptions of PURE people are based on wrong assumptions. Our thinking as we initially approach a PURE person that we do not know is greatly distorted normally with some anxiety and feeling of awkwardness. Is the person going to respond at all? Are they going to be aggressive or violent? What if I don't understand or if I misinterpret what they say or do? How will they respond then? What should I do? Except for the violent part, these are all valid questions. Our problem, typically, when we approach a PURE person is our *own* expectations. We are comfortable talking with normal people because we are comfortable and familiar with their responses which are normally customary and familiar. Even if we are not a great conversationalist, we can control the interchange – we can guide the conversation to safe places and if we don't like the way things are going, we can even walk away. With the PURE person, we don't have the same confidence. We are apprehensive and uneasy. We like to encourage people who are inexperienced with

PURE people, but who are willing to get outside of themselves and do it, with this advice: anticipate a normal response, but don't be surprised if you don't receive one. We tell them further, don't be surprised if you receive an inappropriate response, either, or no response at all – just go with the flow! Depending on the types and severity of the disabilities, a PURE person may or may not be able to speak, use body language, move their hands, or in other ways try to communicate back with us. The scary part is that we are no longer in control! The great part: We realize once again that God is! As we gain experience adapting to each PURE person and being sincere with our attempts to reach out and touch them through words, a pat on the shoulder, or whatever, we will discover that our fear and anxiety will disappear. We begin to see and experience communication, at times seemingly with our being the only one speaking audibly and the PURE person responding as best they can. With other PURE people, there may be no words spoken at all, yet God enables us to communicate with our PURE friend supernaturally. As long as we keep our expectations in check and remember that our attempts to communicate and love that PURE person, no matter how feeble, awkward, or inept those attempts may be, *are always well received* regardless of the response or lack of response we get back. We learn to reach out and touch people for the sole benefit of the recipient and not for the warm fuzzies we may get for doing something *good*. PURE people are so appreciative of virtually anyone who makes any attempt to interact with them. Because PURE people are so frequently only glared at, whispered about, or totally ignored, they most always are overjoyed when any of us takes the time even to acknowledge and speak to them. Know, regardless of response, that they are thankful for your effort. As my good friend and PURE ministry expert, Dr. Jim Pierson, author of *"Exceptional Teaching,"* has said, *"No person is so disabled that they do not respond to our acts of love."* We can't put limitations or expectations on what that response looks like or form that it may take.

E – Eternal: Because There Are No Disabled Souls in God's Eyes

The "E" in PURE is most probably the most important letter. When we get the significance of this letter, the other letters and their meanings become clearer and more understandable. First, let me say that most of us don't necessarily think PURE people have *no* souls –- it's just that we have somehow relegated them to some lesser importance and have not made them a priority of our evangelism. In the next chapter we will talk about just who PURE people are, but as I have stated earlier, the statistics are surprising! We must remember that over 50 million Americans have disabilities. That means that an estimated 10% – 20% of any given community's population is PURE. And they need Jesus, too.

A New Ministry Focus?

If you are a Christian and have been active in a church in America for any time, I would ask you a simple question: have you *ever* seen or heard any promotion or advertisement in your local church, denomination, or in the larger Christian community about *anything* having to do with *taking the Gospel* to PURE people and their families? No? I didn't think so. Another staggering statistic: when the immediate family is included, somewhere between 25% - 30% or 75 - 80 to 100 *million* of our population is *directly* affected by disabilities. Have you seen or heard anything maybe about a workshop on evangelizing the largest unreached people group in America, PURE people and their families? No, again? That's because we, the body of Christ, have somehow felt justified in *not* reaching out to this large population of people. PURE people and their families are in large numbers in our communities, but as a general rule we do precious little to share the Gospel with them, much less include them in our fellowship. Too harsh a statement? Not really – the proof is in the pudding: if we were doing these things to any degree, then the average church in America, statistically, should have among its member's percentages of PURE people and PURE families consistent with the population at large. Sadly, we're not even in the ballpark in this regard.

Again, I believe the reason we don't reach out to the PURE is not necessarily apathy, though apathy is a problem. I believe the real reason is that we individual Christians still subscribe to bad assumptions: PURE people can't understand the Gospel, so why try? We further justify our inaction with a hazy acknowledgment that "Well, since all PURE people *can't* understand, and God makes some special salvation provision for them, we don't need to do anything, plus it really makes us uncomfortable to approach them!" This reasoning is both wrong and right. First, only some relatively small number of significantly cognitively disabled PURE people cannot understand Jesus loving them. However, those PURE people that can't understand the Gospel are most often closer to and more intimate with Jesus than most of us ever will be!

Second, most PURE people *can* understand the Gospel of Christ, but we *assume all* PURE people in wheelchairs, with a limp, a speech impediment, birth defects, or virtually any other intellectual or physical disability, are *also* cognitively impaired. We then take a sweeping, generalized position both individually and corporately as the church and *assume that all* PURE *people are incapable of receiving the Gospel.* Further, we forget the fact that for every PURE person, there is a PURE family composed of people who are not disabled in any way. The PURE family is normally very loyal to one another and when the PURE person is excluded, the PURE family is also excluded. R e m e m b e r, PURE people and PURE family members do have eternal souls. We can never allow ourselves to let our misconceptions or fears keep us from reaching out in the name of Christ to *all* people, especially PURE people.

To illustrate the importance and the impact of the word PURE in referring to people with special needs, I must tell you about an experience I had shortly after The PURE Ministry Project was launched. I was asked to come to a large church in Gainesville, Florida, to preach on a Sunday morning service for PURE Ministry Day. This was in January and in the preceding summer, two wonderful ladies from this church had attended one of our seminars in Atlanta. They realized God was calling them to begin PURE ministry in their church, and went home and did exactly that. This Sunday was a special day of celebration and thanksgiving for what God had done in such a short period of time in ministering to PURE people in their community. Before I spoke, a young PURE dad gave a wonderful testimony of how the church had reached out to his PURE son and his family and what PURE ministry meant to him personally. As I told many others since that day, his testimony was so powerful that we all could have left the service at that point and been greatly blessed. Immediately before I was to speak, the PURE Ministry Project video was played for the audience.

This video is composed of three main segments: the video opens with a number of PURE people of all ages saying "I am a PURE person;" in the second, I simply try to explain the purpose and goal of The PURE Ministry Project; and in the third and last segment, Brent Cochran, pianist and vocalist at my church, Blackshear Place Baptist, performs the song he wrote for our ministry, *"If You Could See Jesus Through My Eyes,"* while wonderful pictures of PURE people are displayed on the screen. Brent beautifully illustrates what is the perspective of a PURE person in the lyrics:

If You Could See Jesus Through My Eyes

Perfectly designed, formed by God's own Hand
PURE gifts from the creator for His plan
All along the journey, we may stumble we may fall
But with God's help, we'll win the race
If you'll answer His call.

If you could see Jesus through my eyes
You'd know the reason for my smile
For a friend who cares, who gives love and shares
For that special touch that only you can give.

If you could see Jesus through my eyes
You'd see much we need your love
If you could see Jesus through my eyes

Oh yes, if you could see Jesus through my eyes.

Although I may seem different, God has a plan for me
And He paints the colors of my life in His master tapestry
If you could see Him through my eyes
You'd see much we need your love
If you could see Jesus through my eyes.

Finally, at the conclusion of the video and as the PURE logo is displayed on the screen, a single PURE child says again, "I am a PURE person." The lights were dimmed in the sanctuary and the video was played. When the video ended, the lights began to come back on and before I could make my way up to the pulpit, six or seven PURE people were standing in the audience and each was saying loudly, "I am a PURE person." "I am a PURE person." The entire congregation erupted in applause and the significance of what had just happened was missed by no one there. I stepped to the microphone and asked a simple question of the people, "Do you realize that this was most probably the very first time that any of these wonderful people have ever been able to stand and proudly proclaim who they are?" True story, true statement.

God had given us the term PURE for us to use to better describe our friends, and in this experience at this church, He not only confirmed PURE for that purpose, but also beautifully and powerfully showed us the power of the word PURE for PURE people themselves. For, you understand, you will not see people proudly proclaim to anyone that "I have cerebral palsy" or "I am developmentally disabled." PURE is a good, positive, and up-lifting identity for the PURE person, both as we use it to talk about them and as they use it to talk about themselves! As our perspective is changed, our new words must reflect the change and PURE does that.

It Really *Isn't* About Me

One final thought as we leave this discussion on perspective. The Apostle Paul says something interesting about our need to identify with or adapt to people in these verses:

> *For though I am free from all men, I have made myself a servant to all, that I might win the more; and to the Jews I became as a Jew, that I might win Jews; to those who are under the law, as under the law, that I might win those who are under the law; to those who are without law, as without law (not being without law toward God, but under law toward Christ), that I might win those who are without law; to the weak I became as weak, that I might win the weak. I have become all things to all men, that I might by all means save some.*
>
> I Corinthians 9:19-22

Paul is stating here the importance of our willingness to adapt to those around us for the purpose of sharing the Gospel. He is saying that flexibility is the key, though certainly not participating in sinful activities with our lost friends; we are to be *made all things to all men* that we may win them to Christ. You all are probably saying to yourself about now, "I've got the new picture, but how in the world am I supposed to do this *adapting* so I can become friends with this little PURE boy down the street? I don't even know what he has and I don't think he is even verbal." Or, "What can I do to genuinely reach out to the PURE man I see sitting on the same corner bench I pass each morning near my work?" The possibilities and opportunities are infinite and if we think too much about what we are to say and do in each and every situation, we'll probably end up thinking of enough reasons not to do anything.

What I am about to say is probably contrary to anything you might have heard or read about relating to PURE people. The world has portrayed virtually all PURE people as intellectually, emotionally, and cognitively impaired. Regardless of their real diagnosis, they are thought of as baby-like, immature, and basically *slow* in every way. All of these worldly portrayals and descriptions of PURE people totally discount and omit the most important fact about PURE people: God has placed something very, very important in them and as we reach out to them in love, Jesus Himself is in the encounter. When we don't care about what people will think, what we need to say to maintain our persona, and are concerned only with touching that other person, *Jesus is there*. Somehow, we are participants in a *divine transaction*. Jesus says when we reach out in His love and power, we have actually and in reality, done *it* unto *Him*!

You're probably still asking yourself, "But how do I get *down* to their level so I can communicate?" NEWSFLASH: As God moves and we begin to see PURE people for the special people they are and the wonderful gifts God has placed in them, we soon discover we don't get *down* to their level – Jesus raises us *up* to theirs.

In conclusion, our perspective, our worldview, should simply be that of Jesus. What He sees, we need to see. What He values should be what we value. Who He loves are those we should love. To do this will cost us. To do this we will have to surrender some of our wrong thinking and give up some of our incorrect presumptions. As Paul said in Phil 3:8 - *I count all things but loss for the excellency of the knowledge of Christ Jesus my Lord*. Paul's words were as true then for him as they are today for us.

As the *PURE* World Turns

I chuckle a little when I think about this, but my mother will do most any anything not to miss her soap operas every day. I joke with her that it would not really be a problem if she missed a day (or week or month, for that matter), she wouldn't have missed much action anyway! One of the most famous popular shows, *"As the World Turns,"* began in 1956 and is still running today. Though I'm certainly not an expert on these kinds of programs, like about all things, I have an opinion. Throughout my life I have occasionally found myself in the room when a "soap" was on TV and before I could gracefully escape, I have watched for a minute or two. I believe that soap operas are popular because they allow the viewer a temporary escape to a simulated, fantasy world. With beautiful actresses and handsome actors playing roles, more often than not of a "professional," for everybody in this world is either a doctor or lawyer, married to one, divorced from one, the illegitimate son/daughter of one, or maybe all of the above! The setting is typically an ideal fictional small town in which things happen *painfully* slow. Consisting mostly only of dialogue and pseudo real life situations, little happens of any significance on any given day without a plot buildup that can last weeks if not months. I believe another reason people watch soap operas is that they can watch for 30 minutes or an hour and if things get too bad or close to home, they always have their real life to reenter. It's all far more complicated than I can understand, but their popularity cannot be disputed.

However, there is another world turning everyday that is not fantasy. It is a world most of us never really think about. It is the PURE world and it is very real and people living in it can't change stations or turn it off. The PURE world (or the world of special needs) is much, much more than any of us have individually experienced. It is ultimately people, just like you and me, born with a disability or who have experienced some disability from an accident, illness, or disease. The words "special needs" or "disability" might make you uncomfortable and this is understandable. We often think of these people in the context of our own perceptions and experiences as we have discussed before.

As we begin to think outside the box of what we believe is normal, we allow God to reshape our thinking, transforming our thoughts to His thoughts, and we see PURE people and their families for who they truly are – and in the numbers that they exist.

Before proceeding, a word about statistics as *fact*. It has been said that you can make statistics prove anything you want, and you probably can. However, statistics regarding disabilities are much, much harder to come by. In fact, there probably exists a subconscious reason that our culture neither wants to nor places a priority on knowing the real statistics about people and families affected by disabilities: if we know, we must act. Further, if we the church knew the real numbers, we would be compelled to do something. In this case, ignorance is truly bliss. Regardless of the reasons, we simply don't have accurate disability statistics available.

The following statistics have been gathered from a number of sources: U.S. census data, various disability organizations, other ministries who have researched statistics like we have at *PURE Ministries*, as well as other secular organizations and associations. We believe that the statistics are as accurate as can be determined given the almost total lack of statistical gathering mechanisms for people with disabilities. Various specific disability groups maintain some types of statistics for people with their particular focused disability, but none for other disabilities. Regardless, perhaps the most glaring error in statistical gathering regarding disabilities is the fact that most published statistics regarding people with disabilities *do not include* children under five years of age or children simply too sick to attend school. In other words, almost all statistics regarding people with disabilities includes *only* people over the age of five, when they reach school age. PURE people do not exist in the statistical world until they reach age five and *rarely exist* if they die before age five! Ironically, it is within this very age category, birth until five, when many children die from disability related causes. Considering this staggering omission as well as other incongruities, I feel the statistics below are nothing if not extremely conservative. We will call them *Realities*.

Throughout the remainder of the book, I will repeat various *statistics*, perhaps even redundantly, in emphasizing certain points. However, I'm not sure any of us can ever really appreciate fully the significance and magnitude of some of these *Realities* that exist in the PURE world. I use them simply to stress again and again: PURE people and their families *do* exist and there are many more people affected by disability than we would ever have first thought or envisioned.

The following *Realities* and *What it really means* about PURE people and their families can be very surprising and sobering:

- *Reality*: Of the 300+ million people in the United States today, over 50 million Americans have disabilities. That means that an estimated 10% – 20% of any given community's population (1 out of 6) will include people who are PURE.

  What it really means: There are many, many more PURE people than most realize. We don't see them in our churches so we assume they don't exist – but *they do in great numbers*. If we take the lowest estimate (10%) to be conservative, and then slice that number in half to 5% to be ultra conservative, we are confronted with a truth, statistically speaking: 5% of the people (1 out of 20) in our churches *should* be PURE people. In other words, a church with 500 members should have a minimum of at least 25 PURE people. It is a very rare church indeed, if one exists at all, that counts among its membership this ratio of PURE people. More about this later.

- *Reality*: When the immediate family is included, somewhere between 25%- 30% of our entire population is directly affected by disabilities.

What it really means: PURE people and their families represent, by far, the largest unreached or unchurched people group in the U.S. today! Cutting across social, economic, racial, and literally all other demographics, PURE people are all around us – except at church!

• *Reality*: Approximately 20% (1 out of 5) children are classified as having some type of disability (in some states this number has reached 2 out of 5 children). Remember, children under 5 are not included in this data.

What it really means: An alarming figure in itself, but particularly alarming when we remember that children under the age of five are not normally counted in any disability statistic. This number would be dramatically larger if these children were included!

• *Reality*: Mostly because of great advances in medicine (particularly with premature births), the PURE population is growing at 3 times the rate of the normal population.

What it really means: Because more and more children are being saved when born prematurely, this number, though seemingly unbelievable, is true. In churches that are serious about reaching all people, we need to consider this when planning for the future.

• *Reality*: When a PURE child is born into a marriage or a child becomes disabled through accident or disease, 4 out of 5 (80%) of these marriages end in divorce – 90% when the disability is autism!

What it really means: Statistics in the United States today say approximately 50% of *all* marriages end in divorce, which makes this statistic even more alarming. As we begin ministry to

PURE people and their families, we will have the opportunity to directly minister to many parents, often many PURE single moms, with PURE children.

- *Reality*: Autism and its yet unknown causes has garnered much publicity lately in America and rightfully so. Autism is somewhat unique in that, since its causes remain elusive, it is considered to be a disability that can be *cured* and possibly even prevented. As of this printing, statistics show that since the early 2000's, the number of children being diagnosed with autism has increased at an annual growth rate of 900%. According to the Center for Disease Control, the incidence of autism has grown from 1 out of 10,000 children in the 1980's, to 1 out of 150 in 2004, and finally to 1 out of 68 children in 2015.

  What it really means: The reality is if autism were a more socially conscious disease, it would be a declared a raging epidemic. Bulletin: IT IS A RAGING EPIDEMIC!

- *Reality*: Stroke is the leading cause of serious, long-term disability in the United States. 28% of people who suffer a stroke in a given year are under age 65.

  What it really means: While most of us assume we are and *will remain* unaffected by disability if we, our children, and perhaps, our grandchildren are normal, this statistic is shocking to most everyone. We tend to think of stroke occurring only with older adults. It is sobering to realize that almost 1/3 of strokes are suffered by people under the age of 65.

- *Reality*: While 70% - 75% of Americans claim to be Christians and statistics regarding disability and faith are poor, we can assume that a much smaller percentage of PURE people (some say less than 15%) can affirm being Christian.

What it really means: We know that confronting someone on the street and asking them whether or not they are a Christian usually results in questionable responses. Most people say they are Christian if they define what it means! At best, if we simply look at the number of PURE people in our churches on any given Sunday, the conclusion is inescapable – we are not reaching them with the Gospel. By default, we are not reaching PURE families, parents and siblings, either.

- *Reality*: Again, statistics are sparse, but by simply observing the church in America and considering the numbers of PURE people, we can safely conclude that the vast majority (perhaps as high as exceeding 90%) of PURE people and their families are not attending any church with any regularity.

What it really means: With so many conflicting, confusing, and many blatantly wrong perspectives of Christianity today in our world, if PURE people and their families aren't in our churches and hearing the word of God, how are they to learn of the real Jesus and His love and mercy?

- *Reality*: PURE children with cognitive impairments are subject to abuse 10 times more frequently than normal children.

What it really means: If we reside in a metropolitan city in the U.S. today, it is a rare week that goes by that we do not hear of a sad incident involving child abuse with the victim being a PURE child.

- *Reality*: PURE people are the group in our society with the highest incidence of poverty, homelessness, unemployment, and suicide.

What it really means: Yes, some PURE people do grow up and it is a sad fact that we find most PURE people on the lower scale of society when measured against other groups of people. In many cases, if and when PURE people move out of their parents' home, we find them in nursing homes, homeless, and/or unemployed. A function of churches serious about PURE ministry is to address these needs as PURE people mature.

• *Reality*: Nine out of ten women, who find out through amniocentesis or other new tests, that their unborn child has Down syndrome, choose to abort the baby.

What it really means: Perhaps no statistic demonstrates more critically the need for PURE ministry and "PURE thinking" (that is, considering PURE people and their God-imputed value) in our churches and culture than this one single fact. The fact that nine out of ten future mothers would choose aborting a child diagnosed in the womb with Down syndrome and would consider this diagnosis worthy of death for the unborn baby, not only should sadden us, but it should alarm and motivate us. We have a huge problem when parents summarily dismiss the blessing of God through this child and the value and worthiness of being that child's mother and father.

• *Reality*: 40% of American pediatricians today view the withholding of nutrition and hydration from infants born with severe disabilities as acceptable practice. The more prominent the diagnosis of mental retardation, the more likely it is that the pediatrician will accept this practice.

What it really means: Though this statistic is difficult to even comprehend, it points up the fact that our culture of doing away with whatever is inconvenient or uncomfortable for us has permeated the medical community as well. It requires little power of prediction to envision what will happen in the future as other people's projected *quality of life* or *value to society* is deemed undesirable, unacceptable, or unworthy - what will happen to these people?

God has so much in store for those who will heed His call and receive unbelievable blessings by becoming involved in the lives of these special people!

WHAT? Christ's Love Lived Out Through Us

What *Exactly* Is PURE Ministry?

PURE people and their families don't want to be viewed as mission projects - but rather, as friends. They want to be treated like everyone else - as normally as possible. For us, as the body of Christ, to treat these precious people as normally as possible, requires us to go beyond what we would normally do. PURE ministry is practical and it need not occur only on Sunday mornings in a formal setting.

As Jesus tells us in the New Testament, relationships are the key:

> *Then one of them, a lawyer, asked Him a question, testing Him, and saying, "Teacher, which is the great commandment in the law?" Jesus said to him, "'You shall love the LORD your God with all your heart, with all your soul, and with all your mind.' This is the first and great commandment. And the second is like it: 'You shall love your neighbor as yourself.' On these two commandments hang all the Law and the Prophets."*
> *Matthew 22: 35-40*

As Christians, we are to love God supremely and our neighbors as ourselves. Jesus loved us *first. But God demonstrates His own love toward us, in that while we were still sinners, Christ died for us. (Romans 5:8)* We have no other option, but to love Him. Having this relationship with the Father is priority #1 for us.

Further, we are to love our neighbor as ourselves. Contrary to popular opinion, we don't get to *choose* who our neighbors are. We are to love everyone God places in our lives. We are to love others as we love ourselves. And, we do love ourselves, don't we?! We never want to look bad, be hungry, be thirsty, be deprived, be unloved … It is with this type love that we are to love those around us — our neighbors.

Genuine relationships are based on needs as opposed to accomplishments. If we look at our intimate relationships, we are only really close to people with whom we can be open and express our hurts and fears. Though in our humanness we tend to form relationships with people like us, real blessing awaits us when we get out of our comfort zone. Yes, we can impress others with our accomplishments and credentials, but true intimacy comes only through transparency.

We Must Be Willing to Get *Personal*

As we begin to consider PURE ministry in our churches, we might find ourselves asking, "Do we really need relationships with PURE people and their families?" The answer in a word is *yes*. PURE interpersonal ministry is nothing if not personal! Though all true ministry involves relationships, PURE ministry *is* relationship. Though we may all not have PURE people in our immediate family, if we are to minister to PURE people and their families, we inevitably will have relationships with them.

We will discuss the personal aspect of PURE ministry in much detail later, but making PURE ministry *personal* simply means valuing the relationships we develop with PURE people and their family members. In many situations, the relationship PURE people have with us becomes the most significant in their lives. Though we are often not aware of this phenomenon, it is not unusual for immediate family members, granddads, grandmothers, aunts, uncle, and even siblings, in some cases, to literally abandon the PURE family. In their inability or unwillingness to grasp and appreciate people in their own family who are confronted with the issues of disability, this abandonment most often manifests by "not coming around" often or "not having time to visit." The results: fractured relationships and the PURE family left wondering where their loved ones are in their time of need. The family members abandoning the PURE family frequently cannot explain or even reconcile their actions to themselves, but unfortunately, it is inescapable that their unwillingness to accept disability in their family is stronger than the love they have for the PURE person and family. The PURE family is left with not only having to deal with these very real issues of living with disabilities, but also having to live with the hurt that often times goes with this abandonment of close family members on which they *thought* they could always depend - and now can't. We obviously cannot make this situation go away and disappear, but we can stand in the gap and become the loving friends that they and their family need and desire *and* can count on. True PURE ministry is *always* personal.

As we will see later, Jesus promises great blessing for those of us who will reach out to people, regardless of how they look, talk, or act. Relating to PURE people especially forces us to learn new ways to communicate and teaches us much about ourselves. In addition to many other benefits, we gain a new sense of thanksgiving. Our patience and new sensitivity to the struggles of others is increased. We find our lives being enriched in inconceivable ways.

Remember,

> *"I can do all things through Christ who strengthens me."*
> *Philippians 4:13*

WHEN? The Time Is Now

What better time to become involved yourself and maybe start PURE Ministry in your church than *now*? Normally, if a church is involved in PURE ministry to any degree, it is because children have been born into the congregation and have grown up among the people. Or, perhaps a teenager in your congregation has had a serious auto accident resulting in severe disability. Or, someone has had a stroke, and they and their families are now facing the new world of disability. The people in the church have become accustomed and have adapted to and love these people and families, and this is in itself PURE ministry. However, as we have looked at the numbers of PURE people and families not in our churches, we propose a revolutionary idea – PURE ministry *on purpose*. Rather than being reactive or responding to PURE people if they happen to attend or if they are born into our church body or if the accident occurs, let us now be *proactive* in seeking these precious people.

In conversations with churches all over the U.S., I have listened to many reasons why churches cannot begin PURE ministry now. These reasons sound perfectly plausible and valid to the church leader explaining why they cannot minister to PURE families at any given time. They generally reflect the prevalent attitude that PURE people and PURE ministry are simply not as important as other people or ministries. Putting PURE ministry in the five-year plan or "we don't have enough room" or "waiting until we get the new building finished" or any other reason or excuse for not reaching out to PURE families now is simply shortsighted and wrong. To check ourselves on these attitudes, we need only ask: would we say this about seniors, adults, teens, or young married couples? It is safe to say we would not, so why then would we feel justified in saying this about PURE people and their families?

Consider also the fact that many PURE children will not have normal life spans. For instance, the mortality rate of children with cerebral palsy is 1800% greater than normal children for the ages one through four, 2700% times for ages five through nine, and 850% times for ages ten through fourteen. Though the mortality rates drop over time for these children, if a person with cerebral palsy lives to the age of fifteen or more, their mortality rate remains much higher than that of the average person[6]. So what does this tell us about many PURE children? We may not have them with us very long and time is precious, that's what! Many of these severely disabled children will only be on the earth a short period of time; this is reality. These PURE families cannot wait for five year plans, space, or new buildings. Perhaps the greatest tragedy in these situations is the fact that so few people experience the blessings of these special children.

Another compelling reason to think more seriously about PURE ministry in our world today is to in some way contend with the callous and unfeeling attitudes held by so many regarding people with disabilities. Disregard of human life is so prevalent in our culture. If we as Christians do not stand up and fight for life, even a life that is judged to have little or no value, who will? In a popular U.S. magazine, we read the following:

The End of Down Syndrome?

Pregnant women are routinely screening for Down syndrome, the most commonly occurring genetic condition. But this year a new non-invasive test will become available that can diagnose Down syndrome and other chromosomal issues with nearly 100% accuracy early in the first trimester. Not everyone agrees on whether this is a good thing. About 90% of those whose fetuses test positive for Down syndrome already choose to abort. With fewer cases being born, parents of children who have Down syndrome worry about support and resources drying up. Parents of children with Down syndrome usually say they can't imagine life without their child. Which opens the question: who decides which genes are unacceptable? Bioethicists note that if you can eliminate Down syndrome, what about genetic alcoholism, obesity, or ADHD, or even homosexuality, shyness, or freckles?[7]

Sadly, we live in a culture that does not value life - particularly, PURE peoples' lives. Given the fact that approximately 1.6 million babies (the vast majority simply for the reason of convenience of the mother) are aborted each year in the U.S., is it really surprising that such articles above would begin to appear *and* be considered advancing our culture? Of course we should make every moral and medically available effort to make the lives of people born with Down syndrome (and every other disability) as normal as possible. But medical science, apart from and devoid of a Christian perspective, has resulted in engineering out what is considered unworthy, and engineering in what is considered worthy and desirable - all in the name of science, and, unfortunately, considered a good thing by most Americans. God, the Creator and Sustainer of all life, is unbelievably and astoundingly left completely out of the formula or debate! With political correctness have come attitudes that, though disguised in moral superiority, are in fact, destructive and disastrous for our country - not to mention those who are deemed unworthy!

In reference to the article on Down syndrome above, the underlying assumption is that this syndrome is bad and people with Down syndrome (or even the potential of people being born with it) are not sufficiently worthy to live. The rational person must ask, "Who gets to decide what is worthy and unworthy?" Has not God already decided, since He *Is* God?

> *Thus says the* LORD *who made you And formed you from the womb, who will help you.*
>
> *Isaiah 44:2*

It is way past time that we Christians stand up to uphold and defend the value of life. Based on Scripture we are being called by the Father, particularly at this point in history, to lovingly, but without apology or compromise, be the voice of reason in a lost and dying world. PURE people and their families are waiting for your help, love, and attention. The Bible says *the fields are white for harvest (John 4:35),* ready for us to act.

WHERE? Right Where You Live

You can start reaching out to PURE people right where you live your daily lives: at the store, waiting for the oil change, at the doctor's office, and in your church! You will be amazed how many PURE people you will see when your heart is open to see them. Within your local body of believers are PURE people or those who have direct contact with family or friends who have need of PURE ministry. Finding these people will not only involve surveys of the church members and the local community, but also being aware as we go about our lives seeing PURE people virtually everywhere we go.

For too long we have fostered a limited and restricted view of just what special needs ministry is and can be. As we have said and will continue to say, PURE ministry is not just on Sunday morning in a special needs classroom. As God opens our eyes to the many possibilities and potential for ministry to these people that we have not traditionally seen in our church pews, we start to see the real meaning and purpose and practice of Jesus on this earth. He did not wait for people who needed healing (physical, emotional, mental, or spiritual) to *come* to the temple - no, He went where they were. As God directs, we begin to physically see PURE people that we never saw before in public places. We see opportunities in that young mother with a child in a special wheelchair at the grocery store, the developmentally disabled young adults from a group home at the car repair shop, or the exhausted and exasperated young mother with an obviously autistic child trying to maneuver the aisles of Wal-Mart. Everyday God begins to present to us opportunities for ministry. We are to touch people where they are and to express His love in places of His choosing. The question remains: will we allow our feelings of being awkward or uncomfortable stop us from being the hands and feet of Jesus? Will we get outside of our comfort zones to touch and be touched by these precious PURE people around us?

There is no need to look very far. PURE people are all around us. Be aware and sensitive and your own PURE ministry can develop within your local church. You'll be glad you did.

WHY? What's the Point?

At the very crux of PURE ministry is the answer to a simple question. "Can't someone else do this?" The short answer to this question is "Sure." But a more important and significant question is, "What blessings will I *miss* if I don't?"

While representing *PURE Ministries* in churches across America, we have the opportunity and privilege of speaking on what Jesus says about PURE people. When speaking to churches, we simply want to help people get a glimpse of what a PURE person is like, what PURE families experience, and how we as Christians can come alongside and help. We try to help people imagine what it's like to be disabled. What is it really like to be blind? What if you could not make sense of all that is going on around you? What if you were trapped in a body that could not respond the way you would like? Or, can you imagine what it would be like to have a doctor come to you in the nursery at the hospital, as you are sharing the news with a joyous and happy family about your beautiful new baby boy or girl, and be told. "There's something wrong with your child?" As you listen to the doctor, you realize that all of your hopes and dreams about your sweet baby will never be what you thought. Your life and the life of your family will never be the same. Or, you receive a call - an accident has occurred, and your teenage son or daughter is involved, and you rush to the hospital. As you enter the emergency room, you are confronted with the news that your child is now paralyzed and will be a quadriplegic for the rest of his/her life. Or, your wife of thirty years suffers a debilitating stroke as you are eating a leisurely breakfast. As you drive away with her and the medical team in the ambulance, you envision the remainder of your married life in a totally different light.

Yes, these situations are only examples, but they are all too real, and they happen every day to ordinary people just like you and me. We can certainly literally thank God that these particular life experiences have not yet touched us perhaps, but what do we do as Christians to those around us who have had experiences like these? Let's look at the Bible and simply see what Jesus says.

Simply Look at What Jesus Did

Without a doubt the clearest reason why Christians today should find themselves interacting with PURE people in their churches and community can be easily found in the accounts of Jesus' life on this earth. For those of us who call ourselves Christians, Christ-followers, the application for us is obvious. If we simply look with whom He chose to spend His time and with whom He chose to invest His efforts, we see it is always the downcast, the poor, and the people in need. In fact, *"When Jesus heard it, He said to them, "Those who are well have no need of a physician, but those who are sick. I did not come to call the righteous, but sinners, to repentance." (Mark 2:17)* Jesus was very critical of the religious people of His day, and chose rather to be with the common man. Though we cannot carry this analogy too far because we do not have the power to actually *heal* people as Jesus did, we can be like Jesus by choosing those who are marginalized in our culture to be our friends and including them in our fellowships.

Evidence of Jesus' strong feelings about our following in His footsteps regarding acceptance of all people can be found in Mark's account of a familiar story. Undoubtedly, we have heard this story about Jesus in Vacation Bible School or in Sunday school. The scene is described in the book of Mark.

> *Then they brought little children to Him, that He might touch them; but the disciples rebuked those who brought them. But when Jesus saw it, He was greatly displeased and said to them, "Let the little children come to Me, and do not forbid them; for of such is the kingdom of God. Assuredly, I say to you, whoever does not receive the kingdom of God as a little child will by no means*

> *enter it." And He took them up in His arms, laid His hands on them, and blessed them.*
>
> *Mark 10:13-16*

Depending on your age, you most probably had this story illustrated on a felt board, whiteboard, or maybe more recently on some other electronic device. Normally, the scene is pastoral: Jesus is sitting on a park bench and surrounded by smiling disciples and beautiful blond hair, blue-eyed children. However, if we look at the meaning of the words that Jesus used and the emotions he expressed, we see a far different picture. The word *rebuked* used by the disciples actually means to "admonish or charge sharply." It is a very strong word, used seldom in Scripture, but used by Jesus when confronting a demon which He cast out of a child in *Matthew 17:18*. The disciples are being condescending towards the parents and forcibly keeping the children away from Jesus. Further, the actual Greek word for "much displeased" (*epitimaō*)) used to describe Jesus' reaction to the disciples is an even stronger word and is never used in describing Jesus' reaction anywhere else in the Scriptures. Not even when Jesus cleansed the Temple was this word used. Jesus was moved with indignation and was extremely angry at the disciples. Why would Jesus be so mad at these men He loved so much? Weren't they simply managing the crowd and keeping a busy Jesus on schedule? Obviously not.

Who were these young children and why were they being brought to Him? In the answer to this question we find the reason for Jesus' anger. If we objectively look at the types of people who approached Jesus to be touched throughout Jesus' ministry, the answer becomes obvious. Could it be that the young children being kept away from Jesus were children with special needs? What type of parents would be bringing their children for Jesus to touch them? Parents of PURE children, that's who!

A disturbing and unsettling parallel can be drawn from this familiar story today. If we liken the disciples' motives and actions to the average church in America today, this scene is unfortunately replayed virtually all over America each Sunday. PURE people and their families try to "come to Jesus" by trying to find a church that will accept them as they are. Sadly, though not intentionally or overtly, we sometimes still find ourselves *keeping* these very same people away -— just like the disciples did. These people are not like us. No, we don't announce it. We don't tell them they are unwelcome, but too often, we just make them *feel* that way by being unprepared. Oh, we tell ourselves we are totally accepting and put it on our signs out front. But again, all too often, our countenances, words, and actions belie our hearts.

If we are to truly be like Jesus in our culture today, it is time to get ready. Being what we must be as Christians, using Jesus as our one and only example, we must be like Him. We must seek the hurting and offer comfort to those in need. PURE people and their families are looking for Jesus. As His disciples, we must commit to lovingly lead them to Him.

Blessing Awaits Us!

Jesus gives us an answer as to what the blessing is in the passage we discussed earlier in *Luke 14:12-14*. In the beginning of this chapter Jesus has been rebuked by the Pharisees for healing on the Sabbath. He has responded with a parable about humility and taking the lowly seat at the wedding feast. He then adds what we read in verses 12 through 14. Again, the dinner invitation is much more than a simple dinner invitation. It is an outward sign of acceptance and friendship and carries with it much more meaning than simply a time together. It is evidence of and a desire for a relationship. If we look closely at this passage, we can easily see the obvious application to us as Christians and our church today.

As he does many times in Scripture, Jesus uses extremes to contrast and make a point. He obviously is not saying literally, *"Do not ask your friends, your brothers, your relatives, or rich neighbors,"* for we know this is not consistent with Scripture. Jesus knows we will do these things: we will surround ourselves with the familiar and remain among those with whom we are comfortable and accepted. However, He is using the extreme to make His point. For example, later in the chapter when speaking on how we are to love Him, Jesus says, *"If anyone comes to Me and does not hate his father and mother, wife and children, brothers and sisters, yes, and his own life also, he cannot be My disciple."* (*Luke 14:26*) Again, Jesus is not saying we must literally *hate* our family, but rather in contrast to how much we should love Him, our love for our family would appear as hate.

So, just who is Jesus saying we should *ask*? And, to where are we asking them? *The poor, the maimed, the lame, the blind* are obviously PURE people – and it should be a priority! In the context of our life and as Christians and in the church, we are asking these people into our fellowship. Because people look, act, or respond differently than we do, it does not exclude them from the love of Christ or His body, the church.

Jesus concludes this amazing statement with an amazing truth: if we do step out in faith and invite the poor, the maimed, the lame and the blind, *we will be blessed!* This is a promise from Jesus Himself. We, who are unfamiliar with the PURE world and PURE people and view it only as tragedy and heartache, at first find this difficult to grasp. However, countless numbers of PURE people, PURE families, and friends of PURE people can attest to the truth of this promise. We are blessed by PURE people through relationships with them and loving them in ways that we never could conceive or imagine. We find ourselves in situations doing things we never thought we would do out of love for people we formerly thought of as nonresponsive or incapable of response. Through these PURE people and families, God blesses us in astonishing ways and changes our lives.

Caution: God at Work

In addition to the promised blessing awaiting us as a result of our befriending PURE people and families, Jesus provides for us another reason of His gift of PURE people to this world. Though we can certainly not fathom the mind, heart, or intentions of God, He does reveal to us just a glimmer of His purposes with PURE people. Recalling the John 9 passage we mentioned earlier, we see God at work:

> *And as Jesus passed by, he saw a man which was blind from his birth. And his disciples asked him, saying, Master, who did sin, this man, or his parents, that he was born blind? Jesus answered, Neither hath this man sinned, nor his parents: but that the works of God should be made manifest in him.*
>
> *John 9:1-3 (KJV)*

Here, as we mentioned earlier, we see Jesus dispelling a myth common not only in his day, but our day as well. When Jesus responds that the man's blindness has nothing to do with either his sin or his parents, He invalidates the common explanation of the day relating to disability; that is, disability is caused by sin. This understanding of disability is sadly too prevalent today as well. In a single sentence Jesus not only destroys the thinking that sin causes disability, but also boldly states that He, God, has created the blind man so that His power can be seen in him. Rather than mistakes, PURE people are specially created by our Father in order to *reveal* His power. Yes, we know Jesus later heals this blind man, but Jesus proclaimed his worthiness *before* He healed him. This blind man, as are all PURE people, whether miraculously healed or not, is a special vessel of the love, mercy, grace, and power of a loving sovereign God.

In summary,

- Jesus *chose* to spend much of His time on this earth with PURE people and we, His followers, should as well.
- We will be *blessed* if we have relationships with PURE people.
- Jesus created PURE people for His purposes and *works through them.*

When Christ returns, He will separate all people into two categories: the sheep and the goats - the righteous and the unrighteous. To be found faithful among the ones who will be rewarded eternally in His Kingdom, He commands us to attend to those who are weak, sick, in prison, and in need. Our calling as Christians, Christ's followers, demands that we care for these PURE people, who yearn for the Bread of Life, and the freedom from sin through salvation that we have found.

It seems that we have no choice in the matter. If our love for Christ is real, we will act upon it joyfully and reach out to everyone we meet! But, there is something else: God has a surprise for those of us who follow Him down this path. There exists a truth about PURE people that is not at first obvious. It is a *truth cloaked in irony* that we examine next.

Truth Cloaked in Irony

But God has chosen the foolish things of the world to put to shame the wise, and God has chosen the weak things of the world to put to shame the things which are mighty; and the base things of the world and the things which are despised God has chosen, and the things which are not, to bring to nothing the things that are.

I Corinthians 1:27-28

A Warning!

You are about to read something that you may not *like* to read. But it is true. In this chapter I will try to deal with probably the most confusing and delicate subject possible when talking about PURE ministry in our churches: why is there so little? The answers to this perplexing question are in themselves also perplexing. What you read may even make you mad when you read it. It also might make you think and reflect a bit. This chapter may also be the most important in the book. If we don't get *this*, there is probably little value in the rest of the book. My difficulty in writing this chapter is this: how do we share with you, our reader, the message we feel we are called to share and, at the same time, communicate the truth that is unsettling at best, and upsetting at worst, to those very same readers?

Vance Havner, the late, wonderful country preacher, is the source of many great quotes. One of his most famous is, I think, appropriate here:

> *Sometimes your medicine bottle has on it, "Shake well before using." That is what God has to do with some of His people. He has to shake them well before they are ever usable.* [1]

Well, it's now time we get shook up! I encourage you to read on - you'll find it interesting. But, if you are easily offended or find it difficult to be introspective, you may want to skip this section and go to the next. If you continue reading, great. But just remember, I warned you.

A Cause *Without* an *Enemy*

In the Beginning ...

I became aware of this issue initially back in 1998 when Zach was born and continued after we started *PURE Ministries*. I have come to a realization and must make a confession: I must admit that I was then and I am now just a little envious and somewhat jealous of most other "causes" and ministries. Let me try to explain why. In 2004, after Zach's death, and after having gone through an upheaval in our own church life, we began *PURE Ministries* because we knew such a ministry was so needed. Naïvely, we set out to reach Christians and churches with our simple message: we Christians have a wonderful opportunity to love a forgotten people in our society, people with disabilities and their families. We never even considered that Christians, once they were made aware of the situation with PURE people and their families not being in our churches, would *not* be eager to hear and receive our message. Surely everyone would respond to this calling once they heard! This was revolutionary stuff we are talking about here - something largely not being currently done in our churches. Our problem, or so we thought, would be how would we manage the great and overwhelming demand of churches for our time - how could we possibly help everyone wanting to start special needs ministries? Man, were we wrong!

It didn't take long for reality to set in. As I said earlier, we began the journey naïvely, and I mean seriously naïvely! However, it became painfully obvious to me after a short while that this was going to be much harder than we initially believed. As my late son, Gabe, once said to a group of people about me, his Dad: "He's not a very smart man, but sometimes he knows what he is doing!" Well, this wasn't one of those times. Over a short period of time I began to notice that phone calls and e-mails to pastors were not being returned. I was told by well-meaning church secretaries (or more perhaps accurately, "gate keepers") too many times that, "We don't need special needs ministry at our church because we don't have any of *them* here." Further, I could literally see people mentally "check out" as I began explaining our ministry when, in doing so, I used those dreaded words, "special needs" or "disability." It became painfully obvious that I had drastically misjudged how the church would respond to *PURE Ministries* and what we were attempting to do. I heard too many times and from too many people comments like, "What you're doing is really great," "What a fantastic ministry," and "This is really needed in our churches." Unfortunately, though not often expressed verbally, because most people were too polite, was an underlying attitude that could basically be summarized by one painfully honest person. She told me, "That's sweet, but I really don't *do* that."

All of this is not to say that God did not bless us with many wonderfully receptive Christians and churches across America in the formative days of our ministry. As a whole, it became obvious most people were just like *me*, before Zach came into my life, when it came to disability ministry. Though I can't remember actually saying these things back then, I know very well now that my pre-Zach attitude could best be characterized by the following:

- Of course I'm a Christian, but I don't know anything about people with disabilities.
- I've never had any real personal contact, much less a relationship, with a disabled person.
- In fact, I don't want anything to do with people with disabilities.
- I don't have any training.
- I'm not a special-needs parent or a special education teacher - they're the folks who are *supposed to do* that.
- I don't even want to *think* about people with disabilities - it makes me feel uncomfortable, because I don't know what to say or do.
- So, I'll just do nothing.

And that's what I did! Until Zach was born and my life and perspective of disabilities were changed forever. What I encountered and experienced then (and continues today) in sharing the message of *PURE Ministries* is simply this: most Christians' understanding, attitude, and *comfort level* with disability was just like mine in my pre-Zach days - I don't want anything to do with it and I don't even want to think about it! This simple revelation was startling and yet comforting to me. I wasn't a *bad* person for thinking this way and neither were these sweet people I was trying to convince. We were simply not *aware* of the blessing God has placed in PURE people!

PURE Ministries' Dilemma

As you can now understand a bit better, we at *PURE Ministries* have a tremendous dilemma, or challenge: we have a message that, on one hand, only comes straight from the heart of Jesus, but on the other, also one that people really don't want to hear. After much prayer and thought, I realized that if I could come to a better understanding of how I perceived disability pre-Zach, then perhaps I could better communicate the need and blessing of PURE ministry to others *like me*. Then it finally occurred to me what the underlying difference was between what we are doing, or attempting to do, at *PURE Ministries* and what other more common causes and ministries were doing. We didn't have an obvious enemy to defeat!

To illustrate, let's consider two very well known, but different organizations/ministries: the American Cancer Society (a secular organization), and Feed the Children (a Christian ministry). If we look at the "mission" (as stated in their own promotional material) of each organization, though initially not obvious, maybe you will see, as I have come to see, a striking, subtle similarity between these (and most every other organization):

The American Cancer Society
"Together with our millions of supporters, the American Cancer Society (ACS) saves lives and creates a world with less cancer

and more birthdays by helping people stay well, helping people get well, by finding cures, and by fighting back. The American Cancer Society is a nationwide, community-based voluntary health organization dedicated to eliminating cancer as a major health problem."

Feed the Children
"Feed the Children is a Christian, international, nonprofit relief organization with headquarters in Oklahoma City, Oklahoma, that delivers food, medicine, clothing and other necessities to individuals, children and families who lack these essentials due to famine, poverty, or natural disaster."

Do you see it? The American Cancer Society, and those that support it intellectually and/or financially, have an enemy: *cancer.* Anybody and everybody are against cancer. Feed the Children, and those that support it intellectually and/or financially, also have an enemy or wrong to right or problem to fix (however you want to view it): *starving children.* Certainly everyone wants every child not to be hungry.

Question: who or what is the *enemy* or *wrong to right* or *problem to fix* for *PURE Ministries?* Before I answer that question, look again at the two organizations. In each of these causes there is an easily identifiable, objective, detached, and *impersonal* adversary! We all might not have had cancer, but probably someone in our family has had cancer. We don't have to have cancer to support fighting it. The opportunities and ways we can participate are most times personally satisfying and pleasant: we feel like we've "done something good." We all have been hungry and have seen the moving pictures on TV of starving children. It is not much of a stretch for us to want to feed precious little children. So why is *PURE Ministries* different? Why can't, generally speaking, "Fighting the Effects of and Issues Associated with Disability" be the rallying cry of *PURE Ministries?* I realize it doesn't have much of a *ring* to it and it wouldn't look good on a t-shirt, but surely, everybody is *against* disability? But, is it a cause that will bring people together arm-in-arm, create warm fuzzy feelings, and find us singing "Kumbaya" in a victory celebration around a campfire? Yes, *everybody* is more or less *against* disability, but that doesn't mean they are necessarily *for* PURE ministry - there is much, much more involved here.

Our Problem

As I have thought and prayed about my attitude in those early days, God has consistently directed me inward to look at my own heart. He has revealed something else about this phenomenon of the natural aversion we all seem to have to this world of special needs and PURE ministry. What is it really that makes it different? I have concluded that it may be too simplistic to blame my envy and jealousy of other causes and ministries only on the reality that they have an objective enemy and we do not. No, there is something else that is more subtle and insidious.

Most probably like you, I will quickly write a check to the American Cancer Society or Feed the Children and occasionally I might even run in a "Breast Cancer Awareness" race. When I do such things, normally I will literally hurt my arm patting myself on the back congratulating myself for doing the right thing and walk proudly away, feeling smug that I have done my duty.

Writing a check or even physically participating in some encouraging, uplifting event doesn't really require much of me - in fact, as I have come to realize, it really requires very little. I can write checks all day, run races, and walk walks when it's convenient, and do other good works that make me feel good and that actually do help the cause. But, again, doing these kinds of things really doesn't affect me *personally* (if I have the money and some spare time) nor do they *enter my personal space*. The longer I talk with Christians about PURE ministry, the more convinced I become that *our* real problem is this *enter my personal space* thing!

You see, when you or I write that check or walk in that fund-raising event with our friends, when it is over, we can walk away and leave it behind. PURE ministry in our churches is fundamentally different. When we start to get even a glimpse of the ramifications of ministering to PURE people and their families in our own church, a realization sets in: "these people" will be walking the halls of *my* church; they might even be in *my* Sunday school class; why they may even sit next to me in *my* pew! See the difference? Most always our support, be it financial or even some enjoyable degree of participation, is really held at a distance from really affecting us and touching our daily lives. It doesn't *enter our personal space*! On the other hand, PURE ministry must and will always be personal!

We certainly understand that PURE ministry in any given church will never involve 100% of everyone who attends that church. However, many times the very prospect of having PURE people around and in *our* own church can stop PURE ministry in its tracks before it ever begins. Our problem is getting beyond impersonal participation to personal involvement - writing checks and attending events are impersonal, while being a PURE child's buddy and friend during Sunday school is personal involvement. Yes, it could stretch us a little. It might be a little awkward. It might even be inconvenient and require some sacrifice of our time, but it would unquestionably be worth our effort.

A great example of this issue of our keeping a distance and the impersonalization of our society is commonly cited as the reason that homes built in America today don't normally have *front* porches. Homes in America used to have front porches - we sat on them and talked with our neighbors as they passed by. Today, many of us don't even know our neighbors two doors down and have only a superficial relationship with our neighbors next door. As Christians we are called to relationships by the great Commandment *(Matthew 22:35-40)*, but how do we actually get there?

"We have met the enemy and he is us"

"Disability" Is *Not* Our Enemy

Pogo was the title and central character of a long-running daily American comic strip, created by cartoonist Walt Kelly and very popular during the 1940s, 50s, and even later. Set in the Okefenokee Swamp in southern Georgia, Pogo and his cast of characters routinely provided a satiric look at the social and political issues of the day. Walt Kelly first used the quote "We have met the enemy and he is us" on a poster for Earth Day in 1970. In 1971, he did a two panel version with Pogo and another character, Porky, in a trash filled swamp. The use of this quote in highlighting the negative human impact on our environment is clear. However, perhaps an even better application of this now infamous quote might better be *PURE Ministries* and its mission to the church.

Consider again the logical premise that *disability issues* should be the common enemy against which *PURE Ministries* should wrestle and convince Christians to fight. Like cancer and children's hunger, *disability issues* seem like a viable and logical target. Much research and many dollars are being invested in finding a cancer cure. Of course, defeating world hunger may perhaps be accomplished in our lifetimes - if enough political despots and dictators are removed from power. Similarly, researchers are busy trying to solve the mystery of such disabilities as Down syndrome and autism. Unfortunately however, unlike cancer and children's hunger, and though research is being conducted in a number of specific disability fields, a cure for all possible disabilities is not likely. One day we may find the gene that causes Down syndrome or even unlock the mystery that is autism, but we will never be able to stop a simple fall which causes a traumatic brain injury. Not to get too theological, but there is something that must be said here about suffering and disability.

No, unlike the American Cancer Society who is fighting cancer and Feed the Children who is fighting world hunger, *PURE Ministries* is *not fighting* something as innocuous as *disability issues*. Disability is not the enemy. Besides, there's not a whole lot we can do about *conquering* disabilities even if we wanted to! Who said *conquering something* was supposed to be the goal of a worthwhile cause anyway? *Defeating* disabilities is not now nor has it ever been even been remotely on the radar of *PURE Ministries*. But then, that's the problem – *who then is our enemy*!?

You may not like the answer, but as Pogo said, "We have met the enemy and he is us!" Note that Pogo didn't say *you* were the enemy - he said "we" (us) are the enemy. Perhaps enemy is too strong a word, but in the case of *PURE Ministries*, we ordinary Christians are the focus of everything we, as a ministry, do. I must tell you that in some of my weaker, less spiritual moments and in my desire to have an enemy, I have actually thought of mounting a marketing campaign with something like the following as our rallying call: *"Help Us Eradicate the Apathetic Christian and Free Up Pew Seats"* or *"Did You Know a Christian Deliberately Ignores a PURE Person in Public Every Two Seconds?"* or *"The Government Just Called Our Church: They're Understaffed and Want to Know if We Could Maybe Help Care for PURE People in some Way."*

No, I agree: a little too much – but, you must admit, these do stress the point even if too convicting - at least it is to me. But, if *we* are the enemy, what are we to do?

The *Illogical* Truth

I'll not even attempt to try to address all of the potential theological issues surrounding a sovereign God and suffering in a fallen creation. For example, is cancer simply a product of a sinful world and polluted environment, are birth defects another example of *rain falling on the just and the unjust*, or is world hunger simply a result of sinful man and corrupt political systems? I certainly don't know the answer to these and other perplexing questions and you probably don't either. But, having gone through the logical steps above and finding no logical answer, God has given me peace and what I believe is the answer relating to disabilities, the *illogical* truth. At the risk of appearing blasphemous, let me present the truth that God has shown me:

> Many times what we encounter and experience on this earth, that we call *bad* or even a tragedy, is, in fact, neither and is, in God's perfect plan, *good*. God is always and forever both sovereign and loving. We certainly will never understand and we can only accept this truth: if God did not want something/somebody to exist/happen, it would not. Therefore it follows, that when anything and everything and everybody does in actuality exist/happen, it has come from the Hand of God - *All things were made by him; and without him was not anything made that was made*). *(John 1:3)* Or, in my more simplistic way of stating this: God has been, is, and forever will be in total control of *everything* - if something isn't, God didn't want it to be; if something is, God wanted it to be.

As discussed earlier, all of us who believe in God will intellectually assent to one degree or another to what we can *understand* and comprehend as the sovereignty of God. Where it gets difficult is when we see, in the world's vernacular, "bad things happen to good people" and are left confused and pondering. We have absolutely no problem embracing God's sovereignty when we get that pay raise, have a *healthy* baby, or perhaps, narrowly escape an accident. God is in control - praise the Lord! No, we have a problem trying to explain a grandson who can't, and never will, walk, talk, see, or do so many other things that we think are essential to a *quality* life. Was Zach a mistake - or worse, was God not in *complete* control of this or so many things we cannot explain in our narrow definition of what is *good*? No, Zach was not a mistake and neither was our God not completely in control of Zach's (or any other person's) creation. Even a passing thought of God not being in control will lead us down a road where we would never want to go. We are left with but one inescapable conclusion: God creates each one of us exactly the way He desires us to be. Wait a minute, you say, *this* is leading me somewhere I really don't want to go and making me think something I don't want to think? You're exactly right, I am. Again, at the risk of sounding blasphemous, let me come right out and tell you that I really don't believe that disabilities are *bad*. Rather, they are simply part of who a given PURE person *is* as a creation of God - how God, in His infinite wisdom and goodness and love, has chosen to make them. He has a plan which is absolutely perfect; who are we to question God?

As I have had the privilege to travel around America, speak in many churches, and meet concerned Christians, many of whom have been PURE people and their parents, over time God has impressed on me a simple truth about His love and sovereignty with respect to disability. This truth initially invoked a great conflict in my spirit and confusion of what I thought I knew about my God. This truth can best be stated as a description of this conflict and confusion God Himself caused in my simple understanding:

- If God is love - and He is!
- He can always only do what is right - and He does!
- If God loves us beyond what we can even conceive or imagine – and He does!
- If God desires only the very best for us as Christians, His children - and He does, as long as we accept the fact that He gets to define what is the very best!
- If God's ultimate desire is to have each of us remain in close fellowship with Him - and it is!
- How do we then explain disability (or cancer or birth defects or many other things we call *bad*) in light of this love?
- Further, how can this loving, sovereign God allow, permit, or using much stronger words (but, nonetheless true), *create* or *cause*: a child to be born with Down syndrome, a young mother

to suffer a traumatic brain injury in a car accident, or, in my case, my precious grandson being born with cerebral palsy, blindness, and a seizure disorder?

Who Are We to Question God?

No, we might not actually admit that we are questioning God, but our actions and attitudes may betray us. A good illustration of this point can be found in the familiar story of Job. However, a simple knowledge of the story does not reveal the depth of the truth that is contained in chapters 38-42 of the book of Job. Job has endured unbelievable hardships and great loss, but has retained his faith. Three "friends" share their opinions of Job's problems and counsel him as to what should be his response. With what appears to be great respect and humility, Job does, in fact, question God (I use the King James because the language is so beautiful and poetic):

> *Therefore I will not refrain my mouth; I will speak in the anguish of my spirit; I will complain in the bitterness of my soul. Am I a sea, or a whale, that thou settest a watch over me? When I say, My bed shall comfort me, my couch shall ease my complaints; Then thou scarest me with dreams, and terrifiest me through visions: So that my soul chooseth strangling, and death rather than my life. I loathe it; I would not live alway: let me alone; for my days are vanity. What is man, that thou shouldest magnify him? and that thou shouldest set thine heart upon him? And that thou shouldest visit him every morning, and try him every moment? How long wilt thou not depart from me, nor let me alone till I swallow down my spittle? I have sinned; what shall I do unto thee, O thou preserver of men? why hast thou set me as a mark against thee, so that I am a burden to myself? And why dost thou not pardon my transgression, and take away my iniquity? for now shall I sleep in the dust; and thou shalt seek me in the morning, but I shall not be.*
>
> *Job 7:11-21 (KJV)*

God, however, who knew Job's heart (and knows our hearts as well), sees through Job's words to his attitude and responds:

> *Then the LORD answered Job out of the whirlwind, and said,*
> *Who is this that darkeneth counsel by words without knowledge?*
> *Gird up now thy loins like a man; for I will demand of thee, and*
> *answer thou me.*
>
>

Job 38:1-3 (KJV)

In other words and in our common day vernacular, God says to Job, "Just who are *you* to question *me?* Buckle up your chin strap, buddy; I've got some questions I need to ask you!" In the next four chapters, and with some of the most beautiful prose ever written, God asks Job some difficult questions concerning creation. For example:

> *Where wast thou when I laid the foundations of the earth? declare,*
> *if thou hast understanding. Who hath laid the measures thereof, if*
> *thou knowest? or who hath stretched the line upon it? Whereupon*
> *are the foundations thereof fastened? or who laid the corner stone*
> *thereof; When the morning stars sang together, and all the sons of*
> *God shouted for joy? Or who shut up the sea with doors, when it*
> *brake forth, as if it had issued out of the womb? When I made the*
> *cloud the garment thereof, and thick darkness a swaddlingband*
> *for it, And brake up for it my decreed place, and set bars and*
> *doors, And said, Hitherto shalt thou come, but no further: and*
> *here shall thy proud waves be stayed? Hast thou commanded the*
> *morning since thy days; and caused the dayspring to know his*
> *place; That it might take hold of the ends of the earth, that the*
> *wicked might be shaken out of it? Where is the way where light*
> *dwelleth? and as for darkness, where is the place thereof, That*
> *thou shouldest take it to the bound thereof, and that thou shouldest*
> *know the paths to the house thereof? Knowest thou it, because*
> *thou wast then born? or because the number of thy days is great?*
> *Hast thou entered into the treasures of the snow? or hast thou*
> *seen the treasures of the hail, Which I have reserved against the*

time of trouble, against the day of battle and war? By what way is the light parted, which scattereth the east wind upon the earth? Who hath divided a watercourse for the overflowing of waters, or a way for the lightning of thunder; To cause it to rain on the earth, where no man is; on the wilderness, wherein there is no man; To satisfy the desolate and waste ground; and to cause the bud of the tender herb to spring forth? Hath the rain a father? or who hath begotten the drops of dew? Out of whose womb came the ice? and the hoary frost of Heaven, who hath gendered it? The waters are hid as with a stone, and the face of the deep is frozen. Knowest thou the ordinances of Heaven? canst thou set the dominion thereof in the earth? Canst thou lift up thy voice to the clouds, that abundance of waters may cover thee? Canst thou send lightnings, that they may go and say unto thee, Here we are? Who hath put wisdom in the inward parts? or who hath given understanding to the heart? Who can number the clouds in wisdom? or who can stay the bottles of Heaven, When the dust groweth into hardness, and the clods cleave fast together? Wilt thou hunt the prey for the lion? or fill the appetite of the young lions, When they couch in their dens, and abide in the covert to lie in wait? Who provideth for the raven his food? when his young ones cry unto God, they wander for lack of meat.

Job 38 (KJV)

Continuing in the next four chapters Job has his ears pinned back by our loving Father. Job is like us: many times, though our words are respectful and dripping with humility, our attitudes and actions about so many things contradict what we say. The truth that God so forcefully and powerfully delivers to Job, and just as importantly to us, is crystal clear: *trust Me; I know exactly what I'm doing and what is best.* This is a hard concept for us when, in what we see or experience, we can *see* absolutely no *good.*

It is exactly this point that I try to communicate at the very beginning whenever I have the opportunity to speak to an audience about PURE people and our ministry. God knows what is best whether we see it as *good* or not. Thinking, but not necessarily saying, that God has made a mistake or was maybe "taking a coffee break" when a PURE person was created, has disastrous effects on our ministry and witness as well as keeping us from the blessing that God has placed in this special person. God is sovereign and that fact is never more important than when we relate to PURE people as His perfect creation.

Please understand that I am in no way trying to minimize or marginalize the difficulties and challenges that PURE people and those who love them and care for them experience 24/7. I can't imagine the frustration and constant aggravation of being a PURE person locked in a body that I can't control, unable to verbally communicate and say what I want to say when I want to say it, or maybe, autistic and incapable of interpreting fully the world in which I live. I really can't imagine these kinds of things. I can only inadequately empathize with PURE people.

Having the privilege of living with Zach for a short time, I do have just a little better understanding of what PURE families experience. I've watched my precious daughter and wonderful son-in-law, though with great heartache and extra burdens, live through it all triumphantly and joyfully. They, like so many PURE parents, brothers, and sisters, as I also, will tell you unabashedly that they would do it all again. That they would not want their PURE loved one to be any other way than the way God created him or her. I have observed PURE people with severe disabilities greatly encourage and inspire other healthy people in amazing and indescribable ways. I have listened as PURE parents have cried before me after losing their PURE child, expressing how thankful they are to God for having had their son or daughter and wishing other people could have been blessed with a child like theirs: PURE!

So what are we to do with all this? Perhaps, it is why many heartfelt and earnest prayers for the *healing* of a PURE person with a disability (be it cerebral palsy, Down syndrome, autism …) are *seemingly* never answered. If you'll grant me a bit of writer's license for a moment, I visualize God, when hearing our prayer to "heal" someone He has perfectly created, respond, *"Heal? Of what? I made him/her this way!"*

An *Adult Spiritual Baby* Grows Up

As I mentioned earlier, if you would have approached me and asked me about my spiritual condition and whether there was evidence of Jesus living in and through my life in 1998, I would have quickly assured you (with as much humility as I could muster) of the following: "I love Jesus with all of my heart, I am chairman of the Deacon Board of our church, I am teaching Sunday school, I am leading trips to the Amazon with mission teams, and I am being the best Christian I know how to be." I would have honestly told you all of these things and I would have been truthful - with the exception of one major caveat which I did not understand or was not even aware of at the time: I was *doing, being, and loving* with the spiritual capacity that I possessed at the time - a capacity and depth that I would soon learn was very shallow. At that time in my life, I am sad to admit it, but for all practical purposes, I was in reality, an *adult spiritual baby*: prideful in my activity, but with not much depth. I was an adult *physically*, but still a baby *spiritually*.

In retrospect, I look back and know that, though I may have been content with my righteousness, God was not. Thankfully, God didn't feel the need to get my permission before He took action. His *way* was to give me a PURE grandson - and to our family, a person who would change our lives and draw us all so much closer to Himself! How, by anyone's definition, could I call or label this situation *bad* or *tragic*?

As I try to explain to anyone who will listen, I am, personally, the absolute best and worst example of a Christian's response to PURE people and their families. Prior to Zach's arrival on the earth, like so many Christians, I thought I was sensitive to His calling and to what He would have me do. As it turned out, I didn't have a clue! Before you dismiss me simply as being a carnal Christian then, I don't think I was appreciably much different than many Christians are today - at least in attitudes toward and perspective of PURE people and their families. Though I might have physically seen PURE people out and about and even knew several PURE persons, I was completely insensitive to them, unaware of what their lives were really like and felt absolutely no responsibility or compunction to reach out to them.

You would think I would be just a little more aware of PURE people, for God gave me an earlier experience that opened my eyes for just a moment, before I shut them again until Zach came along. In my former church, we had annual mission conferences in which some of the missionaries that we supported came for a week so we could get to know them and hear of their experiences in mission focused services. Different church members volunteered to keep the missionaries in their homes for the week and we once had the opportunity to have a vision-impaired young missionary lady stay in our home. She had been totally blind since she was three years old and was serving in Africa at the time. I picked her up that opening day of the conference at church and brought her home to meet my wife and kids. Right before we had to go back to the church, I took her to our downstairs apartment area where she was going to stay. She asked me all about the room and bathroom as I showed her around, and then we went back to church. After the service we all came back home and had a great time of fellowship. At bedtime, I stood and allowed my missionary friend to take my arm to lead her back downstairs to her room. As I opened the door to the stairs leading to the dark downstairs, I reached and turned the light on. My friend kindly said to me, "You don't need to do that for me, I can make it fine by myself." She released my arm and, as I watched her descend the stairs to the darkness, I turned the light off and shut the door. Though I think about this experience often, even this sobering confrontation with blindness didn't wake me up. I *chose* to remain ignorant. I *chose* not to empathize with this remarkable young PURE woman. I *chose* to stay in my comfort zone. God had more work to do on me.

No, PURE people were still truly invisible to me. I felt perfectly justified doing nothing. It wasn't my responsibility. I understood the great Commandment. Or, at least I thought I understood it - as long as I could pick my neighbors! Unfortunately, I can't and neither can any of us who name the name of Jesus. In my life, God used the life of a little boy to help open my eyes to the blessing of PURE people. I realize that everyone will not necessarily be a PURE granddad, grandma, mom, dad, brother, sister, aunt, uncle, or cousin, but we can all experience the blessing of PURE people around us if we will only allow God to open our eyes and hearts.

This brings me once again to *us* as being the enemy. You and I, as Christians, are certainly not the enemies of PURE ministry in any traditional sense. Rather, we are the enemy because of: our unwillingness to really see the PURE; our inability to see their worthiness for our time or attention; our fear of them personally; our mistaken and prideful assumption that we have no responsibility or accountability to God in reaching out to them with the love of Jesus; and, our apathy. These are the real enemies. In a word: *pride.*

I and many others, who feel called to reach and encourage the church to minister to PURE people and their families, are told by far too many well-meaning but unaware Christians, that reaching out to this group of people is not their responsibility. Before Zach, I, like the great majority of Christians in America today who are virtually unaware of the PURE world, felt perfectly justified in my/our position. I am not trained to interact or communicate with these people. Besides, there are not many of them. I feel uncomfortable around them and I might say or do the wrong thing. Somebody else or some other church really should do something about them. And the list of rationalizations goes on and on.

The Age of Entitlement
in the Church

Do any of these thoughts or statements sound familiar? If they do, don't feel like the Lone Ranger. But, if our attitudes and perspectives about PURE people and their families are wrong, what can we do about it? Is our pride, our unwillingness to feel awkward, uneasy, and uncomfortable in even token personal encounters with those unlike us, keeping us from involvement? Rather than being focused solely on PURE people as one would normally think, PURE ministry is actually focused on us Christians. It is the intent of PURE ministry in addressing the often mistaken and erroneous attitudes and perspectives of us Christians that makes PURE ministry so unique. I believe it is this underlying discomfort, apathy, and fear that paralyze most of us from reaching out specifically to PURE people. These same attitudes and perspectives keep us in our comfort zones and in many cases limit our witness to only those around us who are similar to us – only *neighbors* with whom we are comfortable merit our attention and consideration.

Much has been spoken and written recently about the attitude of *entitlement* so prevalent in America today. It is in the news constantly and is cited as the root cause of many ills in our society, perhaps not the least of which is our enormous national debt! This attitude is best exemplified in expressions, sometimes stated but most often demanded, like: "I deserve this," "It's not fair that they have _____ and I don't," "We all should be equal," etc. Much has resulted from this entitlement attitude, and it has even found its way into our churches. David Platt, in his controversial new book, "*Radical*" tragically describes the result of this mindset in the typical American church:

> *Dependent on ourselves or desperate for His Spirit? This is where*
> *I am most convicted as a pastor of a church in the United States*

*of America. I am part of a system that has created a whole host
of means and methods, plans and strategies for doing church that
require little if any power from God. And it's not just pastors
who are involved in this charade. I am concerned that all of
us – pastors and church members in our culture – have blindly
embraced an American dream mentality that emphasizes our
abilities and exalts our names in the ways we do church.*[2]

As Dr. Platt explains, we have been deceived, or rather, deceived ourselves. We talk a good game, but our reasoning is faulty. Tragically, we have convinced ourselves that we *deserve* certain things, *don't* deserve others, and can justify our position with Christian-sounding, but badly mistaken reasons. We may not actually *say* these things, but we certainly *think* like this:

- Since I don't have any training,
- Since I'm not a special-needs parent or a special education teacher,
- Since I've never had any real experience with a disabled person,
- Since even being around these people makes me feel uncomfortable and awkward,
- Since I don't even want to *think* about people with disabilities,
- Since I really don't want anything to do with people with disabilities,
- Then, everything is okay, I don't *have to*, because:
- Somebody else or some other church will do it and, will do it better! That's the government's job - isn't it? The Bible doesn't specifically tell me I need to do this! I'm going to Heaven anyway, so what's the big deal?

Assume for a minute you can identify with me in at least thinking through some, if not all, of the reasons above that we feel justify our attitude of inactivity in reaching out to people. Now, let's ask ourselves honestly: does this reasoning determine the limits of and define our own individual spiritual comfort zones? I truly believe it does. Again, the reasons and conclusions listed above as grounds for the lack of our involvement can be applied to virtually any group of people or individuals in our culture, such as the homeless, people with addictions, etc. Here, we are limiting our discussion to our apparent aversion to PURE people.

The conclusions we reach serve to demonstrate the subtle way an attitude of entitlement has silently crept into the church and affected not only our attitudes, but more importantly, our actions.

If we do come to the conclusion that, "Everything is okay; I don't have to," what are the ramifications of such a decision? Well, let's examine our reasoning and see.

Call Somebody Else!

It is very easy for us to believe that some other Christian or that fictitious church on the other side of town will do what we don't want to do and what we, deep in our hearts, know we should do and do it better than we can do. You know that church: if you go to a small church, it's that big church with all the money and resources; if you go to a big church; it's that small church that can be more flexible and adaptable than your church. You know that church: the church that can surely do *it better*. Unfortunately, that Christian who goes to that other church in town is thinking the same way about your church! The result: we are all feeling warm and righteous that the *other* church in town, because they have Christians who are better qualified, is doing a great job ministering to *those* people. Plus, we don't have to change anything in our church! This is a sad result of us Christians deluding ourselves. The *it* we're telling ourselves we can't do, or are not qualified to do, is simply loving and relating to the people God brings into our lives. As Christians, we have seemingly forgotten that it is not us, but He, Jesus Christ, that is in us. It is Jesus that is to be lived out in our lives! Since when did Jesus, living through us, lack the power to do *anything*!? We comfort ourselves with not only poor reasoning but, worse, false doctrine. Of course, in our flesh and in our own power, and experience, and knowledge, and ... we have no ability or power to do anything. It is only through the power of the Holy Spirit within us that we can be what He wants us to be. It is Jesus who directs, empowers, and lives through us! As Christians, we have everything we need to reach out to anyone in any situation and anytime - particularly PURE people and their families.

Where exactly did we ever get the idea that only the people who can do it *better* are the only ones to do it? And who said they could do it better anyway? If we love, relate to, and care for people with the love of Jesus, who is to say one Christian is doing *it* better than another? It ought to be obvious now that this reasoning is nothing but an excuse for many of us.

This debilitating and fatalistic attitude that is so common among us now is only the tip of the iceberg. The real problem is the entitlement mentality underlying this reasoning. I fear we have reached the point today in our churches where we feel like it is our right *not* to do anything that we feel uncomfortable doing or don't want to do. We are entitled, or so we believe, to do only what we feel comfortable doing, or what fits into our own comfort zones. We now live in a world where many of us Christians feel perfectly justified in establishing for ourselves, apart from any real Scriptural basis, what we will and won't *do*. Of course, God gives us freedom and free will to do whatever we desire, but if we stay in our comfort zones, one thing is sure: we will not grow as Christians. Yes, we can logically explain it all away to each other, but what can we really tell Jesus who has commanded us to be, and might I add, *expects* us to be, the flavoring, preserving *salt of the earth*? We may be comfortable, but we will miss the blessing and joy God has in store for those who are obedient.

Isn't That the Government's Job?

The short answer to the question, "Isn't that the government's job?" is a resounding NO! We as Christians are not immune to the entitlement frame of mind that has so infected our culture. As a society, we have allowed politicians to assume more and more power and authority and with it, assume more and more responsibility that once was ours. Even a quick review of our Constitution will find not so much as an implication, much less mention, of many of the activities, jobs, and overall responsibilities now under the control of our federal, state, and local governments. For example, most Americans believe it is the responsibility of the government to educate our children. Nothing could be further from the truth.

Not to get too political, but with our federal government assuming responsibility for and taking over so many aspects of our lives, I believe even conservative Christians have fallen into the entitlement trap. We have given silent permission and approval with our apathy. For example, we may get incensed when a local public school system prevents our children from singing Christmas carols, but have we ever stopped to question where, when, and why we even have public schools in the first place? Where in the Constitution is the government given the authority and power to educate our children? You won't find it there (or many other functions routinely assumed and controlled by our government either!), and yet, we, like sheep, go right along with the crowd and simply assume that's the way it's supposed to be - in fact, we reason, it makes sense, we don't have to do *it*, it's convenient *this* way, and anyway, we *deserve it!*

Public education in America was mostly localized and rare until the late 1800's. It was during the 1890's that the Progressive Education Movement began and its influence is still so prevalent today. It is interesting to note that John Dewey, perhaps the most well known individual associated with the growth of public schools in America and whose philosophies and values were so influential, was one of the original signers of the 1933 "*Humanist Manifesto*." It is no secret that secular humanists have been not only interested in but have essentially guided America's education system for nearly a century. They have been absolutely successful in teaching children that God is imaginary and contrary to science. Christians, like other Americans, simply accept the idea that it is the government that is charged with educating our children. From a Biblical perspective, there is nothing in Scripture that would give us this idea, but now we believe that we and our children are *entitled* to this education. In education and in so many other aspects of our lives, we have abdicated our responsibilities both as citizens and more importantly, as Christians, to a government more than willing to assume and to use these roles for its own benefit and purposes.

Unfortunately, this attitude of entitlement has so changed our churches that we now commonly expect the government to do many of the things that we should be doing as Christians. Nowhere is this more dramatic than in the area of what is commonly called "social services." Not only is the government in control of education, but we have also blindly allowed the government to feed the needy, care for the indigent, provide medical care to the sick, house the poverty-stricken, and perform virtually all other ministry that formerly would be our responsibility as the church of Jesus Christ. In so doing, we have not only abdicated our role in our culture, but we have, though unintentionally perhaps, greatly reduced the scope, depth, and the impact of Christianity in our culture. What a tragedy and indictment against us as Christians!

Though most government supported and operated mental institutions have now closed, once viewed as the epitome of the government doing something we, as a society, did not want to do, we still look to, expect, and depend on the government to care for these and other PURE people in our communities. Question: "How did we get here?" The easy answer is pragmatism. It is more *practical* for a large entity like our government to do the heavy lifting than it is for us at the local church. Or so we think. Once again, try as we like, we will find nothing in our Constitution that dictates that the government is to do all that we now expect it to - especially in the area of PURE ministry. With all of their money and infrastructure, can't the government do a better job, we may ask?

First of all, it is not their money, it is ours; and second, no, they can't do a better job. How can an impersonal, detached, dispassionate, government do a better job of caring for and loving those in need in a local community than Christians in our churches, empowered by the Holy Spirit? "That would take so much work, money, and time, and *we* would have to do it. How could we ever do such a thing?" Yes, it would, and that is a much bigger issue than can be addressed here. Can you imagine our communities if our local churches were being what we are called to be in ministry vastly beyond what we are currently content with doing? It is something to pray about, think about, and work towards – and it's biblical!

More practical and pragmatic, however, is what we can realistically do today, both individually as Christians and corporately as churches, in ministering to PURE people and their families in our communities. As we have discussed the *Luke 14: 12-14* passage earlier, we Christians are not to be isolated or segregated unto ourselves. Rather, we are to be inclusive and all-embracing as we *invite the poor, the crippled, the lame, and the blind.* It is not only our responsibility, but it is our opportunity to be Jesus in our flesh. Embracing them with the love of Christ by becoming their friends, providing respite for the PURE family, and welcoming them into our fellowship is something *only* we, as the body of Christ, can do. Neither the government, secular organizations, nor any other entity has the power, ability, or the Person to do this – only we do! We are uniquely positioned, have the necessary infrastructure (there are churches on virtually every corner), well staffed, financially able (God owns *all* the money), and supernaturally empowered to do this - the government doesn't come close.

The Bible Doesn't "Tell Me So"

This is an easy one - no, it doesn't specifically tell me I must do this. However, the Bible also *doesn't* specifically tell me to love my children or drive within the speed limit. The Bible is God inspired and is the inerrant Word of God. *All Scripture is given by inspiration of God, and is profitable for doctrine, for reproof, for correction, for instruction in righteousness. (II Timothy 3:16)* The Bible is completely sufficient and correct in specific do's and don'ts. However, if we attempt to live our lives solely by the specifics and not by its *principles* as well, we could find ourselves committing many, many sins of omission as well as commission. In our attempt to keep only the explicit do's and don'ts, ignoring the principles of Scripture, we will also invariably become legalistic and judgmental of others.

No, the Bible doesn't tell me (or you) specifically that we must love, befriend, speak to, or even acknowledge a PURE person. However, how could a Christian defend *not* loving anyone when we are told to love even our *enemies - But I say to you, love your enemies, bless those who curse you, do good to those who hate you, and pray for those who spitefully use you and persecute you? (Matthew 5:44)* How can we allow our unwillingness to subject ourselves to a situation that may be initially a bit uncomfortable, uneasy, or awkward, when we claim to follow the One who doesn't even have a place to *lay His head? (Luke 9:58)*

I'm Going to Heaven Anyway, So What's the Big Deal?

This is an easy one too. I won't even begin to address the many issues of eternal rewards as mentioned prominently in Scripture. Too many of us find the whole idea of rewards too confusing and hard for us to understand. This entire concept of inequality in Heaven based on our finite and inadequate understanding of what Heaven will be is beyond us. Here's the deal. Contrary to some unsound Bible teaching being espoused by some in pulpits today, and though Jesus has no *requirements* for being saved other than simple faith in Himself as expressed in the ABC's of salvation: (A) Admit to God that you are a sinner; (B) Believe that Jesus is God's Son and accept God's gift of forgiveness from sin; and (C) Confess your faith in Jesus Christ as Savior and Lord. He does have *expectations* for His children.

No, we won't lose our salvation if we have placed our trust in Jesus Christ as our Savior and don't get out of our suffocating comfort zones and love PURE people, but we will miss out on unimaginable blessings, both here now and in Heaven later, if we don't. Guaranteed! It is very difficult to explain to someone who has not experienced the wonderful gifts God has placed in PURE people, but based on my limited but profound experience with them, I have personally discovered, as will you, that:

- God never moves among us more powerfully or beautifully as He does through crippled or stilled legs.
- God never touches us as tenderly or as profoundly as He does through frail or unmoving fingers.
- God never speaks to us more clearly and lovingly as through seemingly unintelligible words or silenced lips.

Missing this *is* a big deal.

At the end of the day, it is apparent that most of us Christians have bought into entitlement in one way or the other. We are perfectly content to volunteer to do things in our church that make us feel good, require little effort, not take too much of our time or money, and somehow check the fictional box in our minds that says we have met our spiritual obligations. As long as we feel righteous and meet our own self-defined standard of doing *enough*, we're happy. Until we search the Scriptures, that is.

When we do, we will not find the word *volunteer*. However, we will find the words *servant* and *serve*. In fact, depending on your preferred translation, a more accurate rendering of both the verb and noun forms of *minister* is *serve* and *servant*, respectively. When Jesus' time on this earth was measured in hours and He entered the upper room to speak to His disciples for the last time about the most important things He wanted them to understand, He did something that caught them all by surprise.

> *Jesus, knowing that the Father had given all things into His hands, and that He had come from God and was going to God, rose from supper and laid aside His garments, took a towel and girded Himself. After that, He poured water into a basin and began to wash the disciples' feet, and to wipe them with the towel with which He was girded.*
>
> *John 13:3-5*

Even in His last minutes on this earth Jesus Himself was a *servant.* He modeled servanthood in the upper room as He washed the disciples' feet before He went to the Cross.

Paul certainly didn't *volunteer* either. As he said to King Agrippa as he was recounting Jesus' words to him on the road to Damascus,

> *Now get up and stand on your feet. I have appeared to you to appoint you as a servant and as a witness of what you have seen and will see of me.*
>
> *Acts 26:16 (NIV)*

No, Paul thought of himself as a servant to the Lord Jesus from the time he met Jesus until he took his last breath. *Servant, not volunteer.* He refers to himself as he writes in his epistles not only as *apostle of Jesus Christ,* but also *a servant of Jesus Christ.* Not one time does he describe himself as a *volunteer.* Further, he tells us this:

> *This mystery is that through the gospel the Gentiles are heirs together with Israel, members together of one body, and sharers together in the promise in Christ Jesus. I became a servant of this gospel by the gift of God's grace given me through the working of his power. Although I am less than the least of all the Lord's people, this grace was given me: to preach to the Gentiles the boundless riches of Christ,*
>
> *Ephesians 3:6-8*

If Jesus considered Himself a servant, and since Paul, perhaps the most influential Christian to ever live, also considered himself a servant, then why would we think of ourselves any differently? Why do we think it is okay to volunteer *only* when it is convenient, when we have the time, etc, when our Lord counts Himself as a servant? Are we entitled to something less demanding?

Our impression is that we are not so much entitled *to* something, but rather we are entitled *from* something. It's not that we see ourselves entitled *to* a comfortable, nurturing, secure Christian fellowship with requisite inspirational worship services (music and worship style to our liking, of course!) No, we are more subtle than that. We don't say it, but our actions, or in this case, our inactivity betrays us. In some strange way, we assume that we are entitled:

> *Not* to *have* to do anything that we don't *want* to do or
> *feel* inadequate or uncomfortable doing.

This is a sad state for us who worship the Creator of the universe and our own personal Savior whom we also profess to be the Lord of our lives. He waits, desiring and willing to empower us, to do literally anything and everything He has planned for us. What *are* we thinking?

The Christian's Response and Responsibility

So, if Pogo is right (and I'm afraid he is) and we are in fact the enemy that keeps us from reaching out to PURE people and their families, then what can we do? It's much easier to just do what we've always done or what is comfortable and familiar than it is to take a risk and do something beyond what we thought we could or should do. What is it that causes us to stay in our comfort zones and keeps us from taking that risk?

Perhaps it is not true about all ministries, but for PURE ministry the single most powerful barrier to our reaching out to PURE people is *fear.* We will discuss this barrier now and later, but fear alone is undoubtedly the most significant and troubling obstacle we commonly face. In most cases this is not a physical fear of PURE people, for many PURE people are but children. It's not so much that we are fearful of the PURE person himself, but rather it is the *imagined situations* we fear. It is a fear of envisioning ourselves in situations where we would not know what to do or what to say or how to respond. When fearful, we all can tend to think in worst-case scenarios. In reality these *imagined* situations seldom develop. For most of us this fear is rooted deeply in our pride: it is a fear of our becoming *transparent.* Let me explain it this way. If you choose to get genuinely involved in PURE ministry, it is almost a certainty that you will find yourself in situations dealing with people who literally don't care about the many accomplishments, status symbols, or reputations on which we believe our very identity is based. In a normal setting we can impress people with our educations, where we live, what we drive, or our job. You may find this hard to believe, but the great majority of PURE people could care less about these things - they care only about being your friend and relating to you as best they can. Oh, that the rest of us could be like this! However, it is this prospect of discovering ourselves in the presence of a PURE person who sees us so transparently that is often so threatening to us. As we learn quickly, we cannot impress them with our stuff nor can we control the situation; this is what, in reality, keeps us in our comfort zone.

Ironically, one of the greatest blessings of being around PURE people is this transparency! For the most part, God has made them this way. It may at first scare us, but if we persevere and stay for a while, their transparency causes us to become transparent as well.

Fear is a powerful force in our lives, whether we will admit it or not. Boyd Bailey, in his inspirational *"Wisdom Hunters"* devotional book, describes this fear and the biblical solution to being victorious over it:

> *Do not let divorce, death or disappointment exclude you from the Lord's strength. Work will get you down. People will let you down. Failure will knock you down. Your greatest fears may cause you to wake up in the middle of the night in a cold sweat. Fight fear with fear. Let the fear of God strengthen you, as it fortifies your faith in Him. "Teach me your way, LORD, that I may rely on your faithfulness; give me an undivided heart, that I may fear your name" (Psalm 86:11). The greatest energy drainer may be serving God in our own strength. This is one of Satan's most effective schemes. He wants to occupy us in good activity void of eternal energy. Serving God and others in our own strength means we are driven by what we can do for God, rather than what He can do through us. It's the difference in being energized in our service or being drained by our service. Christ's strength comes from being still. He strengthens your soul in daily quietness before Him. His whisper of affirmation motivates you to walk with Him. It is learning to trust in Him and not strive for Him.*[3]

There are many things, both real and imaginary, that can cause great fear in us. I can remember many times waking in the middle of the night worrying - can you remember worrying like this, too? I thought so. Fear is a common emotion in all of us, but God does not want us to live fearfully. *For God hath not given us the spirit of fear; but of power, and of love, and of a sound mind. (II Timothy 1:7)* Fear can literally knock us down and keep us less than God desires for us to be. Boyd Bailey's recommendation as the solution for our fear is not new, but it's true. Our only real solution to rid us from this that can paralyze us is to fear or simply lovingly depend minute by minute on the strength of the Lord.

What then is required of us to reach out to minister to, and to be ministered to, by all those God puts in our path who are different from us and, in times past, from whom we would turn away? Is there a magic book somewhere that will give us instructions - that will tell us what to do, what to say, how to respond? In a very real sense there is, and it is the Bible itself.

Our Wake-up Call

As mentioned above, when we first publicized The PURE Ministry Project as our main ministry focus, we began using the following tag line to describe what it all meant: *A wakeup call for Christians - Transforming the way we think - A Christian Awakening, a Nationwide Project to Increase Awareness of and Ministry to People with Disabilities and Their Families in our Churches.* Besides the notion of a wake-up call and a Christian awakening, by far the most important phrase is *transforming the way we think* as we discussed above. The apostle Paul states this principle like this: *I beseech you therefore, brethren, by the mercies of God, that ye present your bodies a living sacrifice, holy, acceptable unto God, which is your reasonable service. And be not conformed to this world: but be ye transformed by the renewing of your mind, that ye may prove what is that good, and acceptable, and perfect, will of God. (Romans 12:1-2)* Much has been written about this wonderful chapter in Romans and more particularly these two verses and we will not take time here to delve into all the riches contained here. Let's look for just a moment at verse 1.

Paul first tells us that we must *present* our bodies as a living sacrifice, which is in itself an intriguing statement. I think we can all commonly agree that throughout all of the Old Testament where sacrifices are mentioned, though the sacrifices spoken of may be different animals, there is one common characteristic about all of them: they end up dead! Now here in the New Testament, similar to Jesus as being our sacrifice, Paul is instructing us to be *living sacrifices*. A question: *What* actually is to be sacrificed that is *holy, acceptable unto God?* I believe Paul's meaning is clear as we read on to verse 2: *We* are to be living sacrifices. It is simply saying that:

- Based on what Jesus has done for us with His atoning love on the Cross in the past,
- What He is doing for us today as we live in the present,
- And what He has done in preparing a place for us in Heaven to be with Him someday eternally in the future,
- Then, we are to sacrifice *our* desires, *our* goals, *our* pride, and *our* very lives for Him and His kingdom. This is our *reasonable* service or worship.

What does this type of sacrifice really look like in our lives today? Once again, I turn to a PURE person for an example of true sacrifice as best we can understand from the human perspective. My friend David Nasser, a wonderful pastor, speaker, author, and truly visionary theologian, recalls a story in his book, "*A Call to Die*," that sheds some light on sacrifice.

> *My little brother Benjamin (I say "little," but he outmuscles me by about twenty pounds), has Down's syndrome. He is very, very special in many ways. Benjamin, much like other people with Down's, is very routine-oriented. Breaking a habit for him literally takes a miracle. One of his most deeply rooted habits was his love for country music. He was an Iranian redneck! He has the three-pound belt buckle; starched wranglers; numerous cowboy hats; a full country stage complete with drum set, guitars, lighting, and sound equipment; and just about every country CD out there-you get the point. Needless to say, for his high school*

145

graduation gift, he asked me and Jennifer to get him tickets to see his favorite country music stars at an all day festival. $400 got him the best seats in the house. For days and days, all Benjamin could talk about was the festival. The problem was that the only person available to take him was Mom, who happens to be the Iranian version of Grace Kelly - sophisticated and reserved-not your typical country music fan. However, she loves Benjamin so much that she gladly volunteered.

The day after the concert, I called Benjamin to see if he had a good time and if Mom had survived. When he picked up the phone, Ben told me he could not talk now because he was saying goodbye. Before I could ask, "Goodbye to what?," Mom picked up the phone. Excitedly, she began to tell me what was going on. Apparently, after having been at the concert all day, on the drive home Ben looked at Mom and said' "God didn't like some of the stuff that happened at the festival today, did he?" As Mom and Ben reflected on the behaviors they had seen-the cursing, drinking, suggestive clothing, drugs, etc. - Ben came to the conclusion that it broke the heart of God. Some of it had even happened on stage. To Benjamin it was simple, what he saw broke the heart of God, so it broke the heart of Benjamin. He decided right then and there that he didn't need to have anything to do with country music.

That morning when I called the house, Ben was putting all his country CD's into a box and was going to get rid of them. As someone ingrained in the habit, this was a major sacrifice, probably one of the toughest of his life. To some, this might sound like legalism, but in the crucible of the choice, Ben followed the Father. He didn't see the point in offering anything to God that cost him nothing. (II Samuel 4:24) [4]

As Benjamin Nasser so trustingly exemplifies obedience in the above story, we, too, have a decision to make. Based on what Jesus has done for us, *everything*, it is then reasonable that we give up *everything* for

Him. Simple concept, difficult living. This means we keep breathing, but it is Jesus who gives us breath. We keep hearing, seeing, feeling, and living, but it is Jesus who gives it all meaning. We keep loving, but it is Jesus who gives us the capacity to love. Though we continue to live physically, we also die to ourselves, that is, sacrifice ourselves, our desires, our pleasure, our prideful perspective, everything we are for Him and His Kingdom. Again, Paul says this beautifully in his letter to the Galatians, particularly in *Galatians 2:20 - and the life which I now live in the flesh I live BY the faith of the Son of God*. Yes, we keep living, but it is Christ who is living through us. This ought to give us incredible confidence in living our lives! Though important and seemingly insurmountable to us, our daily trials and tribulations are minor to our indwelling Savior. These same trials and tribulations which we do our best to avoid serve as the platform on which He demonstrates His power, His love, and His watch care over us. Even the faith that we need *in* Him is supplied *by* Him. We have no fear of failure for Jesus is all powerful. We need not fear anything because we have been given and now possess the actual *faith* of Jesus Himself. How our lives would change if we could fully comprehend what Paul is trying to tell us.

Comfort to Confidence

This brings us now to what exactly our response and responsibility are in regard to PURE ministry. Have you ever found yourself in a situation of being profoundly blessed by God only to realize that, if truth be known, you wouldn't have even been in the place to be blessed if it had been solely up to you? It's happened to me many times. I don't want to go back to church on Sunday night because I am just too tired, nobody will notice or care that I'm not there. Then, I decide to go despite all the good reasons not to, and God touches me there in a new and wonderful way. What a blessing I would have missed if I had chosen to stay in my own little comfort zone! It's probably happened to you when you didn't want to help with Vacation Bible School or teach a Sunday school class or go on a mission trip to a strange land. We always have a choice to make: security or risk. The question is do we want *all* of God or just a little?

> *I would like to buy $3 worth of God, please.*
> *Not enough to explode my soul or disturb my sleep,*
> *But just enough to equal a cup of warm milk, or a snooze in the sunshine.*
> *I don't want enough of Him to make me love a black man, or pick beets with a migrant worker.*
> *I want ecstasy, not transformation.*
> *I want the warmth of the womb, not a new birth.*
> *I want a pound of the eternal in a paper sack.*
> *I would like to buy $3 of God, please.*[5]

This whole concept of comfort zones is addressed brilliantly by Dr. John Ortberg, in his wonderful book; *"If You Want to Walk on Water, You've Got to Get out of the Boat,"* explains how subtle entitlement thinking can cripple us as Christians in the area of evangelism:

> *Most of us have an area that might be called our "spiritual comfort zone," which is the area where we feel most comfortable trusting God. When God calls us to go beyond our spiritual comfort zone, we begin to feel nervous or uncomfortable. We would prefer not to go outside the zone until we feel better about it.*
>
> *For example, we might be comfortable talking about God with church friends, but nervous about explaining our faith to someone who does not believe. We might be comfortable in our current job, but anxious about the possibility that God wants to do some vocational realignment. We might feel enough faith to pray for people we are in relationships with, but actually confronting someone who has been behaving badly toward us would make us cringe. We might discuss past problems smoothly enough, but the idea of honestly naming our current struggles to a trusted friend would send us running.*

There is only one way to increase your spiritual comfort zone, and acquiring more information alone will not do it. You will have to follow the Path of God, which requires taking a leap of faith.

You need to get out of the boat and overcome them. For instance, one of the most exciting spiritual adventures in life is helping another human being find God. What keeps us from getting out of the boat evangelistically? The number one reason is fear. Fear of what? Historically, people have risked their livelihoods and even their lives for their faith. In many parts of the world, Christians still do. But for most of us, the worst-case scenario is that the other person will not want to talk about spiritual matters. We may experience a brief sense of embarrassment or rejection. When we ask, "Would you like to talk about spirituality?" the other person may say, "No, I don't think so. Not today. Thanks anyway." That is about the most pain we face.

On the other hand, look at the upside potential. We might actually be part of God's redemptive purposes on earth. But if I wait until I'm feeling 100 percent certain about having a spiritual conversation with somebody who is far from God, I may never have it. I will have to take the risk first. I have to get my feet wet.[6]

Dr. Ortberg's use of the term *spiritual comfort zone*, I believe, could be applied to all of us who are Christians living in the Western world today. Perhaps the best application of living in this spiritual comfort zone is our reluctance to acknowledge and befriend people in our communities who are not like us - people who are different, like PURE people and their families in our midst. We remain comfortable and satisfied in our cozy and sheltered groups comprised only of people like ourselves. Sadly and unknowingly, we have accepted and become content living in our miniscule comfort zones. This acceptance is probably best reflected in the reasoning we most commonly use to defend our lack of sensitivity and involvement with PURE people. Similar to my pre-Zach attitude of PURE people described above, this thought process allows us to feel better and even justified in our fear of entering the PURE world, or sometimes even acknowledging its very existence.

As we have said before, *getting out* of our comfort zones is the common vernacular. We at *PURE Ministries* choose not to use that phrase. *Getting out* implies that, after rarely doing something or going somewhere not familiar to us, we then *go back into* our *comfortable* comfort zones. The human tendency is to stay in our comfort zones, the comfort zones that we ourselves have each defined. When we are prodded and poked enough, we sometimes will step out of our comfort zones with the understanding that this is a one-time thing. We will feel very proud of ourselves for our actions, and then we will quickly retreat back to the security of our own little world. We are told by an unbelieving world that this is natural and it is. Unfortunately (or in reality, fortunately) we Christians have a supernatural God living within us with supernatural power on a supernatural quest. God leaves the decision up to us: we can stay familiar, secure, and comfortable *or* we can take a risk and *extend* our comfort zones to be God sized. Too often we choose the easy way only to miss great blessing. The late Dr. Adrian Rogers, pastor and author, says it this way: *"Most people want to serve God, but only in an advisory capacity."* [7]

We would be hard-pressed to find in Scripture where God states His desire for us to live a comfortable and pleasurable life, as we would define it. He desires that we grow closer to Him and become like Him and we can't do that when we choose to remain safely in our spiritual cocoons. I believe we are not called to just do what we want to do or feel capable of doing. Rather, and more importantly, we are called to do the things we may not, at first, want to do and the things we feel incapable of doing. How can God bless us on a mission trip if we don't go? I have heard people say, "I don't do mission trips," "I don't like the food," "I may get hurt," or "I don't know the language," and feel justified by saying it. Yes, we always have free choice, but when did we, the *creature*, get the right to tell the *Creator,* what ministry we would or would not do? How can we ever explain to our loving Father God that we did not do what He wanted us to because we loved our pleasure, comfort, and security more?

God is constantly giving us opportunities to grow. Our response and responsibility are to face the challenges and seize the opportunities, not in our own strength, but His. With complete assurance that God desires for us to mature as His children, we can confidently, boldly, and yet, humbly grow in these situations. God makes what is unfamiliar, familiar; uncomfortable, He makes comfortable; and in our insecurity, He brings divine security. He does this every time, every place, with each of us who love Him, and though we may not even be aware as it transpires in our lives, that what we once knew as our comfort zone has been greatly extended.

As we are transformed by the renewing of our minds and our thinking changes, our comfort zones are enlarged or they may very well disappear altogether. In a very real sense, if we really believe *Romans 12:1-2*, one of two things is true for us who name the name of Christ: either (1) we have *no* comfort zone in that in the power of Christ, we, at long last, realize and accept that we can do *anything* or (2) stating it in a different way, our comfort zones are *boundless*. There are no limits or borders to God's reach through us! If we really believe God is active in our lives, and we see Him in everything that happens in, to, and around us, then we should be confident and comfortable in literally every opportunity God brings across our path. *Trust in the LORD with all your heart; and lean not on your own understanding. In all your ways acknowledge him, and he shall direct thy paths. (Proverbs 3:5-6)* The bottom line is if we are obedient, God will bless us. If we trust totally in the Lord and solely on His wisdom and acknowledge Him and see Him in everything, every situation, every circumstance, then He leads us where He wants us to go. And, we are blessed.

At this point you most probably are in one of three different camps – you might be saying (a) "I don't have any idea what you're talking about and I'm just not interested," (b) "PURE ministry sounds good, even logical, but I really don't need another 'blessing' right now- I'll just pass on this one," or (c) "I want to do this, but I just can't - I don't have it in me; I just don't have whatever it takes to do it!"

Let me reiterate something very important at this point. Please understand that I am not only talking about what we perceive PURE ministry to be, but rather *any* personal ministry to any people or group of people who are commonly not present in our church fellowships. It's *any* ministry that will involve us personally in the lives of others who are unlike us in some way. With that said, let me speak as gently, honestly, and frankly as I can to each of the three groups.

Let's take group (a) first, because it is the most difficult, but quickest to address. What I've been talking about may seem foreign to you and you're wondering how any of this could apply to you. You've heard the arguments, read the Scripture, but still don't see any pertinence at all to you in your life. In fact, if we go back to *Romans 12: 1-2*, you're probably not worried too much about being conformed to this world or the renewing of your mind - you're pretty much okay with this. Whether you sense a calling to PURE ministry or any ministry is between you and Jesus. However, if I may be so bold in speaking to this group, I would simply say, maybe my words have been confusing and I've done a poor job communicating my message, but Scripture is very clear. If there is absolutely no impulse, no inclination, or no yearning whatsoever to recognize and at least empathize with those around us who need our help and friendship, a person calling themselves Christian should probably ask, "Why don't I feel anything?" I would also simply ask that you reread the Scriptures presented here and pray that the Lord will extend your comfort zone as only He can. Our response and responsibility as Christians are simply to live this out in our lives however God moves. We are who we are in Christ, not for what we do or have done, but for *Who* lives in and through us and is evidenced in our lives. Finally to group (a), let me point out that nowhere in *Romans 12:1-2* does it say or imply that our transformation is ever complete. Ironically, like other Christ-like characteristics given to us (humility is probably the best example), if we ever *think* we have attained it, we definitely have *not*! That's our pride deceiving us once again.

Let's now address the group (b) persons, those really not in need of *another blessing*. At the risk of simply implying that Scripture means exactly what it says and it does, then "We've got a problem here, Houston." The real truth is you and I now know too much! And, if I'm reading my Bible correctly, we really don't have a choice if we want to do what God says! James says it like this: *Therefore to him that knoweth to do good, and doeth it not, to him it is sin. (James 4:17)* Please understand that I'm not saying everybody has to get involved formally in PURE ministry (but you will be blessed if you do!). I am saying if we want to obey the great commandment, we are to *love* them – our neighbors, PURE people and their families, just like Jesus did. I predict that they won't be invisible to you any longer when you are out and about. Besides, who really is not in need of another blessing from God? Can we seriously say that?

Finally, to group (c), those who just can't do it, those that just don't have it in them, those that think they just don't have what it takes to do it - let me just say one thing: *You're right!* If I can add, join the club! I'm right there with you - I can't do it and neither can anyone else in and of themselves. To make matters worse, our fear keeps us from doing what we know we should do and we might end up doing (or saying) the wrong thing. We don't have the ability, capacity, talent, skill, or power within us to do it - but God does!

If you are like me and are saying that if this all depends on me, it's not going to work. Thankfully, it doesn't depend on you or me, but rather on the power of God working through us - if we let Him. God will empower you and me to do more than we could ever imagine. Yes, it is likely we will find ourselves in situations that we could never have dreamed. As John comforts us in his epistle: *But as many as received Him, to them He gave the right to become children of God, to those who believe in His name: who were born, not of blood, nor of the will of the flesh, nor of the will of man, but of God. (John 1:12-13)* The truth is that in reality, it is only in God's power that we do anything and, if we belong to Him, we have that power! He has us just where He wants us when we admit we are powerless (maybe even a little scared and anxious even) to do what He asks. We are ready for PURE ministry or anything else God wants us to do!

The Three Essentials for Extending Our Comfort Zones

Getting past our fear to reach out to a PURE person will invariably require that most of us will indeed need to extend our comfort zones. However, God promises great blessing if we do. We can still choose to stay in our comfort zones, but rather than enjoying the security we believe it affords, staying in our comfort zones carries a great price - much greater than we realize. We miss the special blessing that God has placed in these people. It cannot be received vicariously through others - we have to experience it ourselves. But, it will not happen if we do not extend our comfort zones.

Can't we just make up our minds to be braver and bolder and consequently extend our comfort zones? Yes and no. Yes, extending our comfort zone is a choice we must make. No, we can't just do it ourselves - we've already admitted we don't have what it takes. So, how *do* we extend our comfort zones and, just as importantly, how do we know how well we are doing it, i.e. *proving* what is that good, and acceptable, and perfect, will of God?

I believe there are three Scriptural *essentials*, or principles, that, if followed, will guide us as we seek to remove the barriers around our lives that keep us secure, but less effectual than we can be. These three essentials can also serve to measure or evaluate our progress and effectiveness as we expand our comfort zones and touch others with greater impact. These three essentials are just that, basic fundamentals in how we must think and not simply steps or mere phases that we pass through on our journey. We don't accomplish one step and move to the next, but rather Jesus works through us in growing us in each principle simultaneously. Again, it is a matter of our will also. In His grace and mercy, Jesus only knocks; we must open the door.

Each essential is not only Scriptural but practical in that it is necessary if we are to be authentic Christ followers to those around us. These are the three essentials:

1) Making it personal
2) Committing to remember

3) Cherishing relationships

These three essentials are by no means original with me. Each is firmly supported by Scripture and applicable in all areas of our lives, not just as we reach out to PURE people and their families. However, I have observed time and time again how when these principles are lived out, do work! They have worked and are working in me, many times in spite of myself, I have seen them work in others, and they will work for you.

1) Making it Personal

Though we have discussed earlier the personal aspect of PURE ministry, being *personal* is at the top of the essentials list. A brief survey of Scripture reveals many truths, some not immediately apparent to the reader, particularly for those who don't want to see them. For example, in the account of the creation in Genesis, did you ever stop to think that since God is *the* creator, He could create the earth with age and not necessarily brand-new as we would understand? This causes great consternation for some. Excuse me for my irreverence, but sometimes I can just visualize God chuckling at today's evolutionists as they try to calculate the age of the earth or things found in it: "This ought to keep them befuddled for a century or two!" Even the technique and process by which they must use to measure the age of objects, carbon dating, was also *created* by the very God they deny exists! I certainly don't know the mind of God, but sometimes He seems to have a great sense of humor. If He wanted to create certain aspects of the earth aged with millions or billions of years when He spoke them into existence, he could and maybe he did – lest we forget, He is the Creator of *all* things – and that includes time itself!

Another truth that is not initially obvious in Scripture, but true as we live daily, is that our God is very personal. He doesn't care much for committees, task forces, or teams of people. We see time and time again that when God had a specific job, He always called and used a person and not a group or a crowd. Yes, there are a few exceptions: the Jewish nation is dealt with commonly as a group; the disciples are sent forth as an advance band to establish the church; and perhaps a few others. But even in these cases, God personally relates to each person and saves each individual as He desires.

God proves His personal nature in sending His Son, Jesus, to this earth as a sacrifice for each one of us. Though Jesus was God-Man, we can relate to Him, identify with Him, and empathize with Him because He was a man. More importantly, God in the person of Jesus can relate to you and me, identify with you and me, and empathize with you and me *personally*. Need to free His people? God used Moses. Need to save a nation from annihilation? God used Queen Esther. Need to save His people from starvation? God used Joseph. Need to demonstrate His faithfulness and protection? God used a harlot woman, Rahab. Need to institute His church? God used 12 hand-picked workmen. God always uses people.

A prime example of the personal nature of our God in the person of Jesus Christ can be witnessed every day in our pseudo-religious atmosphere in America. It is very acceptable to use the word "God" in conversations and discussions, as long as we are not too dogmatic. We can talk with Christians, Jews, Muslims, or virtually anyone about "God" as much and as long as we desire and not really be talking about the *same* God - it doesn't matter. However, if you really want to change the tone and the mood of the discourse from congenial to divisive, merely mention the name *Jesus*. You see, God for unbelievers is not particularly personal; in fact it is more of a concept. But with Jesus, it's *all personal*. Use the name, Jesus, in a conversation (with virtually anybody and sometimes even with people who call themselves Christians) and you will immediately be branded intolerant, bigoted, prejudiced, and fanatical – the discussion comes to a screeching halt all because you mentioned the name Jesus. Why is this? Because Jesus is a person and He is personal with us His children.

If we are to minister to, and be ministered to, by any person, it will always be personal. However, if we are to minister to, and be ministered to, by PURE people, it will only be truly meaningful when we do it on a *personal* level - and this is precisely the point. Yes, we need organization, structure, and roles to fill in our PURE ministry effort, but it will always be reduced down to two people: you (or me) and a PURE person. This fact is virtually certain about any ministry we undertake, but it is *literally* true when we talk about PURE ministry. As we will see later, PURE ministry requires relationship and relationship is personal.

Am I saying that one cannot participate in PURE ministry without being directly involved in interacting with PURE people and their families? No, not necessarily - like in other ministries, we can always participate and be involved *at a distance*. By *at a distance* I mean we can send a snack for a PURE event, write a check in support of our church's PURE ministry - anything that does not require us to interact personally with another person. These *at a distance* deeds have value, but they don't normally move us or touch our hearts like personal involvement. It is only when we get personally involved, one on one, that God's blessings become so evident. Being personal certainly does not mean that we don't do things in, with, or through groups of people - it just means that PURE people are blessed with an ability or capability that many of us aren't; they can normally relate to people more easily, transparently, and in many ways, better than we typical people.

I mentioned earlier the experience that I had at Eagle Eyrie with a group of PURE people. If you remember, I was shocked when confronted with the reality that, though I was warmly greeted and accepted by my PURE friends, they didn't show deference to or respect me more because I was a normal person. Couldn't they see that I was different from them? Better even, than they were? After all, I was normal while they were all disabled in various ways. As I recall this event once again, I remember that I felt more ashamed than anything else – how could I have ever thought this way? Now, before you get too critical and judgmental of me for my prideful attitude, you might want to examine yourself as you have dealt with PURE people in your past. Though you or I don't come right out and verbalize it, in some perverted, prideful way we often do think we are better than our PURE friends because we can perhaps talk, walk, and think better. We actually believe that we must somehow *lower* ourselves in some way to communicate with PURE people when the real truth is that we must somehow be *raised up* to their level for our interaction to have meaning. PURE people are blessed with a transparency, innocence, and purity that we can only admire and envy. They seemingly don't make judgments of people the way we do - they really don't care what we look like, the way we are dressed, our ability to speak, or so many other things that *we* think are absolutely necessary. Whether we like it or not, we invariably make snap judgments about people based on these and other superficial factors – typically, PURE people don't. PURE people get personal quickly because they are not impressed, nor put off, with the superficial. My initial exposure to these wonderful PURE people years ago opened my eyes to this amazing transparency, and I have marveled and desired to be more like them ever since.

If I can allay any fears you may have as you begin to approach and attempt to communicate and relate to PURE people, let me assure you need not be too concerned with "saying or doing the right thing" - your attempt to communicate lovingly will be well received. Two important things to mention here are (1) though PURE people are normally loving and extremely transparent, unfortunately they can easily detect our prideful attitudes, and (2) you may not be able to discern or recognize that your interaction was well received. PURE people can almost instantly tell when we are condescending, looking or talking down to them, or treating them in some patronizing way. I have found that if I can remind myself often enough, as I think about my PURE friends and the fact they are especially blessed of God with this uncanny ability to recognize my lack of authenticity, I can relate to them with humility rather than pride. I like to tell people we must be willing to lay down our fear and pride and enter the PURE world; "You'll need to check your pride at the door - it won't work in here and besides, it's not needed anyway!" I encourage people to "unzip and remove it and the masks that we hold so dear," yet get in the way, when loving on PURE people.

Another aspect of our pride rearing its ugly head in our quest for personal relationships with PURE people is that our expectations of how they should react and respond to us are defined and limited to that which we call normal. Fortunately, PURE people don't necessarily think that way - and that's a good thing! Don't necessarily expect the earth to move just because you conquered your fear and finally approached a PURE person and said, "Hi." They may say "Hi" back at you, they may ignore you, they may hug you, or they may do absolutely nothing, not acknowledging you at all. We should approach PURE people expecting a normal response, but not be surprised or disappointed if we don't get it. Because a PURE person doesn't respond the way we think they should, that in no way means that our attempt was not received and appreciated. In our encounters with PURE people, we cannot allow our expectations for us to receive appropriate responses and reactions (as we define them) to hinder us. Empathy with our PURE friends can really help us here. PURE people may have difficulty speaking; they may not speak at all; they may be unable to control their arms or legs appropriately; they may have impaired or no vision; their ability to process language may take more time, etc. When we learn to think in these terms, our expectations become more realistic and unimportant and we, like our PURE friend, become more transparent.

Unlike other ministries or programs in a typical church, we can choose to become involved in support roles. As we discussed earlier, this doesn't mean that there are not valuable and worthwhile support roles in PURE ministry. There will always be a need and opportunity to bring food, send cards, etc. and these are important tasks that must be done. If we purpose to *really get involved* in ministry to and with PURE people, it will always be based and enmeshed in relationships. We may believe we can be impersonally involved, but our PURE friends will make it personal. Most PURE people don't do impersonal! A wonderful gift God has put in most all PURE people is the ability to relate to others on a personal level. Most PURE people know no other way. Unlike us, they are not clever (in our case, manipulative and deceptive) enough to try or see the need to impress us or wise (in our case, dishonest, prideful, and guarded) enough to be anything other than completely authentic, open, and transparent in everything they do or say. For some reason, God has obviously blessed PURE people with these traits - even people with autism. Don't believe me? Then, answer these simple questions especially if you've had any experience with children with autism. (1) When was the last time this PURE child was *ever* concerned in any way with impressing you? (2) Has he/she *ever* been hesitant or restrained in letting you know what they liked or didn't like, for fear of your thinking less of them? These motivations normally govern our actions and reactions, but they are not even on the radar of the typical PURE person!

If we choose to get close to a PURE person, not only will they force us to literally strip away our masks and tear down our prideful perspectives, but they will most likely dictate the terms of the relationship. I realize this is new ground for most of us used to controlling the terms of our friendships, but it is reality if we are to have PURE friends. This does not mean that the PURE person will do these things or have this effect on us on purpose, for they are not even aware of their influence. It is simply a matter of fact that their honest, straightforward, and, yes, innocent manner of relating gives us no other option as we began to connect and relate to them.

However we choose to be involved in PURE ministry, it will require us to do it personally. We will be blessed beyond belief for our efforts, no matter how awkward or meager we may think them to be.

2) Committing to Remember

A funny thing has happened to me as I have been busy living my life, being married, having children, and now grandchildren: I have gotten old! Though only in my early sixties, I'm starting to understand just a little about what I thought would never happen to me. All during my business career my partners and I always tried to stay active by playing basketball and running at lunchtime. I can remember times in my younger days when several older men would occasionally join our games at the church gym where we played. Afterward in the locker room, I can also remember joking with my friends about how awkward and clumsy these old guys were as we all had a good laugh. Fast forward a few years (or so it seems), sitting in the same locker room with the same friends, and the situation was decidedly different. Winded and exhausted, we were talking with each other about how we just couldn't do the same things we could do on the court as we could in our younger days, when a good friend, Bruce Brooks, uttered the classic remark about us, "We have become what we used to laugh about!"

I also have another problem: I even forget God sometimes. Maybe you suffer from the same problem. My life gets so busy, I just don't have time for a quiet time; or so I justify it to myself. As Pastor Francis Chan puts it, all of us have spiritual amnesia:

> *There is an epidemic of spiritual amnesia going around, and none of us is immune. No matter how many fascinating details we learn about God's creation, no matter how many pictures we see of His galaxies, and no matter how many sunsets we watch, we still forget.*
>
> *It may sound "un-Christian" to say that on some mornings I don't feel like loving God, or I just forget to. But I do. In our world, where hundreds of things distract us from God, we have to intentionally and consistently remind ourselves of Him.*[8]

Or as the great pastor, D.L. Moody, said, most times it is *good things* that make us forget:

> *We can stand affliction better than we can prosperity, for in prosperity we forget God*[9].

Another common malady that strikes most of us as we age is memory loss. Even though I suffer from an occasional *senior moment* from time to time, I have learned that I can remember what I really want to remember. I may not remember certain details about things that happened long ago, but I can remember most of the important things. I understand that certain horrific diseases such as Alzheimer's and dementia can and do sometimes literally erase our memories, but God has spared me of these to this point. My wife accuses me of *selective hearing*, of which I (as are most married men) am surely guilty. But, I also like to think that I still have the ability to *remember* selectively, too - what I want to remember and, most importantly, what I commit or purpose to remember.

Why do we remember wedding anniversaries, birthdays, etc.? We obviously want to remember these important days, but in reality we remember them because we love the people associated with the dates. In the busyness of life we may sometimes forget one of these days that are so important to us, but normally we don't. We don't *forget to remember* - we are committed to remember because we love the people and value those relationships.

Here is that second essential principle: *committing to remember.* So often in our busy world, most of us stay so wrapped up in the things of life that directly affect us on a daily basis that we don't take the time to remember the important things. None of us are immune. A funny but sobering experience occurred to me recently that emphasized once again just how quickly we can forget to remember the important things – and people. Our church has a wonderful monthly PURE respite for adults on Friday evenings and children and their siblings on Saturdays. Mrs. Lori Millwood runs the ministry at our church and is simply amazing in what and how she does what she does. I have been privileged to be a worker at respite now for well over ten years. For the last five years I've been the caregiver for a precious little boy named Sam. Lee and I have grown so close to this sweet family that we consider Sam's mom and dad, Pete and Maria, our adopted children and Sam and his sisters, Grace and Emma, like grandchildren. Our treasured relationship with Sam and his family is what happens as a result of in-church respite and we will talk more about this on another day.

I must confess two things here. First, I was initially attracted to Sam because when I first met him, he looked a lot like Zach. Second, since that day when I first met Sam, I've become pretty jealous of my time with my boy! In fact everyone at respite knows Sam is mine! Only if I am out of town or sick and not there, does anyone dare to even think about keeping him at respite. Sam and I are buddies!

Sam has infantile epilepsy which manifests in many ways like cerebral palsy. Sam continues to make great developmental strides, but infantile epilepsy is bad stuff. His mom and dad take wonderful care of Sam, and he is improving everyday in many ways. We all long for the day when he will speak and walk. Recently I was caring for Sam at respite. Just so you have the picture, Sam is a *big* 8 year old and probably weighs close to 100 pounds. Though I'm certainly not a giant by any means, Sam is quickly growing to be as big as I and soon will also be as big as his mom or dad! As we were having a good time doing what we do at respite, an overwhelming thought struck me: Maria and Pete do what I am doing every hour of every day. It's fun for Sam. It's *fun* for me. Sam and I spend three hours tussling on the floor, going to the gym, going to the playground, and participating in the special, fun activities Lori has planned each Saturday. Though we were having a good time, something was nagging me. It was not until later that night that the Lord revealed the truth to me.

Despite all I know and have experienced, I had allowed myself to forget what my PURE friends and families' experience 24/7, 365 days a year. It was not until the Lord said, "You forgot, again" that it all made sense.

I know better. I had *forgotten to remember*. As I put the diaper bag back on his wheelchair, I had forgotten to remember how my friend Sam must feel in having his family members care for his most basic and personal needs. I had forgotten all the things Maria, Peter, and the girls do every day in caring for Sam. Yet, these precious people go on living daily without complaining, rarely asking for help or special consideration, and are stronger and better people for it all.

How could this happen? In reality it's pretty easy and I must confess it wasn't hard for me at all. Just let yourself get so wrapped in your own life, what you are doing, where you are going, where you ... and, it can happen to any of us. I love these people. They are my dear friends. I talk with and see them frequently, yet I had *forgotten to remember*. This experience is now branded on my mind and heart: I must choose to remember or else, by default, I have *chosen to forget*. Not committing to remember people who are hurting, homeless, poor, destitute will deceive us into thinking everyone is living the way we are living. For most middle class Americans, nothing could be further from the truth. Through PURE people, God teaches us yet another lesson: do not forget others, do identify with others, and do empathize with others. When we do these simple things, our focus begins to change to others rather than ourselves.

Reflecting on the life of my grandson Zach, I am so thankful that God permitted me to see and spend time with him almost every day of his short life. Through no planning of my own, God made a way for me to retire early from my business. I considered myself blessed, but I really didn't know why the Lord did this in my life until a year or two later. It was then that Zach was born, and God's blessing of giving me virtually unlimited time with my grandson became evident. Because of the severity of Zach's disabilities (cerebral palsy, blindness, and more), all of us in the family who loved him and cared for him were constantly trying to make sure that he was comfortable and enjoying himself. Because he could not speak, we were forced mostly to guess what he would like to eat, play with, sleep with, etc. Sometimes we guessed right and sometimes we guessed wrong, but Zach, in his wonderful way, always seemed to appreciate our efforts and to know that we loved him.

As Zach grew, I found myself becoming almost obsessed about whether he was happy and content not only while I was physically with him, but even more so when we were separated. I was constantly thinking of him, wondering what he was doing and whether his needs were being met moment by moment. Walking through a mall, spending time with friends, or in a worship service, I was consciously remembering Zach, even though I *knew* without a doubt that his mom, my daughter, and his dad, were caring for him as only a mom and dad can. Rather, I consciously chose to remember him virtually every minute of every day. We had a close relationship, I loved him and he loved me, and I wanted him to *always* be happy, comfortable, and content.

I tell this story only to illustrate the importance of our committing to *remember* PURE people as we go about our daily routine. We need not be obsessive, like I was, but simply making it a point to regularly think of our PURE friends and their families. Most PURE people and their families have so many challenges, so many hardships, and so many issues to overcome on a daily, even minute-by-minute, basis and, as we allow ourselves to get to know them beyond the superficial, we begin to empathize with them. As our friendships grow and we become more aware of ways that we can help, remembering them becomes habitual, sometimes even unconscious. We begin to discover that we are *considering* them and we're not even aware of it. It is not realistic or possible for us simply to purpose to remember every PURE person we may have encountered at the grocery store, in the sense to which I am referring. I have experienced, and have observed in others, that committing to remember becomes an attitude and mindset that we choose to embrace only when genuine relationships have been lovingly developed.

As we look closer at the lives of PURE people and their families, we will notice a common characteristic that is always present which I will call *limitation of life options*. This characteristic and the impact it has on the person and the family is in most ways directly dependent on the type and severity of disabilities of the PURE person. It is also greatly influenced by the personalities of each family member as well as the dynamics of the family itself. By the phrase, *limitation of life options*, I simply mean that the basic, everyday life *options*, many that we take for granted, of PURE people and their families, are *limited* for them in various ways. The degrees to which these limits are manifested vary greatly. For example, one of the reasons that I was so compulsive in my concern for Zach was that, as I said earlier, he could not communicate with us in a normal way to tell us what he wanted or if he felt bad, good, sad, or hungry. Also, because of his vision and the effects of cerebral palsy, so many of the educational and entertainment options, such as books, TV or games were not options for him. His life was limited or narrowed in significant ways. My worry for him was how well his family and I could substitute other things in his life that he could do to fill the void and provide other options that he would enjoy.

Another illustration of this limitation would be a ten-year-old with moderate autism. From our perspective, the assumed option of adapting his behavior to be liked and accepted by his peers or be perceived *normal* in public is once again denied for this young boy. For example, this young boy does not weigh the consequences of how he is being viewed by people when he impulsively acts out in a restaurant. It is not a conscious choice he makes, but rather a *limitation* as a result of the autism that he is *unable to make* a choice. His autism prevents him from taking advantage of such an option and his world is limited in that way. Further, it would not be uncommon in a situation involving autism that the disability of the PURE person would limit other members of the family in public settings as well. Perhaps emotional outbursts in public by the PURE person in the past and the fear that these experiences will occur again, many times limit opportunities for not only the PURE person, but for various members of the family as well. It is easy to see how other physical, intellectual, and emotional disabilities can limit life options for PURE people in varying degrees.

When we broaden this concept of *limitation of options* to the family, we see other ramifications. Those of us without a PURE person in our family think nothing of choosing from a myriad of churches in our communities that we might consider attending. We look at such factors as doctrine, preaching quality, music style, children and youth programs, and friendliness of the people. Sadly, this option is greatly limited for a PURE family. If the family chooses to become involved in a church at all, they must choose one first that can accommodate their PURE family member - this normally is, by necessity, their one and only prerequisite and *must have*. The PURE family will have, in the best case, a single or just a few church options, and in the worst case, *none*. Also, compounding this are the inherent health issues associated with any disabilities, behavioral issues in many cases, and other factors too numerous to mention. All PURE people and their families have a limitation imposed on them to some degree.

What can we do in light of this *limitation of life options* for our PURE friends and their families? We can choose to remember them. As we enjoy the many benefits of living lives with virtually unlimited life options, we can remember others who can't be where we are, do what we're doing, and otherwise benefit from a freedom to do as we desire.

You may have never even thought about the basic human options most of us enjoy every minute. Joni Erickson Tada, the inspirational founder of Joni and Friends, who became a quadriplegic as a teenager, once remarked that one of the simple pleasures she missed most due to her condition was scratching her nose! Again, if you are like me, you probably never give a second thought that you can feed yourself (whatever and whenever you want to eat), walk outside to sit on a bench and read a book, drive a car, or press the remote to change the station. I think you're probably getting the idea.

Choosing to remember PURE people and their families as we go about our daily lives not only makes us more thankful for these simple abilities that God has given us, it also causes us to empathize more with our PURE friends and families. We will start to think of ways to include them in activities that may not have been open to them formerly. We will come to appreciate and admire them so much more for overcoming the challenges that they have. From a church fellowship perspective, when we commit to remember them, our church will change. When we worship, fellowship, or serve, we will discover that these PURE people and their families have so much to give. We realize that not only have they missed out by not being in our church, but just as important, *we* have missed out on not having them with us in our fellowship! Lovingly including PURE people and their families into our churches certainly removes some of the *limitation of life options* that they experience, but it also blesses the local body of Christ in incalculable ways.

In the Gospel of Mark, in the first 5 verses of Chapter 2, a moving story of an encounter between a paralytic man, his friends, and Jesus is recounted:

> *And again He entered Capernaum after some days, and it was heard that He was in the house. Immediately many gathered together, so that there was no longer room to receive them, not even near the door. And He preached the word to them. Then they came to Him, bringing a paralytic who was carried by four men. And when they could not come near Him because of the crowd, they uncovered the roof where He was. So when they had broken*

*through, they let down the bed on which the paralytic was lying.
When Jesus saw their faith, He said to the paralytic, "Son, your
sins are forgiven you."*

Mark 2:1-5

We have a story here of four that remembered. They could have so easily gotten together and decided to go see the Master Teacher as he came to the town, but somewhere in the deep recesses of their heart, they *remembered* their PURE friend and his need. They not only remembered him, but be sure to catch this, they *acted*; they did something about it! Even when they were deterred by the crowds, they found a way to get their friend to Jesus. Perhaps nowhere in Scripture is a better illustration of our obligation (yes, I used that word again that we are so fearful of using in Christendom) to evangelize, particularly to PURE people. However, it all starts with simply remembering them.

3) Cherishing Relationships

Mention any ministry in the church today and you will invariably hear the word relationship as a factor in the impact, growth, and vitality of the ministry. This is also true about PURE ministry, but even more so. I believe it is more correct to say that *relationships are everything when we talk about PURE ministry*. In actuality there is no PURE ministry where there are not relationships. This is a strong statement, so let me explain.

Let's revisit the 22nd chapter of Matthew once again. Jesus reveals once and for all how we as Christians should be living - that is, what should be the one thing we should be concerned about most as Christ lives through us. Strangely, this revelation is given as an answer to a modern day skeptic of his time, a lawyer who is trying to embarrass Jesus with a trick question, "What is the great commandment of the law?" Unfortunately for the lawyer, and fortunately for us, Jesus gives the memorable answer and establishes forever our priorities for living. In these few short sentences, Jesus tells (in reality, commands) us how we should live. First and most importantly, He says, we are to love Him with every fiber of our being, with all that we have. Then, abounding and overflowing with the love that He has so graciously provided in our hearts *"because the love of God is shed abroad in our hearts by the Holy Ghost which is given unto us." (Romans 5:5b) (KJV)* We are *commanded* to love others, our neighbors, as we love ourselves. These two commandments, He says, are everything. All of us have heard and read this passage many times before, but do we really comprehend what He is trying to tell us? Though we don't fully understand what *"love the Lord thy God with all thy heart, and with all thy soul, and with all thy mind"* really means, each of us has a good idea of what loving someone means to us. We love our wife/husband, we love our children, and we *really* love our grandchildren. So, we can relate in some fashion, to loving our Heavenly Father with a deep, sacrificial love we have for those that are closest to us. Further, I believe most of us get the idea of loving our neighbors with some lesser version of the love we reserve for those in our families. Of course, we remain really confused on exactly who our neighbors are, but we get the concept.

Sadly, most of us walk away from this passage with only a shallow understanding of not only what it means but how it should impact and literally change how we live. Again, it is God who has given us the capacity to love and has placed those special people in our lives for whom we care so much, and we will do and sacrifice anything for their good. I think we get the first part of the passage as best we can in our finite minds with the experience we have on a human level with those in our families that we love. The *loving our neighbors* part is where we fail, or at least where I fail, so often in fulfilling Jesus' command. The zinger that Jesus uses to make Himself clear and to bring it all down to our level is most often dismissed as unimportant by most of us. The phrase, *"Thou shalt love thy neighbor as thyself,"* is the key to the entire passage. Loving our neighbors *as ourselves* instructs us on how we are to love them and, at the same time, sets the standard of that love. If only Jesus would have used another phrase, to describe His love: anything would have been easier! What about "as we love our mothers and fathers?" Respect them, yes, but not love them always with this type of love. That wouldn't work because all of our mothers and fathers aren't always that lovable. What about "as we love our spouses," or "as we love our children or grandchildren?" No, we don't necessarily all even have spouses, children, or grandchildren. Jesus knew exactly what He would say and what it meant.

Usually when we hear the expression, "loving ourselves," in false humility we quickly argue, "We really don't *love* ourselves; we love others *more*." We might think we don't love ourselves, but Jesus knew the truth: we not only love ourselves, we *adore* ourselves! Need convincing? We may occasionally diet and deprive ourselves of goodies that we like to eat, but when was the last time you didn't make sure you had enough to eat? Don't we always spend the time necessary to look as good as we possibly can before we go out in public? If we, especially us men, are sick or not feeling well, the world essentially stops spinning until we see the doctor, take our medicine, and moan and groan until we are feeling good again. We each have certain obligations to job, family, church, and friends, and we may occasionally do something we don't want to do, go somewhere we really don't want to go, even eat something we don't like. However, if we will be completely honest, we spend most of our time each and every day doing exactly what we *want* to do to make ourselves happy and content. And perhaps the best proof of all, when was the last time you had to teach a toddler to be selfish - to take all the toys, even if he made all the other kids cry?

No, the unavoidable truth is that Jesus was right and He should know. He made us. We do love ourselves and it is with *this* love we are to love everyone else. This *agape* love of which He speaks is the deepest love of all. It is not only the same love that He commands we have *for* Him, but it is also the same type of love He has *for* us and drove Him to the cross to die for us. Jesus is not telling us we are to love others with some kind of reduced or "fat free" love, reserved for those who are less important in our lives. On the contrary, He is telling us to love others with the most intense and powerful love we know and experience as human beings: in actuality the way He made us - the way we love ourselves. He tells us this is the way we are to love others and this is the also the benchmark by which we are to measure that love. "*Love thy neighbor as thyself*" is not a throwaway axiom at the end of a profound passage, but in reality it is fundamental to our really understanding what Jesus is saying. We can live our lives arguing with Jesus that we think we should have other priorities or other things should be more important to us: we all inevitably define and pursue our own selfish priorities. Yes, we can argue, but we will be wrong. Jesus gives life and He alone gets to set the parameters and the rules.

If we could summarize *Matthew 22:35-40*, that Great Commandment passage, condense it down to one word, the one thing Jesus says is most important above all other things, it would basically be *relationships*. Our lives have meaning only in the context of relationships with our Heavenly Father and with others. It is through relationships that Jesus lives through us most mightily and movingly. As with all other commands, or requirements that Jesus gives His children, we can only respond with four short words, "I can't do it!" And, once again we're right, but Jesus can through us. It is then that we realize that in ourselves, we really can't do anything. It is only through His power that we live and do anything.

So Jesus has set the stage. How can we take this truth and apply it to relationships with PURE people and their families? In the lives of so many PURE people, relationships are in reality all they have. Because of limited life options, they normally do not have the distractions or alternatives from which to choose. Friendships are everything for PURE people.

I certainly don't pretend to understand this, but PURE people seem to have a capacity for relationships that most of us do not have. They have an ability to actually *be* authentic and genuine. This is not a temporary mind-set demanded by a particular situation as we non-PURE people might understand. No, most PURE people *are* authentic; what you see and hear and love is who they really are! In some divine way, this capacity is somehow related to their disability, their utter transparency, and the limitation of life options we discussed earlier. Again, I don't pretend to understand it. I've just experienced it over and over again. While we are concerned with the outward facade, PURE people have the gift of looking beyond the outside to get to the inside.

We are so often distracted by the many impersonal, glitzy enticements of life when most PURE people only want to be friends.

This quality has never been better illustrated than in the life of my good PURE friend, Will. Will is now in his mid-teens, and I have known him since he was just a young boy. Will has an undiagnosed condition, but could be broadly labeled developmentally disabled. When Will was only small a child and until just a few years ago, all he wanted was to be with anyone who would take the time to be with him and blow bubbles. If you saw Will, he had his little bottle of soapy bubble solution and the little wand that you use to blow bubbles - and he wanted *you* to do it with him. If you were going to relate to Will, you were going to have to blow bubbles - period. Oh yes, you could try to impress Will with how important you were or that you had more important things to do, but all he cared about was whether you were going to blow bubbles with him: not childlike selfishness, but rather proof of friendship in his world. If Will was going to be your friend, you had to do it Will's way. Again, Will was not being selfish; he didn't necessarily want it to be this way; he certainly didn't make it this way, but it was the way he was made and the only way he knew. It wasn't so much the bubbles, it was whether or not we were willing to take the time to relate to him in a way that was required if we were going to have a relationship with Will. I could choose not to blow bubbles and not get myself totally soaked with bubble solution, but I would have missed out on knowing Will.

Like Will, most PURE people quickly cut right through the superficial and get right to the heart of relationships. Most of us have only a few deep relationships. Perhaps a spouse, children, a close friend or two comprise most of these types of relationships in our lives. When we choose to get involved in PURE ministry, this will likely change. Relationships with PURE people don't necessarily look like typical relationships, particularly superficial ones: they are PURE.

When we men meet another man for the first time and begin to establish a rapport, it is normally built on the ability of each guy to out-impress the other. We use jobs, positions, make of car we drive, past athletic feats, size of fish we caught, and other weapons in our arsenal to establish our superiority and dominance. I can't speak for all women, but I've been told they do the same thing, but they use the exploits of their children and grandchildren as their weaponry of choice to accomplish the same goal in a more feminine way. Whether man or woman, we have quickly learned this art, though most often subconsciously, to control and manipulate others and protect our self image. Harsh and brutal appraisal, I know, but honest. As mentioned earlier, we have mistakenly and erroneously learned that relationships are built on an *accomplishment* level when, in fact, they are built on just the opposite: a *needs* level. Think about it: are you closer to people that you are trying to impress with who you are and what you've done *or* with the person you love with whom you're willing to be transparent? If you consider the person on this earth with whom you are closest, it is almost certainly with this person that you most likely are the most open, transparent, and honest; your self-image is not nearly as important to you as the other person. A sacrificing attitude becomes normal in this relationship. It extends beyond typical sacrifices of time, attention, and effort onto sacrificing our need to wear masks and hold back our true feelings. You are not afraid to share your innermost fears and concerns with this person.

Would it shock you to learn that PURE people are just this way *naturally*? They just don't seem to let pride (or what they think you are thinking about them) get in the way of relating to people. PURE people may be physically, intellectually, and/or emotionally disabled in some ways, but we can learn much from them in the area of relationships - most are *relationally gifted*. Again, our relationships with PURE people are different than our other relationships with non-PURE people.

As with my friend Will, *I must lay down my expectations* of how my PURE friend should act, react, and respond. Not to discourage you, but sometimes this is easier said than done. As we would normally define it, many PURE people are by nature loving and responsive while others are not, just as non-PURE people are. The key phrase here is "as we would normally define it." If we are going to relate to PURE people in a meaningful way, we are not going to have the privilege of defining what loving and responsive means. They, PURE people, do.

We must adapt to them and their world or there will be no relationship. This is why surrender of our pride is so important. If we live our lives saying things like, "I would never___," "I don't do___," or "If someone is going to be my friend, they must___," we will find relating to PURE people difficult, but not impossible if we're willing to change. In relating and learning to love your PURE friend, you may very well find yourself doing things you never thought you would do, all for the sake of friendship.

Friendships with PURE people are different also because the ways we typically believe we must communicate and relate are different. Our PURE friends may be verbal or they may not. How will we communicate if we can't use words? As I mentioned before, Zach really never said a distinct word. He could only squeal, grunt, and laugh, no matter how much he wanted to say *real* words. I could talk to Zach but he could not talk to me, at least not in any traditional or conventional way. Yet somehow we found a way to be closer than I could ever describe. I can't explain it, but it was true. Our PURE friend may not even make eye contact with us - ever. What are we to do? I can only answer this question about this challenging situation and other complex questions about equally challenging circumstances this way: I'm not sure. I do know this, it is in these relationships we will find Jesus and He will provide a way.

In a nutshell, relationships with Jesus and others are what matter on this earth. Relationships with PURE people can be the most precious, if we dare get personal, choose to remember them, and cherish relationships. The question is: will we surrender our pride, forget our preconceived ideas, and get real?

The *Real* Truth Cloaked in Irony

Have you ever noticed that when we read Scripture, we always identify with the *good guy*? Think about it. It may be subconsciously and we may not even know we're doing it, but we do. Maybe it's just me, but I don't think so. For example, when we read in *Luke 18:10-17* of the

Pharisee and publican who went into the temple to pray, who do you identify with? The Pharisee who pridefully told God how good he was and how glad he was he wasn't like the sinners? Or the lowly publican, who stood afar off, who would not even lift his eyes towards Heaven in his humility, and simply prayed, *"God be merciful to me, a sinner?"* Why, we're the humble publican, of course!

What about the story of the parable of the talents in *Matthew 25:14-30*? Do we see ourselves as the fearful, risk-avoiding person who was given one talent, buried it in the field, and then blamed his lack of fruit on the perceived wrath of the master (Jesus)? No, we are the person given two talents who increased it to four, at those times when we haven't had a quiet time in a week or so and not feeling very spiritual. But, more frequently in our phony super-spirituality, we are the guy given five talents who increased it to ten; give me more and I'll do it again (excuse the rhyme)! Why, we are even good *dirt*; certainly not hard, stony, rootless, or overcome with thorns kind of dirt we read about in the parable of the soil in *Matthew 13:1-23*.

The *I Corinthians 1:23-28* passage is another one of those passages in which, I believe, we may identify with the wrong character.

> *But we preach Christ crucified, to the Jews a stumbling block and to the Greeks foolishness, but to those who are called, both Jews and Greeks, Christ the power of God and the wisdom of God. Because the foolishness of God is wiser than men, and the weakness of God is stronger than men. For you see your calling, brethren, that not many wise according to the flesh, not many mighty, not many noble, are called. But God has chosen the foolish things of the world to put to shame the wise, and God has chosen the weak things of the world to put to shame the things which are mighty; and the base things of the world and the things which are despised God has chosen, and the things which are not, to bring to nothing the things that are, that no flesh should glory in His presence.*
>
> *I Corinthians 1:23-28*

We don't necessarily want to say we're the *wise, mighty,* or *noble* in this passage because we'll look prideful. We'll profess to be the *foolish, the weak,* and *the base things* because it sounds and looks good to our Christian friends. If we are perfectly open and honest, in our positive self image we *think* of ourselves as more or less wise, mighty, or noble. However, it is truth cloaked in irony; God doesn't use the wise, mighty, or noble, but rather the foolish, the weak, and the base things. To be used of God we must acknowledge ourselves foolish, weak, and base. If the real truth be known, we are; we just don't like thinking of ourselves in that way. We are left with a choice: recognize who we really are and be used of God or keep thinking that we are wise, mighty, noble, and be essentially useless. Could it possibly be, just maybe, that God is using the PURE ones around us, who have no struggle with bogus self images and know that they are *foolish, weak,* and *base,* to help us realize that we aren't who we think we are! To be used of God we must become spiritually like them, like trusting children.

As we end this chapter, may I close with one other controversial opinion and attempt to explain this truth cloaked in irony? During this latest phase of my life (the post-Zach years), I have been blessed to spend a lot of time with PURE people. I have also spent some time in churches with people genuinely moved by God to start PURE ministry in their churches. During this time, I have also met some people who actually felt it was their duty to crush any PURE ministry movement in their fellowship: not needed or too costly – all the standard, false, erroneous, and inaccurate excuses that are used. But mostly during this time, I've been around people who like the idea of PURE ministry, *conditionally* - as long as it didn't directly involve them. In my *PURE Ministries* experiences in being in churches across America, I have cherished knowing and been inspired with the PURE ministry movers and shakers; tolerated the PURE ministry opponents, and remained perplexed at the multitudes in between.

When thinking of these experiences and people, I am always taken back to the account of the paralytic man in *Mark 2:1-5* which we looked at earlier. We understand the basics: these four men cared for their friend enough to get him before Jesus so that he could be healed.

Conventional evangelistic teaching of this passage is normally reduced or condensed to something like this: we Christians should *bring* our friends to church. We conveniently leave out the fact that these guys are bringing a *paralyzed* man to a type of church, unless we're talking about miracles. If we're talking about miracles, we conveniently omit the church part and just talk about the healing.

As an aside, did you ever wonder why Jesus, when presented with a person in need of physical healing, *always* forgives them *first* of their sin? Then, He heals them of their *physical* problem. He did that here and He does it each and every time a miracle healing is recorded in Scripture. In fact, here it is not until six verses later and after a confrontation with the scribes in attendance that He actually physically heals the man who then walks away whole. Based on this and the other similar healings in Scripture, I can come to only one conclusion: Jesus is primarily concerned with our spiritual condition and secondarily concerned with the physical. He is more concerned with our being forgiven and clean, than being healthy, wealthy, and wise. Since we can only be close to Him (now and in eternity) when we are forgiven and clean through His own shed blood, being healthy, wealthy, and wise seems relatively unimportant to Jesus. Rather, Jesus is more concerned with our "brokenness" so that we can be truly healed. As Vance Havner once said:

> *"God uses broken things. It takes broken soil to produce a crop, broken clouds to give rain, broken grain to give bread, broken bread to give strength. It is the broken alabaster box that gives forth perfume. It is Peter, weeping bitterly, who returns to greater power than ever."*[10]

Returning to the story, so much is taught in this passage, yet we are left with many questions. In whose house was Jesus teaching? What caused the man's paralysis? How big was the house? What was the room like? How did the four get their PURE friend on the roof? How did they uncover the roof and let down the bed without falling through themselves? All good questions, but there are others even harder to answer and left to conjecture. Maybe the most important question in relation to us is who exactly were the four? Male? We assume so because of the physical worked involved, but not necessarily. Young? Probably so, same reasons. Were they actually friends of the paralytic? Again, we assume so and it is most likely true, but we are not told explicitly. Bottom line: we just don't know much about them.

Has it ever occurred to you that these four could have been PURE people themselves bringing their PURE friend? Intriguing, yes? Maybe this explains why the crowd wouldn't let them into where Jesus was speaking. Who knows? Honestly, the possibility of the four being PURE has occurred to me, because I've seen it happen many times. Obviously, not exactly the same setting and characters (except One), but I have seen this: dads, mothers, sisters, brothers, grandmothers, granddads, aunts, uncles, cousins and yes, friends of PURE people being *brought close* to Jesus simply by being around and involved in the life of the PURE person. The PURE person in these miraculous situations may or may not have been able to verbally witness to their own relationship with Jesus. Most didn't have to, for their very lives spoke louder and clearer than words ever could.

In his book *"The Power of the Powerless: A Brother's Legacy of Love,"* Christopher De Vinck writes beautifully and powerfully about the impact on his life of his brother, Oliver, who was severely disabled.

> *I grew up in a house where my brother was on his back in his bed for thirty-two years, in the same corner of his room, under the same window, beside the same yellow walls. He was blind, mute. His legs were twisted. He didn't have the strength to lift his head or the intelligence to learn anything. Oliver was born with severe brain damage that left him and his body in a permanent state of helplessness.*[11]

Pretty dire and hopeless situation, wouldn't you say? Yet, Christopher De Vinck goes on to describe the impact his brother had on him:

Oliver still remains the most helpless human being I ever met, the weakest human being I ever met, and yet he was one of the most powerful human beings I ever met. He could do absolutely nothing except breathe, sleep and eat; yet he was responsible for love, courage and insight.[12]

In my experience, I've seen rough, tough PURE dads made meek and gentle in loving and caring for their PURE son or daughter. I've seen Jesus do extraordinary things in the lives of brothers and sisters, touched and inspired by being there as their PURE sibling simply lived among them. I've seen men serve as pallbearers in the funeral of their PURE friend, forever changed, simply by being in the PURE person's presence for a time. Finally, being one of those granddads brought closer to Jesus, words of witness were not needed -— I experienced Jesus in the relationship itself just like *Matthew 25:40* said I would. PURE people might just very well be the finest of evangelists. They can *bring* people to Jesus in ways we normal people can't. I'm certainly not trying to make Scripture fit my purpose and saying that the four were PURE. The account doesn't say they were, but it also doesn't say they weren't.

I have come to a conclusion, and this is my controversial theory. Let me state it in a question: Who, in reality, is more disabled: (1) a PURE person with his/her limitations plainly visible and open, but with an ability, willingness, and desire for authentic personal relationships with their Lord and literally anyone else; or (2) a normal person who actually *is disabled* by being so self-consumed, inhibited, unwilling, and unable to identify and empathize with those around them who don't meet their own definitions of worthiness? I have seen far, far more disabled in the latter case than I have the former. As we discussed earlier, in our own anxiety and angst to say something, it is so patronizing and trivializing to say to a PURE person something like: "Well, we all are disabled in some way." True, but equating having thinning hair or big ears to a person with Down syndrome or spina bifida rings pretty hollow to a PURE person. What is critically important is this: there are many, *many people, many of them Christians, suffering with the disability of pride that, in reality, results in lives guarded from being touched by those who can bring meaning and therefore remain almost impossible for God to use.* So, in a very real sense, many of us normal people are more disabled than PURE people. We can see their disabilities pretty easily -– ours are much more obscure and concealed, or so we think. Jesus, who really matters, sees it in each of us, is patiently waiting for us to see it too. When we do, we're usable.

When we finally get the courage to surrender, commit to get involved with or at least expose ourselves to PURE people, and actually do *it*, most of us do *it* with visions of how righteous and noble we are. We think we are blessing them (and we are); in reality, however, they are simply blessing us more! Jesus alone can empower, enable, and raise us up when we realize this.

I leave you with my final question:

> Is it not ironic that many times, PURE people are the kind of people that God uses in his Kingdom and our being their friends is as much for *our growth* as it is for their good?

My prayer is that we all know the answer to that now. But, knowing this, what do we *do*? How do we respond to this truth cloaked in irony? The next chapter will help us as we move from simply thinking and talking about it to acting on it.

Practical PURE Ministry

"Therefore whoever hears these sayings of Mine, and does them, I will liken him to a wise man who built his house on the rock: and the rain descended, the floods came, and the winds blew and beat on that house; and it did not fall, for it was founded on the rock."

Matthew 7:24-25

Just Turn Right at the Paradigm Shift - A *Radical* Ministry

The phrase *paradigm shift* has received much press in the last few years. For example, the term was used and applied more frequently and perhaps most appropriately, in describing the effect of the internet on our world: the internet was a paradigm shift in how most all of us view and interact with our world. The word *paradigm* originally meant simply an example or pattern, but is now generally accepted, and maybe overused, to mean: *A set of assumptions, concepts, values, and practices that constitutes a way of viewing reality for the community that shares them, especially in an intellectual discipline.* In other words, a paradigm is all the factors and assumptions involved that affect, influence, and constitute how we look at, think about, interact with, and value something. As we apply it here, our paradigm with respect to ministry, how we view and know it, is what we are now proposing as what we can and should *shift*.

The entire concept of what ministry is in the western world has been conventionally based on Scriptural dictates, culture, and, to some lesser extent, tradition. So, in other words, what we are about as Christians in the U.S. today is following the Bible consistently and without fail in spreading the Gospel in meaningful, relevant ways to the lost people in our culture, with only scant consideration of our religious traditions. Huh? Are we really doing that? Makes for great mission statements, church slogans, and bylines on church websites, but is it the truth!? (*Acts 1:8b - ye shall be witnesses unto me both in Jerusalem, and in all Judaea, and in Samaria, and unto the uttermost part of the earth.*)

If you could travel with me as I speak in churches across this land, you might have a completely different view of the ministry occurring today in our typical, post-modern United States church. Keep in mind, most always I am asked to come to churches where some awareness of PURE ministry has been awakened in some of the people and where

God is actually moving in some way (the *only* prerequisite for my coming); these ought to be the *strong* churches. However, there have been times when I have sat waiting to speak in churches, enduring lifeless worship devoid of any emotion or passion, and all the while saying to myself, "Just how *weak* can a church be that *I* am going to be the highlight of the service!?"

Strong or Weak?

If you believe that the typical church today in America is doing and being what I described above, you are either a member of one of the *strong* churches or, far worse, you are not and have become acclimated to a *weak* one. By *strong*, I simply mean a church that is alive, growing both spiritually and in number, and outwardly focused. Conversely, a *weak* church is spiritually on "life support," stagnant with little or no growth, frequently strangled by tradition, and focused inwardly on themselves. Unfortunately, when we evaluate churches solely on the most basic and fundamental scale, that is people being saved and Christians growing in their faith, a clearer picture of the church landscape in America emerges. It becomes obvious that, contrary to our assumptions, the *strong* church is undeniably the *exception* and certainly not the norm. Numbers, obviously, are not the only measure, but we can point to statistics of our largest denomination in America, the Southern Baptist Convention, as being at least empirically valid and troubling.

> *The 2010 Annual Church Profile showed dips in baptisms, total church membership, worship attendance and participation in Sunday school and other Christian education programs. Declines were also reported in giving categories, but some of that was attributed to the fact that not all Baptist state conventions asked churches for information in ways that make for year-to-year comparison. Southern Baptists reported 5 percent fewer baptisms in 2010 than in 2009 – 332,321 compared to 349,737. Total membership was counted at 16,136,044, a drop of 0.15*

percent and the fourth straight year of membership losses. "I pray that all of us will see the urgency of the moment," said Thom Rainer, president and CEO of LifeWay. "We must make the Great Commission the heart of all we do and say. These latest numbers should be received with a broken spirit and a God-given determination to reach people for Christ." One area that did show increase was the number of churches, which rose 1.59 percent to 45,727. Rainer said he was encouraged by a church-planting trend that could help stall the membership decline. In 2009 baptisms increased after four straight years of decline. The record year for baptisms was 445,725 in 1972. While there are far more Southern Baptist churches now, observers say baptisms have essentially been plateaued since 1950. In 2010 there was one baptism for every 48 members of a Southern Baptist church. Sixty years ago the ratio was 1:19.[1]

Though the spiritual growth and the changed lives of its members would be an equally good measure, it is also obviously much, much harder to assess. The trouble with those of us who are not even aware of what real ministry looks like is that we have, in our apathy, settled for so little when God has promised us so much. This occurs only if we surrender everything to Him, including our notions of what church and ministry should be. I submit we have not only, in many cases, reversed the priorities of Bible, culture, and tradition, but we have also in many ways perverted our mission as stated by Christ. We have often deceived ourselves by following man-conceived, successful church growth models that can and do fill beautiful buildings, but do precious little to really impact the lives of those who attend, much less the world around them.

All this talk about *strong* and *weak* churches based on impactful and meaningful ministry leads to us to the question, "What then is *real* ministry?" If we can answer this simple question, we can then be confident that what we as the body of Christ are being and doing in our communities is just what He has charged us to be and do. In the next chapter, we will make an attempt to answer this question as well as identify the important role that PURE people and their families have in our churches in realizing that ministry.

When we start to get a vision of what we are proposing to be and to be doing in our churches and realize that it does *not* revolve around meeting our own needs or preferences, we start talking about something *radical*! If we use *Matthew 7:21-23* as our standard, *Not everyone who says to Me, 'Lord, Lord,' shall enter the kingdom of Heaven, but he who does the will of My Father in Heaven.* [22] *Many will say to Me in that day, 'Lord, Lord, have we not prophesied in Your name, cast out demons in Your name, and done many wonders in Your name?'* [23] *And then I will declare to them, 'I never knew you; depart from Me, you who practice lawlessness,* we probably have many lost people attending our churches on any given Sunday morning.

Real, genuine ministry has nothing to do with the color of choir robes (whether there are choir robes at all), worship styles, building architecture, service times, number of services, Sunday school or home group organizations, large church or small church, or any of the more conventional ways we think of church. We at *PURE Ministries* refer to this all-encompassing concept as a *total church ministry.* Ministry is not based on me or you or what we like, want, or feel comfortable or able to do. No, it is ministry driven, directed, and empowered by the Holy Spirit, focused not on programs or even people in general. It is ministry focused solely on him, her, or them – people with *names.* Ministry is people with whom we have relationship. Think about this: ministry to and with PURE people, if only we recognize the gifts God has placed in them, is not only real, Scriptural ministry, it is the very model for *all* ministry.

What must we do as the church as we not only accept, but also ride the crest of this paradigm shift *wave* when we start thinking about PURE ministry in our churches? Though I obviously cannot speak for God in listing all the purposes He has for placing PURE people among us, I can identify some of the purposes fulfilled by His placing one PURE person, my grandson, Zach, in my life: to cause me to learn how to get outside of myself more, to learn to relate better to people in different ways, to think more about them than me, and other lessons too numerous to mention. Please understand that I am certainly not saying that I have arrived or that God is through growing me, but I can say that through a *personal relationship* with a young PURE boy, God has taught me something that I would not have learned in any other way. What He taught me is something that I really believe is applicable to all of us who name the name of Christ as we seek daily to make a difference in this world.

A *Total Church* Ministry

As we said above, most ministry programs within the typical church are conceived of, planned, and implemented by an interested and motivated group of people and aimed at serving or addressing a specific group or need. PURE ministry is similar to these other ministry models in some ways, but if it is to reach its God-intended potential, it must be drastically different. For example, everyone in church knows that it must have a vibrant youth ministry for many reasons: most of us have children; we all were youth once and know how important it was to us; in general, it's just something we do as *the church*. Every person in the church is not directly involved at any given time, but everyone is aware of it and generally supports it. A smaller, focused group of people within the church is involved in implementing the youth program whose focus is the youth.

Consider now PURE ministry as going deeper still. We must change the way we typically think of, respond to and interact with, and otherwise view this meaningful ministry to and with PURE people and their families. For any church to have a truly meaningful ministry to PURE people and their families, it must learn to look at this ministry as something much more than what is typically offered. Though many churches claim to have special needs or PURE ministries, most have a one hour PURE Sunday school class with very few members and staffed by a few brave souls, while most of the church does not even know that such a ministry even exists in their midst. I offer for your consideration a completely different way of approaching and actually living PURE ministry.

If your church body is going to truly include the PURE family, the ministry must be a *total church* ministry. By *total church* we mean the entire body, that is, ministry staff, church leaders, and people of all ages, are supportive and involved in ministering to and with these special people.

First, the ministerial staff (from senior pastor on down) must understand that ministry to PURE families should be a top priority of any church that is attempting to genuinely fulfill and live according to Christ's teachings. Jesus spent the majority of His time on this earth ministering to the needs of the lame, blind, and infirmed – why should His church today be different? Jesus saw their needs and met them. Further, these families have needs that we as the Body of Christ are uniquely qualified and empowered to meet – we have the love, compassion, and understanding of Jesus to share with these wonderful people. We can come alongside, become their friends, and truly help them as they live their daily lives. However, none of these things can be accomplished in a local body of believers if the shepherd(s) of the flock does not understand, actively support, and believe in this concept of PURE ministry. The ministerial staff must first believe that the ministry is vital to the life of the church and then convince and encourage the sheep that this ministry is essential to the very life of the Body.

Second, church lay leaders must also buy into the concept of *total church* and PURE ministry. It is these leaders, at the urging and encouragement of the ministerial staff, who will actually organize the church body for action. The leaders must implement the various ways the church will respond to the call and lead the people, as the church actively ministers to people in situations of which we are so often completely unaware.

Finally, though every single person in the church may not be actually directly involved, every person must have the *right* attitude. When the call is given for people to become involved in PURE ministry in a church, it is typical that many people will answer with the reservation, "I don't think this is my gift, but I'll try." It is also typical that most of these people will experience blessing of which they could not have conceived when they began – virtually no one ever gets involved in PURE ministry and then abandons it because they are uncomfortable or don't sense belonging. Rather, they begin to see life differently, appreciate simple things much more, and receive far more than they give. Again, everyone does not get involved, but everyone must change his or her preconceived notions of what church is or should be. Contrary to what many think, church is not necessarily a people, homogeneous in age, social status, intellect, or physical appearance, strengths, or weaknesses. In fact, church as defined by Jesus Himself is very inclusive – it must be *loose* enough to let anyone in, and *tight* enough not to let anyone slip away. The church is not to relax its doctrine in any way, but must not overtly or subconsciously require people to meet its standards of behavior, dress, or whatever before they are welcomed into its fellowship – it must be remembered that it is Jesus, and Jesus alone, who changes hearts. More pointedly, most PURE people cannot ever meet these superficial standards because of the way that God made them and it is supremely important that they always feel welcomed and a part of the Body. For example, if a church member thinks there is something wrong with an eighteen-year-old PURE person with Down syndrome being a greeter or usher or if they have problems with making allowances in worship to include PURE people, there is a serious heart attitude problem which must be addressed.

As discussed earlier, when Jesus gave us the *great commandment of the law* in *Matthew 22:25-40*, His response is revealing and convicting. Jesus' response is simple: love Me first and most with everything you are; love others as you love yourself. Again, Jesus said relationships, with Him and with people, are what we as Christians are to be primarily concerned. Further, it should be noted that Jesus commands us to love all of our *neighbors* – everyone, not just people who look, talk, dress, and respond as we do. According to the Word of God, an authentic body of believers will ultimately be concerned with fulfilling this commandment as Jesus instructed and will be a church based on relationships.

We believe that for a church to be a sweet savor to Jesus Christ, it is imperative that it reaches out in new and meaningful ways to PURE families. The caring, total ministry church must think of PURE people not only for one hour on Sunday morning, but must commit to think of PURE people and their families each and every time the church doors are open for anything or whenever or wherever the church body is worshipping, ministering, fellowshipping, or serving. "What needs to be done, what can I do, to allow them to be with us as we ...?" must be the question that we who care must constantly ask and affirmatively answer. When we do, we will experience *total church* ministry.

The Critical Factors: Understanding and Empathizing

Without question, the most critical factor in growing genuine PURE ministry is our willingness to become more aware of the everyday life of the PURE family. It is only through some degree of understanding and empathizing that we can become friends and be sympathetic and perceptive of how they live. What are the family members thinking and what are the feelings associated with being a PURE person or being related to a PURE person?

Perhaps one of the greatest blessings and benefits of PURE ministry for the average Christian is the opportunity to get to know and become friends with an amazing group of people - the PURE family. However, as we begin to see them, talk with them, and become more aware of who they really are and the challenges they face daily, we discover much more than we would have ever thought.

A common misconception, that all PURE parents are supermen and superwomen, begins to crumble once we get close to the situation, but frequently becomes reality as we become their friends. Somehow we think that PURE parents received individualized and extensive training about their newborn child with a disability, but soon realize this *never happens*! PURE parents, gifted with the birth of the PURE child, must learn on the job. Coping with the emotions that we will learn about later in this chapter, they are forced to pick up the pieces, bury many of their hopes and dreams, and care for their child. Moms and dads who become PURE parents as a result of an accident or debilitating illness are no different - perhaps brief instruction is given on a feeding tube or medical device, but like the PURE parents *by birth*, they have *no disability training*. As we become friends with these precious people, and begin to learn about them and all they have done, continue to do, and are, we start thinking that maybe they are supermen and superwomen after all!

However, PURE families are not living in fairytale settings. To learn a little more about these PURE parents, let's ask and answer some questions. If PURE families don't receive "disability training" (and they don't!) and they still must raise their child while dealing with the accompanying heartbreak, grief, etc., we began to ask: "What are PURE families thinking?" and "How can we, as individual Christians and corporately as the church, really help?"

What are PURE Parents Thinking?

As we gain better understanding, we learn that most PURE families are very similar to most other families with some *major* differences. These differences could not be more stark than when we consider common concerns that normal or non-PURE families are asking and then compare them to the PURE family's daily issues. For example, the typical non-PURE or normal family might be thinking:

- How do we get Johnny to his game and Mary to her dance class? They're at the same time!
- Where are we going to go camping this weekend?
- When are we going to have time to shop for that prom dress?
- How about a romantic little getaway, just you and me without the kids?
- Let's all go see a movie!
- Son, are you sure this is the girl you want to marry?

Typically the average PURE parent would literally give anything to have a life characterized by the thoughts, concerns, and questions listed above. However, the questions that the PURE parent is asking are drastically different and typically describe an entirely different situation:

- How are we going to survive?
- What will happen to my child after I am gone?
- How can I do this? I can't do this!
- Why did God allow this to happen to us?
- Will the next doctor tell us something different?
- Will he ever be able to walk?
- Will she ever be able to say she loves me?
- What would ever drive someone to make fun of him?
- How are we ever going to afford this?
- Why has my mom forsaken me now when I really need her?
- Why does no one ever ask us over?
- What am I going to do now after he's left me and I am a single mom?
- How can I keep from screaming if those people keep staring at my daughter?
- Is it really true that this all happened because of something we did, and now God is punishing us?

Yes, the PURE parent is thinking about things about which most normal parents never have to think; they are concerned about different things and spending time and effort doing different things. Yet, they have many of the same hopes and dreams for their children as do normal parents. In fact, the number one desire of PURE parents is simply to be viewed, treated like, and included as normal parents and for their PURE child to be treated as normally as possible.

What do PURE Families Really Need?

As mentioned above, PURE parents don't want to be treated as *special*. However, there are simple things that we can do to help PURE families that express the love of Jesus and show them that we do care. Perhaps the number one need of the typical PURE parent is simply a friend - someone who will listen, just be there, be a shoulder to cry on, be a person who will rejoice in seemingly small accomplishments of the PURE child. A friend who will come alongside and experience life with them. This seems like a small request, but it becomes crucial when coupled with the fact that in most PURE families at least one, and frequently more than one, immediate family members like grandmothers, grandfathers, aunts, and uncles of PURE children, *cannot handle* disability and virtually abandon the PURE family. The tragic effect and burden this places on the PURE parents not only adds to the loneliness, isolation, and alienation they are experiencing, but forces them also to accept and deal with a broken relationship with a loved one that they heretofore believed to be unshakable – "Surely, my mother is not abandoning me at this time when I need her most?" In many cases a good friend is all the PURE parent has. Particularly if the PURE family lives in a different city from the immediate family, the need for a close circle of friends is imperative.

How can this happen if we continue to operate under false assumptions, that is, the PURE family is similar to mine. We assume they've just had to make a few *adjustments* and now they're pretty normal, just like us and our friends. Special announcement: they aren't normal or average and neither is my family or yours! No, if we are really going to connect with and befriend PURE people and their families, we've got to know a little about where they're coming from, what their lives are really like, and most importantly, what they are thinking and feeling about it all. How can we become friends with someone if we won't take just a little time to know what they may be experiencing? Especially, if it is far different than what we assume to be true.

The church body is the one obvious place where the PURE families' circle of friends should be found, but sadly it is most frequently absent in the life of the PURE parent. This fact was underscored to us a few years ago when we were producing our first *PURE Ministries* video. We taped a number of PURE parents describing their experiences in raising a PURE child and they mentioned the friendships they had and help they had received from their church. However, one young PURE unchurched mom was describing her day as a mother of a PURE child when she began crying as she said, "I look forward to the therapists coming in during the day because it's the only time I get to talk to another person." The loneliness and isolation reflected in her face and evident in the words of this sweet young woman were heartrending and heartbreaking.

Just like all of us, the greatest need of the PURE person, parents, and siblings is the Savior. Just like all of us, PURE families need the close friendship of Christians willing to share the love of Jesus with them in practical, everyday ways. We cannot fix the situation, we cannot heal their child, and we cannot make everything all right, but we can care and that means more to these precious people than we can understand. What do PURE families really need? Jesus. Put very simply, Jesus, in and through us.

What Is The PURE Person *Feeling*?

All PURE people, parents, and siblings do not necessarily experience all of the emotions we will present below. Further, they all don't experience them with the same intensity nor at the same times or seasons in their lives. However, most PURE families are dealing with some of these emotions to some degree every day. Knowing them and trying to empathize can make all the difference between a shallow acquaintance and a deep friendship.

In this chapter we will explore the feelings of PURE parents and PURE siblings and offer practical things we can do to help. However, here for PURE people themselves only, I will not suggest those types of things that we can *do*. Because the disabilities of our PURE friends may be such that they cannot verbally communicate, cognitively understand, physically respond, or be limited in various other ways, the typical ways we may help them may be virtually useless. However, just because they don't communicate the way we do or respond in appropriate ways, that should not stop us from loving them. Because each PURE person is so unique, our help may take the form of a warm smile, playing a game, a touch on the shoulder, or maybe just being there with them. If we learn that the PURE person is cognitively aware at some level, then we communicate with them at that level - it is we who must *adapt* to our PURE friend, for they would do the same to us if they could.

Though it is difficult, if not impossible, to know for certain what many PURE people are feeling, some emotions experienced by even the nonverbal person or young child do not require words to be said to be understood by us. While a person with only physical disabilities with no cognitive or emotional issues can tell us how they feel, we can only project or empathize how others who can't verbalize must be feeling at any given time.

Emotions experienced by the PURE person can change over time, depending on cognitive and emotional development, severity of disabilities, and many other issues. We must realize that we cannot fix the situation by what we say or do, but we can be sure that loving them with the love of Jesus Christ will help in ways that we may never know. Just as we appreciate having someone come alongside us when we are sad or hurt, the PURE person needs and appreciates us when we attempt to relate. Though in many cases we will not be rewarded with helpful verbal feedback as with our typical friends ("I really appreciate your coming to the hospital to visit – you really cheered me up!"). By the promise of the Word of God, we can trust that He has blessed our efforts - no matter how feeble.

> *Who comforts us in all our tribulation, that we may be able to comfort those who are in any trouble, with the comfort with which we ourselves are comforted by God.*
>
> *II Corinthians 1:4*

In an attempt to describe these emotions of the PURE person, we will now discuss each by endeavoring to "get into the mind and heart" of the person. We'll do this by making objective statements and observations (without quotes) and by making statements that the PURE person might make in describing their emotions if they could (with quotes). I realize attempting to identify with a PURE person may very well be considered presumptuous, but if we don't even attempt to project how they feel, how can we relate and gain some sense of empathy? With the realization that our task is risky at best and with an understanding that our perspective must be very broad (certainly each and every observation is not true about every PURE person), we must at least try to understand what our PURE friends may possibly be experiencing. How else can we be their friends if we aren't willing to at least try to know them better?

Grief

- At times, it can be felt an intense, tearful, and overwhelming hurt.
- At other times, can manifest as an undercurrent, subtle sense of sadness and depression.
- "My life is not going to be like others."
- It can be prompted by the awareness or realization that "I am not like everybody else."
- This type of grief can occur and reoccur at any time and at different stages of life.

Depression and Despair

- It can be very general or specific.
- "Everything is so hard, so why try?"
- This feeling of depression can become a way of life.
- It can cause isolation, seclusion, withdrawal.

Fear and Anxiety

- It is particularly true with PURE people with cognitive disabilities.
- Lack of understanding of surroundings can cause great fear and anxiety.
- "I don't understand - what is happening?"
- "How do I fit in?"
- "What is my future?"

Anger

- It may be directed at oneself, others, or God.

- It may cause acting out and inappropriate behaviors.
- "Why am I this way?"

Different

- It is based on awareness level and cognitive ability of PURE person.
- "People don't look, act, or talk like me."
- "I'm odd."
- "I am a mistake."

Confusion

- It is similar to emotions of fear and anxiety in that it is more prevalent in PURE people with cognitive disabilities.
- "How do I fit in to what I'm seeing and experiencing?"
- "Who am I?"

Frustration

- It is more often than not, a result of exasperating life experiences.
- "If I could just ... –- but I can't and I never will."
- "Why can't I ...?"
- "No one understands what I feel."

Hopelessness

- Many times it is a result of the cumulative effect of other emotions and lack of encouragement from others.
- "Why try?"
- "My life has no meaning."

Inadequacy

- Constantly observing others do things he/she do or do easily.
- "Since I'm different, I am unworthy and useless."
- "I can't do what 'they' do, the way 'they' do it."

Lack of Fulfillment

- Success in virtually all areas of life for the PURE person must be measured differently. If not, fulfillment for the PURE person is elusive.
- "I can't be what I want to be."
- "I can't do what I want to do no matter how hard I try."

Loneliness

- The one emotion we can best address: we can't totally eliminate it, but our friendship and presence can make a huge difference!
- "Why do people pretend I don't exist?"
- The PURE person does feel literally invisible!
- "Where are people who will accept me?"
- "Why did this happen to me?"
- Particularly in the situation of a debilitating injury or accident, "Where are my old friends?"

Acceptance and Understanding

- With maturity, the PURE person grows to become thankful for how God has made them (*I Thessalonians 5:18*).
- Understanding that their disability is in God's perspective, it becomes a mark of ownership and an asset.
- They again recognize that their life has an impact on others: family members and friends have derived strength, insight, and a greater ability to love and accept unconditionally from this experience.
- Many PURE people have special abilities to pray so sincerely and praise God so authentically, that we non-PURE people can only envy their transparency, honesty, and intimacy with God.
- "I'm perfect just the way God made me."

What Are The PURE Parents *Feeling*?

The PURE parent's life is characterized by many different issues, stages, and situations, but ever-changing emotions are a constant amidst it all. From the shock of the initial diagnosis to the joys of simple life successes for their child, the PURE parents are constantly faced with their own feelings. It must be emphasized that these emotions are frequently exacerbated by the fact that many PURE parents are *single* parents. Unfortunately, with the high divorce rates in PURE families, PURE moms often find themselves severely stressed in their valiant attempt to be both parents to their children.

The value of support groups to the PURE family cannot be overestimated. Forming friendships with others in similar situations is typically a great encouragement to the PURE family. Also, activities specifically focused on and geared to PURE families can reduce the tension and anxiety normally present when involved in activities in more traditional settings. Simply having a shoulder to cry on or receiving a word of encouragement from someone who knows what is being experienced or is in the future can become vital to most PURE families. As concerned friends, helping our PURE family friends in locating a support group or possibly helping start one in your church, is always appreciated.

Below are some of the most common emotions experienced or *lived out* by parents, either temporarily or constantly, and some practical suggestions of how we might *help* in a meaningful and much welcomed way. Again, as for the PURE person, these comments and observations are very broad and general in one respect, but many, if not all are commonly experienced at some point by the typical PURE parent. Needless to say, our greatest help is to pray consistently for the parents and to ask God to show us individually how we can become involved in their lives.

Grief

Lived out:

- It is not caused by death alone – it starts at birth and/or diagnosis and never ends in a PURE family.
- This is a general and pervasive feeling of sadness – a sense of loss of dreams and hopes.
- The five traditional stages of grief (denial, anger, bargaining, depression, and acceptance) are inadequate to completely describe this grief that virtually never goes away completely.
- Perhaps a better, alternate grief theory best expresses this kind of grief:
  - Shock – It comes with the diagnosis, with the prospect of a different life altogether than planned, with what is required of them as a PURE parent.
  - Emotional Release – It is characterized by alternating periods of "We can do this" and overwhelming depression and helplessness.
  - Panic - "How am I going to do this?!"
  - Guilt - This is the most common of all emotions of PURE parents: even among Christians who know better, the universal thinking is "If I had not done ... when in college" or "God is punishing me for ..."
  - Hostility - It is an easy and immediate release of emotional energy to get angry at oneself, others, or even God. Later, hostility can become a common defense.
  - Inability to resume business-as-usual activities - Sometimes the PURE parent is simply overwhelmed with the entire situation and withdraws from family and friends and can be triggered by life situations in loving and caring for a PURE child and all of the demands placed on them as a PURE parent.
  - Reconciliation of grief, hope - Though sometimes fleeting in the course of daily living, the PURE parent accepts their

PURE life as a gift from God as opposed to His wrath or punishment.

- Every PURE parent is different and experiences and lives through this special grief in his/her own way – the spectrum ranges from some PURE parents expressive in their grief, some ostensibly feeling no grief at all, and everything in between.
- Not all stages (especially of the five traditional stages) are ever, in fact, experienced nor are the stages necessarily experienced sequentially.
- For the normal PURE parent, the stages of this grief are virtually never experienced only once on some theoretical passage to the next stage. Rather, grief can reoccur at any moment prompted by major events such as the first day of school, a confirmed diagnosis, or other milestones. It can also be unprompted and spontaneous realizations of family life. While attending a wedding of a friend, the parent abruptly and unexpectedly realizes for the first time that their PURE child will never get married; with other moms watching other children play on a playground, the sudden realization that their PURE child will never have that simple pleasure; and seemingly insignificant events like overhearing friends innocently discuss weekend plans for their children's ball games, piano recitals, and other common activities, the PURE parent is overtaken with grief knowing that their weekends will most likely never include such normal circumstances.
- Grief can overwhelm the PURE parent when least expected – a familiar smell, a glance at a photograph, a trip to a convenience store, or a harmless and innocuous comment by a friend can trigger grief in a PURE parent. It is seldom anticipated and little, if nothing, can stop it.
  - It is characterized by such comments as: "I wish I would have …" or "I wish I didn't …" This is part of the life for the PURE parent.

We can help by:

- Listening.
- If the parents are not Christian, presenting the Gospel of Christ to the hurting PURE parent and encouraging a forgiving spirit and acceptance of forgiveness.
- Being willing to just listen and not correct or attempt to solve the problem.

Loneliness, Isolation, and Alienation

Lived out:

- Regardless of the appearance or perception of their level of participation, their involvement, or their activity levels, *know* without a doubt that every PURE parent experiences some degree of loneliness, isolation, and alienation. The extent to which PURE parents feel this way is normally based on four major factors:
  - The type(s) of disabilities of the PURE person,
  - The severity of disabilities,
  - The emotional make-up of the parents themselves,
  - And, perhaps most of all, us! We cannot obviously eliminate the other three factors, nor can we totally prevent these emotions in our friends who are PURE parents, but our willingness to enter into genuine friendships with them can certainly help.

- PURE parents often feel totally alone because people don't know or understand what their lives are really like every minute of every day. We visit with them at church, and then we go home and have a normal night's sleep. They go home to a PURE child who doesn't sleep at all or requires care on the hour, every hour. The PURE parent is all too aware of this misconception -- we seldom are.

- In our nervousness and uneasiness in communicating with PURE parents we often tend to heap praise and adoration on them for lack of anything else to say. The PURE parent must then deal with a difficult, confusing, and perplexing dichotomy: they are constantly told how *special* and *blessed* they are, yet they feel so inadequate and ill prepared to be a PURE parent. For example, they struggle on Sunday morning to get to church and then are told "God chose you to be a special needs mom. I don't see how you do it all." What only the PURE mom knows is that she had "lost" it earlier that morning and thrown a bowl of oatmeal across the kitchen in utter frustration!

- Because of our fears and feelings of awkwardness and being uncomfortable around PURE people, we don't know what to say or do – so we say and do nothing and the PURE parent is, again, isolated.

- Even friends, not sure how to deal with a PURE situation, sometimes withdraw, fade way, or vanish completely by conveniently being *too busy* to be involved with the PURE family.

- As discussed earlier, in almost every PURE situation some immediate family members abandon the PURE family.

- Feelings of loneliness, isolation, and alienation never totally disappear for the PURE parent. Like grief, they reoccur at the least expected times.

We can help by:

- Empathizing with them as best we can.
- Phoning just to say Hello.
- Making personal visits.
- Inviting them to be included in each and every activity - even if you already know they can't attend. Our asking means we care to the PURE parent and will inevitably lead us to become more involved in the PURE family's life, perhaps leading us to, "Let me stay with Johnny, and you go to … in my place."

- Treating the parents as normally as possible. Along with a respite break, this is perhaps the number one need of the PURE parent!

- Offering to help in meaningful ways, not just saying "We'll pray for you." Though the PURE parent should constantly be in our prayers and if our prayer is real, God may call us to get involved. *James 2:14-17* addresses these hollow prayers - *What does it profit, my brethren, if someone says he has faith but does not have works? Can faith save him? If a brother or sister is naked and destitute of daily food, and one of you says to them, "Depart in peace, be warmed and filled," but you do not give them the things which are needed for the body, what does it profit? Thus also faith by itself, if it does not have works, is dead.*

    o Not simply accommodating, but including the PURE family socially. It is easy to accommodate, "Sure, you can bring your daughter if you have to – we'll find someone to look after her if we can." But it is much harder (and much more rewarding and beneficial to everybody concerned) to genuinely include, "We're so glad you're coming and especially glad Susie can come! She'll have so much fun with the other kids – they've missed her while she's been in the hospital."

<u>Guilt</u>

Lived out:

- As discussed earlier in the section on the sovereignty of God, many if not most PURE parents suffer from feelings of unfounded guilt. It is easy for any of us to identify something in our past as the *reason* God is doing something to us in the present.

- Except in the rarest of circumstances (child abuse, substance abuse, or the like), PURE parents' guilt is baseless. However, the guilt can sometimes be emotionally crippling to the PURE parent stressed with raising a PURE child.

- Like all of us, PURE parents think they must have a *reason* to explain their PURE child. The need to have a *reason* often leads to wrong thinking, especially about the character of God. Shocked and bewildered with the reality of having a PURE child, PURE parents many times initially view their child as something *bad* that has happened or even a *tragedy*. Fortunately however, most PURE parents perspective of their PURE son or daughter changes over time as they realize their child is actually a gift from God, never punishment for sin.

We can help by:

- Remembering not to judge, but to lovingly affirm and tenderly explain why the feelings of guilt are irrational.
- Helping alleviate their feelings of inadequacy, even though they are doing their best.
- Refusing to validate feelings of guilt.
- Encouraging self-forgiveness.

Confusion

Lived out:

- Contrary to common misconceptions, PURE children are not born with a "toe tag" listing their disabilities. Except in certain disabilities, the actual period of making the diagnoses as well as the short and long term effects of the diagnosed disability(s), is normally months and years rather than days and weeks. In fact, a definitive diagnosis for many PURE people is never confirmed. This delay, whether temporary or permanent, combined with the other uncertainties surrounding a PURE child results in a sense of confusion for the PURE parents.
- Most often no firm information is given as to how the PURE person's disability will affect their development.

- Extended periods of testing, evaluation and study many times conclude with little or no answers.
- Long term expectations and prognosis are unclear.
- In addition to confusion regarding diagnosis, the spectrum of treatment options for any given disability can be overwhelming for the PURE parent, leading to even more confusion. For example, though the internet is an amazing tool, if one Googles "cerebral palsy treatments," 1,900,000 results are instantaneously returned. To add to the confusion, treatment regimens are ongoing in countries all over the world; some must have started with children at certain ages; some require months if not years of on-site care; and virtually all are extremely expensive. To make matters even more confusing, this dilemma is only for the one disability, cerebral palsy. Cerebral palsy, like many disabilities, is rarely a solitary issue – usually, more disabilities accompany it. Faced with so many choices and not knowing with any certainty if any will work or any are appropriate for their child, parents are confused and unsure which direction to take. Should life changes be made to accommodate necessary travel for possible treatment? Somebody must keep a job to pay for treatment and, in most situations, insurance won't pay.

We can help by:

- Going along with our friends to medical appointments, assisting with transportation, or physically helping the PURE person.
- Only if asked, gathering and organizing information. The last thing a PURE parent needs is a well intentioned friend suggesting 20 different websites to visit concerning their child's issues or treatment.
- Caring for children while parents attend appointments is always a practical and welcomed gift.

Shock, Fear

Lived out:

- For many parents, receiving a serious diagnosis about their precious new baby can best be described only as shock. They are literally stunned with the news and realization that their lives, as they had believed and assumed they would be, are now forever changed. Though they cannot fully imagine what their lives and the life of their son or daughter will be, they know enough that everything will be different and certainly not what they had expected or planned.

- This shock sometimes can cause people to be totally unable to go about their daily lives – living, simply doing the mundane things we automatically and routinely do every day, virtually stops. The prospect of raising a child with his/her issues is simply too much to bear. The PURE parent suffers from an ambiguous sense of numbness to life as they know it.
  - Along with the shock, comes fear, both imagined and real:
  - "I don't know anything about _____ - how can I possibly ever care for my child?"
  - "Will my child ever be able to _____?"
  - "How will this affect our marriage?"
  - "What about our plans for our family?"

- Special Note: Though, obviously, none of the emotions that arise in the hearts and minds of new PURE parents are a surprise to God, it is at these times that God is especially merciful to family members in the grasp of this debilitating shock and fear. Like any of us facing a seemingly insurmountable trial or challenge in our lives with which we are unaccustomed and unprepared, the Lord, in His infinite mercy, does not reveal the future in its *entirety*. Our vision into the future is very limited and clouded with both real and perceived obstacles. No, the Lord lovingly and gradually reveals His plan to us on a minute-by-minute, day-by-day basis. In most cases we cannot even *see* what the very next day holds. God protects us by not showing us our lives in a panoramic way, for, most likely, few of us could take it all in. Regardless, in this situation of PURE parents facing life for which they feel unprepared or any other life situation that we might find ourselves, God is encouraging us to simply lean and depend only on Him.

We can help by:

- Being patient with our friends and not minimizing what they are feeling.
- Accepting how this is affecting their daily lives and helping them with practical daily activities.
- Understanding that the shock and fear will fade over time – this situation in its intensity is temporary, but the emotions will linger and reappear at times.

Denial, Unrealistic Hope

Lived out:

- Because PURE parents are just like non PURE parents, their reaction and response to their child's disability issues can run the entire emotional gamut.
- Many PURE parents live in a constant state of denial: the doctors are wrong, the diagnosis is wrong, something like *this* just isn't happening to them. They cannot believe that there is really a problem with their child. "We need to get another (and another, and another …) opinion." Regardless of the signs, clues or actual evidence these parents experience or receive, they cannot bring themselves to accept the reality of their child's issues. They will excuse any abnormal behavior or telltale signs, explain away or rationalize anything atypical in their child, and generally are unreceptive to suggestion from

anyone to the contrary. These PURE parents will sometimes *shoot* the messenger. If a nursery worker or teacher mentions some abnormal behavior he or she has observed, it is easier to deny than to accept the very thing they are trying so hard to avoid. It is not unusual for these parents to put their children in untenable situations, such as he/she is placed in a normal classroom with no extra help or assistance, even though the child is not ready for that environment.

- At the other extreme are PURE parents who have *accepted* the fact of their child's disability, but believe unrealistically that their child can be *cured*. They believe that if they can go to the next doctor, clinic, or treatment facility, that they will find the elusive cure. Obviously, this is not to say that PURE people cannot live *normal* lives within the context of the severity of their disability. It is not that these PURE parents are not happy with the accomplishments of their PURE child; they just believe that somewhere, if they keep looking, they will find the cure.

- Most PURE parents find themselves somewhere in the middle of the denial/hope emotional spectrum. Many vacillate between the two extremes from time to time based on real life experiences. For example, after listening to their young autistic child read a book flawlessly, the PURE parent might try to convince themselves that the diagnosis was wrong -- he/she is normal after all! It is not until later that same day that the child has an embarrassing, unprovoked, emotional breakdown on a trip to the local shopping mall that the PURE parent is again faced with the reality of their child's issues and their own emotional roller coaster. Balancing between the two emotional limits is the typical PURE parent's challenge of accepting the reality of the diagnosis and its inherent limitations, yet being hopeful and content with their child's progress, development, and accomplishments.

We can help by:

- Being a good listener which is, perhaps, how we can help the PURE parent the most. There is little we can say to change their mind – this is the work of the Holy Spirit.
- Trying to understand the emotions that PURE parents are experiencing and how they are trying to make some sense of their world.
- Encouraging the PURE parents as they gain insight into how their own emotions are affecting their child.
- Avoiding making suggestions or recommendations on how to "get over this problem." We can't help if we become *part* of the problem.

Anger

Lived out:

- It is not uncommon for the typical PURE parents to find themselves angry. The shock of the diagnosis begins to wear off, the reality of the situation starts to sink in, and they feel vulnerable and unprepared for what they see that lies ahead. They begin asking the question, "Why me?" Not receiving a clear answer, they can easily to fall into a general state of frustration which sometimes gives way to anger.
- Normally, this anger is not open hostility toward others, but in some cases it may be. The PURE parent may be shunned repeatedly enough by family and friends by conveniently not being invited or included. Though most times unintentionally, friends and family *reject* them by saying, "We didn't think you could come so we didn't ask." A simmering resentment can be and often is the result. This type anger can be manifested in quietness, coolness, aloofness, and even withdrawal.
- Couple the isolation inherent in the PURE family with hearing too many well-meaning family and friends make comments

like, "If you would just discipline him/her, your child would behave" or "We heard about a nice home for people with _____" can send a PURE parent over the edge.

- Even lashing out at loved ones is not uncommon -- being angry feels better than being afraid.
- The Christian PURE parent isn't immune to anger. "After all I've done for you, Lord, why this?" can be a common plea for the Christian parent who has yet to acknowledge and appreciate the blessings God has placed in their PURE child.

We can help by:

- Not taking our friend's occasional short temper or outburst personally - we don't really know what they're going through at any particular time.
- Conveying that anger can be a positive emotion if well-directed.
- Being a good listener.
- Commending family members for efforts to use anger in a positive way.

Bargaining with God

Lived out:

- We've all done it: "If You'll just let me pass this test, I promise to study next time;" "If You'll just let me marry him/her, I'll promise to give up _____;" or "If You will get me out of this one more time, I'll live my life for You, Lord." Yes, none of us are above trying to bargain with God: if God will do X, then we promise to do Y. Unfortunately, God isn't into bargaining - He is into obedience. The PURE parent's bargaining might go something like this: "If You will just let him walk, I'll not ask for anything else" or "If someone would just ask her over to play one time, I promise not to ask again." Though the PURE parents' requests are in most cases not for themselves but for their child and they are normally more poignant and heartrending than our "get me out of this test" types, they do reveal an incorrect perspective of who God really is. Despite what we sincerely believe to be best for us or even our PURE child, God *knows* what is best, and that is what will be done. We cannot negotiate or bargain with the Creator of the universe and our loving Heavenly Father. He already knows what is best for us, how it all fits into His plans, and what the results will be.

We can help by:

- Lovingly sharing our own unfruitful bargaining experiences with our PURE parent friends and helping them see God not as an arbitrator but as a loving Father.
- Encouraging the correct view of God. He is not out to *get us* nor is He punishing us. He loves us and only wants the best for His children.
- Discouraging bargaining behavior and encouraging simple trusting in God. He is listening and will respond, but maybe not like we think He should.

Sorrow and Depression

Lived out:

- It is a rare PURE parent who does not from time to time suffer from a sense of sorrow and depression. It may be triggered by an event or simply the fact that everyday life is so very challenging and hard, but sorrow and depression can come like a rogue wave and engulf the PURE parent.
- Based on the emotional makeup of the individual and the closeness of their support, sorrow and depression can become a way of life for the PURE parent if he or she is not careful. Because, in many cases everyday life can become overwhelming, a heaviness of spirit can become ever-present. It is very

important for those of us who are close to these PURE parents to be sensitive and observant and do all we can to empathize, help, and encourage them. In some cases, professional help may be required.

- It should be noted that many times these feelings of sorrow and depression are heightened and more intense when the PURE parent is fatigued.

We can help by:

- Allowing family members to cry, and crying with them - sharing the loss of dreams and expectations.
- Gently offering encouragement by pointing out all the things the family members are doing well in coping with the disability.
- Sharing the load by giving practical assistance and providing pleasant diversions such as offering to give the parents a date night.
- Offering to come over to vacuum or cut grass can do amazing things for the tired PURE parent.

Acceptance / Understanding

Lived out:

- As we have discussed earlier and we will discuss further in the last chapter of this book, PURE people, when we get a glimmer of what God has placed in them, can literally change our lives. This is nowhere more evident than in the life of PURE parents who accept God's plan of having a PURE child.
- With this acceptance of what God is doing both through the life of their child and through themselves, they see their PURE child the way God intended - not as a person with a disability, but as a person especially gifted and talented.

- Through life's experiences, PURE parents develop a sincere appreciation, respect, and admiration for their own PURE child as well as other PURE people and families.
- Though unsure and anxious when the journey began, a more relaxed attitude is evident in the life of the PURE parents who have successfully navigated through so many life challenges.
- Regardless of the number and severity of disabilities, PURE parents experience growth and an indescribable joy in the relationship with their PURE child.
- They begin to view the opportunity of having a PURE child as a special blessing rather than dwelling on hardships that arise.
- Perhaps most of all, the perceptive PURE parent begins to recognize the effect their PURE child has had on their family as a whole. Again, it becomes obvious that both immediate and extended family members have derived strength, insight, a greater ability to love, and unconditional acceptance from the experience of living with the person.

We can help by:

- Taking a genuine interest in the accomplishments of the PURE person – not patronizing, but seeing the accomplishments for what they really are in the life of the PURE person and family.
- Being sensitive to the times when depression re-surfaces and continuing to offer practical assistance.
- Encouraging family members to share their experiences with others – we all have so much to learn from these people!
- Joining with the PURE parent in thanking and praising God for the blessing of disability!

What Are The PURE Siblings *Feeling*?

PURE siblings are without a doubt the one group in the world of disability that is most often forgotten. Yet, both the positive and negative effects of being raised in a PURE home are life-changing and profound. Those closest to a PURE family mistakenly assume that the younger brothers/sisters are unaffected by the dynamics of the PURE family - but, everyone is affected. These emotions can be more easily observed and detected with older children, but are a constant with the siblings beginning with their first awareness that something is different about their PURE brother or sister. An aware, informed, and sensitive church family can do much to bring balance and encouragement to these children living in a world filled with confusing medical discussions, visits by therapists, necessary absence of parents, and many other disruptions and confusing events. Though life is hard for PURE siblings, the character built is most often one of a very loving, sensitive, caring and strong person. In training sessions we often shockingly state, "A sibling growing up with a PURE brother/ sister will normally either grow up to be a wonderful person or a jerk." Pretty strong language, but most often true nonetheless. We go on to explain that only the most self-absorbed person can live through and observe the challenges and struggles faced by their PURE brother/ sister and parents and not become a more caring and loving person. The church body has great opportunity to make an enormous impact on the life of the PURE sibling. In fact, many churches who believe they have no disability ministry in place are unaware that they have PURE siblings already in their midst. The special attention of a youth worker, caring Sunday school teacher, or family friend can many times fill a void that the PURE sibling often experiences.

Let me emphasize again, just as for PURE people themselves and for PURE parents, not all PURE siblings experience each and every one of the emotions below. Neither do they all experience them in the same ways, same intensity, or even at the same ages. Young PURE siblings aren't as adept at hiding their feelings. It must be remembered that just because feelings are not expressed verbally or not evident in behaviors does not necessarily mean that the older siblings are not dealing with these very emotions. My attempt is to take a broad look at some of the common and most frequently experienced feelings of a typical PURE sibling. With that said, what are PURE siblings feeling?

Resentment / Jealousy

Lived out:

- It is quite normal, regardless of age, for virtually all PURE siblings to feel some amount of resentment and jealousy toward their PURE brother or sister. Obviously, this is more prevalent in young children, but resentment can linger into adulthood if not addressed by the PURE parent. This entire subject of resentment and jealousy as being problems with PURE siblings may seem strange initially, but a closer examination of what is involved may shed some light on the reasons for such feelings. Imagine being a five-year-old and having your mother spending most of her time with another sibling. You know that there is something special about your PURE sibling, but you certainly cannot understand all of the issues involved. All you know is that your brother or sister gets more time with your mom and dad. In this case and so many like it, it would actually be unnatural for the PURE sibling not to feel some resentment or jealousy of their PURE brother or sister. Though the dynamics and life situations of the family change over time and as the children grow up, still some feelings of resentment can linger even for teenagers. For instance, PURE siblings may not be able to do what their peers are doing because of the demands, though unintentional and not deliberate, placed on the family by the PURE brother or sister. For example, "Why can't I go to the game with my friends?" is answered with "Because you know you have to keep your baby sister while your dad and I are at the hospital tonight." Logical, reasonable, and perfectly understandable - except if you're a teenager wanting to go out with your friends and *again,* unable to do so.
- Feelings of being *left out* are common, particularly in young PURE siblings, who watch their parents spend so much time and energy on their PURE brother or sister. Young PURE siblings don't necessarily understand all that is happening

in their lives. Further, it doesn't really matter how well it is explained, for like all young children, they are simply resentful of the time and attention they're missing.

- In most all cases regardless of age, the PURE sibling knows these feelings are wrong, but they can't help what they feel. As a natural result, these feelings often cause guilt which is another emotion common to PURE siblings.

We can help by:

- Doing our best to stay knowledgeable about what is currently happening in the PURE family. With this knowledge and with sensitivity, including the PURE sibling in your family's activities - sharing a meal, watching a game together, or going to get ice cream can be a wonderful diversion for a PURE sibling.
- Purposing to spend extra time with PURE siblings of whom you are aware in your church. If you are a family close to the PURE family and are called on occasionally to keep the PURE siblings while the PURE parents are caring for their PURE child, make the visits fun and do all you can to make the PURE siblings feel special and part of your larger family.
- Individually, or corporately as the church, taking PURE siblings on special outings – a ball game, a movie, or a picnic.

Guilt

Lived out:

- Frequently, guilt, as discussed previously, is a direct result of other feelings, common in PURE siblings, namely resentment and jealousy of a PURE brother or sister.
- In younger PURE siblings, guilt is often caused by a child's imagination, lack of information, confusion, and misunderstanding. As they try to make sense of their PURE

brother or sister's issues, they sometimes wrongly assume "Something I did caused this." It could be as innocent as calling their brother a name while playing or taking his/her cookie while they weren't looking - the imagination of children is fathomless and as their conscience are being developed, illogical consequences for certain actions are sometimes the result.

- Another real type of guilt is common to us non-PURE people, but particularly to PURE siblings: we feel guilty for being healthy. We can't seem to accept the fact that God has made us healthy while our PURE brother/sister (or friend) has many issues, health and otherwise. Granted, this is a common problem for all of us in many areas of life -- why are we: wealthy or poor; tall or short; thin or heavy; born in America or in a third world country; and the questions never end. We will never be able to answer or understand the answer to any of these life's dilemmas, but if we are Christians, we know the One who does and we must only trust completely that He knows what He is doing.

We can help by:

- Being sensitive to the PURE sibling's concerns and treating them as real problems.
- Avoiding minimizing or making light of their emotions.
- Doing our best to confirm God's sovereignty in all things. As Christians, we are not called to live with guilt, which in essence questions the wisdom of God Himself. Further, PURE siblings need not live under the cloud of some obscure, misplaced guilt for something for which they bear no responsibility: the disability of their PURE sibling. But, many do. It is right and good to thank God for being who we are, that is, healthy, male, female, tall, short, thin, heavy, left-handed, etc. It is sinful to thank God that we *aren't like somebody else* – a certain race, poor, or particularly, PURE. This is a very fine line for certain, but

remember Jesus' parable in *Luke 18:9-14* of the two men who went up to pray, illustrates the point perfectly. It is fine, for example, to thank God that we haven't had a stroke, as long as our trust is in Jesus. "But, if You allow it for me, I know You'll be there with me, it is part of Your perfect plan, and You will receive glory through it all." No, we aren't to live our lives guilty and ashamed because God has blessed us with health, families, or jobs. Besides, everything, all situations and circumstances, on this earth are temporary – just because we haven't yet experienced bad health or a wayward daughter doesn't mean God might not allow it for us if it is in His plan sometime in the future. What do we do then? Will we be like Job and trust Him - *Though he slay me, yet will I trust in him? (Job 13:15)* We are always to thank Him for good things He has given us, but all the while knowing that He alone knows what is really best for each of us at any time.

- Remembering that even without us receiving or possessing certain perceived *good* things, God is still God – loving, merciful, just, and sovereign.

<u>Sadness</u>

Lived out:

- The kind of sadness we mean here is not the superficial sadness of a very young PURE sibling who is sad that he/she cannot do something or go somewhere because of their PURE brother or sister. That type of sadness is really more akin to resentment. However, much like the PURE parent, sometimes the PURE sibling is simply overwhelmed with a deep sense of sadness in the normal course of life. In a human sense this sadness is very real and, in many cases, justified. For instance, when a young teenager leaves to pick up his prom date and glances back at his young PURE brother looking proudly out the picture window, he will suddenly realize (perhaps even for the first time) that probably his young PURE brother will never be able to do the very thing he is doing. Sadness in this situation and in so many others is a common and natural emotion for the sensitive PURE sibling.

- As the PURE siblings mature, more awareness of the plight of their PURE brother/sister can be a good sign of spiritual growth as the siblings empathize more and more with their parents and PURE brother/ sister. Sadness is a natural result of this growing awareness. "My brother will never be able to marry" or "My sister will always be in that wheelchair."

We can help by:

- Recognizing that the situations creating these sad feelings are indeed real and that the PURE sibling's emotions are natural and justified.
- Depending on the age of the sibling, we can use these situations as teachable moments to encourage the PURE sibling. We want to help the PURE sibling not to focus on what their PURE brother/sister can't do or suffers from, but to encourage the PURE sibling in how they bless their PURE brother/sister when they spend time with, give attention to, and do whatever brings joy and fulfillment to them.
- Realizing that in some rare cases, professional help may be needed to keep the PURE sibling's feelings of sadness from worsening into depression, or, equally troubling, pity.

Embarrassment

Lived out:

- Similar to feelings of resentment are those of embarrassment. Even the most loving PURE siblings can find themselves in situations where they are embarrassed by their PURE brother or sister. This can happen at any time, but is more common when the PURE sibling is not fully aware of the condition of their PURE brother/sister and during their formative years when they themselves are more concerned with appearances and being accepted by their peers. Most all of us can recall our teenage years when we were embarrassed even by our parents because they weren't sufficiently *cool*. In this case, the PURE sibling knows he/she *shouldn't* be embarrassed by his PURE brother/sister out in public, but like any of us, other emotions take a back seat when our self-image is threatened.

- Like the emotions of sadness, a personal confrontation with one's own embarrassment can lead to serious reflection and soul-searching for the sensitive PURE sibling. As they work through their feelings, they gain understanding and realize that their PURE brother/sister is not trying to embarrass them, but rather their looks, behaviors, and abilities are part of who they are. Dealing positively with embarrassment can be a good sign of spiritual growth as the sibling empathizes to a greater extent with their PURE brother/ sister and parents.

We can help by:

- Assuring them that feelings of embarrassment are sometimes natural and normal for PURE siblings, but not something that they should accept of themselves as they mature.
- Helping them work through their feelings of embarrassment by listening and encouraging them to empathize with their PURE brother or sister.
- Encouraging a sense of humor in dealing with many of these life situations.

Fear and Concerns About the Future

Lived out:

- With a lack of information and frequently confused with the information they have, children's imaginations generate their own childlike and frequent frightening misunderstanding of their PURE sibling's situation. Complicated medical terms take on different meanings. With this confusion often come wrong assumptions for the typical, young PURE sibling - "My brother is dying," or "I may catch what she has."
- Another real concern of PURE siblings that can occur as early as five or six years old is the realization that they possibly will be caring for their PURE brother/sister after the parents are gone. This is a heavy burden for young children to contemplate, yet it is common in the minds of even the youngest perceptive PURE siblings and stays with them throughout their lives. Based on the types and severity of their PURE brother/sister's disabilities, this is a very real possibility for PURE siblings.

We can help by:

- Supporting the parents in explaining to the younger PURE sibling, in age-appropriate ways, confusing situations to help alleviate their fear and apprehension.
- Comforting, affirming, and counseling the PURE sibling as he/she matures with regard to possible options regarding extended care for their PURE brother/sister, if the situation arises.
- Stressing dependence on and refuge in our loving Lord in whom we can fully depend, regardless of what life may bring to even the youngest PURE sibling.

Isolation and Excessive Responsibility

Lived out:

- A natural result of the life of many PURE families is that non-PURE children are often apart from parents for extended periods of time. In the life of many PURE children are many doctor visits, therapy sessions, and often frequent stays in the hospital. With dad working or absent, mom is responsible for most of the PURE child's care and must rely on family and friends to care for the PURE siblings while she is away. With this unintentional separation and disjointing of the family, the PURE sibling can feel isolated and alone. Even within the warmth of another loving family, whether extended family or friend, a PURE sibling can feel isolated from other members of their own family.

- Also with the frequent times of being left with family or friends and particularly when old enough to be left alone, the PURE sibling sometimes has greater responsibility than would be appropriate for their age otherwise. Most PURE siblings are extremely mature for their ages and have learned much about making it on their own. These unfortunate but unavoidable situations of isolation for the PURE sibling can be character building if handled appropriately.

We can help by:

- Praising the PURE sibling's self-reliance, affirming the positives and downplaying the negatives of the situation.
- On the other end of the situation, supporting the PURE parents by being one of those families to which they can confidently entrust their children as the need arises.
- Helping alleviate feelings of abandonment by filling the time void with activities that the PURE sibling enjoys.

Pressure to Achieve

Lived out:

- If there is a number one feeling of the astute PURE sibling, it is the increased pressure they feel to achieve. The reasoning goes something like this, "Mom and Dad have sacrificed and struggled so much with my PURE brother/sister, I've got to make them proud." Though these feelings are admirable and evidence of a loving son or daughter, sometimes the pressure these PURE siblings place on themselves is unbearable and impossible for them to ever achieve. As a result they can become frustrated in not reaching their unattainable goals and further feel as if they have disappointed their mom and dad.
- It must be remembered that this pressure that the PURE sibling is experiencing is almost always self-imposed – it is extremely rare for a PURE parent to put these unrealistic expectations on their children.
- Like so many of the feelings of the PURE sibling, the pressure to achieve can also be a great character motivator if properly controlled and channeled.

We can help by:

- Sincerely praising the real accomplishments of the PURE sibling. Depending on the emotional makeup of the PURE brother or sister, some will need more encouragement than others. All people, especially PURE siblings, need the constant encouragement that can be so impactful and meaningful coming from a good friend.
- Building self-confidence with helpful and encouraging comments. Not only are our positive comments needed to communicate our concern, care, and love, they also are extremely important in building the self-confidence of the PURE sibling. Most of us need only to think of situations in

our own lives when friends, or perhaps more meaningfully, parents of our friends, complimented us on something we had done or accomplished.

- Assisting and encouraging the PURE sibling in setting realistic goals and expectations. A difficult task for sure and a fine line to walk, but if we care, we may need to come alongside and bring realism with a good probability of success to a PURE sibling. Otherwise, they may live their lives laboring under unrealistic goals and expectations sure to bring failure. Ever mindful of not damaging their self-confidence, we sometimes must be a voice of reason to a PURE brother or sister suffering with his/her inability to reach expectations that are too lofty and unrealistic.

Independence, Maturity, Loyalty

Lived out:

- A natural result of the life of the PURE family in many, if not most, situations is a more mature, independent, and loyal person. Because the PURE sibling must deal with circumstances and emotions that most of us never encounter or if we do, much later in life, they are forced to grow up more quickly. As they grow up faster, PURE siblings are frequently more mature than their peers. This greater responsibility often results in an earlier and exceptional maturity.
- Coupled with this maturity is often a greater sense of loyalty. Though not always the case, the PURE sibling develops a faithfulness and loyalty not only to their PURE brother or sister, but to the family as a whole. This heightened loyalty is evident from the first time the PURE sibling takes up for his/her brother sister on the playground and continues throughout their adult lives. Loyalty becomes an integral and prominent characteristic of the typical PURE sibling.

- Again, because of what become normal situations in the PURE family (hospital stays, therapy sessions, doctor visits, etc.) necessitating PURE siblings being left to stay with friends and family, the PURE brother or sister develops a greater sense of self-reliance than what would be typically expected. The PURE sibling learns how to cope with these difficult circumstances and normally grows from the experience.

- Perhaps the most important result of a person being raised in a PURE home is that drastically different perspectives are gained. For example, thankfulness in a PURE family can be genuinely expressed for the simplest of things: a full night of sleep, an uninterrupted meal, or the seemingly small successes of their PURE brother or sister. A genuine appreciation of family, the worthiness of all people, and real love are but a few of the perspectives positively attained in a PURE home.

How Can We, the Church, Help?

Besides genuine friendship, what can we, the church, do to actually help PURE families? As the church family, we need to understand that as a PURE child grows and matures, his/her needs change and new, unanticipated ones surface constantly. Similarly, our ability to respond and meet these needs changes as well. It must be remembered that our willingness and commitment to stay close to PURE families, who want to be in church each Sunday but frequently cannot be due to the issues with their child, are crucial if we are to be aware of these needs as they arise. In other words, we must be good friends to *know* what our good friends are going through and need - we simply can't know these things seeing people occasionally and infrequently at church - we must make a concerted effort to know.

The key word for helping PURE families is *practical*. Whatever the specific need of a given PURE family, our approach as Christians, if we truly love as Jesus would love, will always be practical. In so many examples of Scripture, when Jesus is confronted with a need, His response is always practical. When confronted with the need for more wine at the marriage in Cana of Galilee, He created more wine - He didn't condemn the host for his lack of preparedness, nor did He build a winery! Throughout Scripture Jesus went about meeting the needs of people He encountered. He was most concerned about people's souls, but He met their physical needs as well. No, we cannot create wine from water nor can we heal people like Jesus did, but we can show His love in practical ways to those around us who need it - PURE families.

As authentic Christians genuinely concerned with meeting the needs of PURE families in our communities, we must first know generally what those needs are. Obviously, all of these needs, however broad, are not applicable to all PURE families, but they are a starting point from which we can begin to become involved and engaged.

Let's look at some practical needs and concerns of the typical PURE family from the perspective of the age of the PURE person in the family and what we can do practically as the church.

Pre-Natal

With the tremendous advances in medical science, many parents are being made aware today of issues with their new son or daughter who is still in the womb. Though these opportunities to know about families in this particular situation may be uncommon, it can and will occur in churches sensitive to PURE people and families in their communities.

What We Can Do:

- Help the family in adjusting to the prospect of having a PURE child.

  Affirm that you and the church will be with them and help them. Encourage and pray with them that they continue to be excited about the birth of their new baby. Offer to do practical things to help them in their preparation for the new baby: help decorate the nursery, or buy some new baby clothes. In many cases it is often very helpful for other PURE parents from the church to take the prospective PURE parents out for coffee and encourage them with their own experiences. Sometimes, people will appreciate and value hearing from those who have been there.

Infancy and Childhood

After the baby is born, PURE parents are confronted with a brand-new world. Important facts concerning disabilities' diagnoses are commonly unknown to the average person, including the new PURE parents. As mentioned before, in many, many cases the diagnosis of the issue(s) of the PURE child is not immediately known at birth. Remember, typically the diagnosis occurs over a series of weeks, months, or even years and, in some cases, never known. Contrary to the common notion, that a baby is born and all of the medical issues are diagnosed while in the nursery of the hospital, is the reality that in most cases the physicians know something is wrong, but determining the actual diagnosis takes time.

With this information in mind and simply not knowing what the future holds, the PURE parent is often overwhelmed. The type and severity of the disabilities obviously are significant factors in how the PURE parents are impacted, but regardless, they understand that their life has forever changed. As the child grows from infancy and childhood, new opportunities for us, the church, to love the PURE family constantly emerge.

What We Can Do:

- Make *certain* that *all* activities and events are open to and *welcoming to all* PURE children.

  Unless special attention is given to PURE children and their needs, they will inevitably be left out of many children's activities. The leadership of children's ministry must constantly make allowances for PURE children in the planning stages of classes, events, and special activities; not after the fact. For example, we have heard far too many stories of PURE children not being allowed to be in children's choir because there was no ramp to the platform, they sang too loud, and other inane reasons. Why mature Christians in these situations don't simply pick up and move the wheelchair onto the stage or place a worker next to the "loud" singer to help or whatever else is required says more about hard hearts and programs than love and acceptance. We must make a way for these children to participate, no matter the costs. Why? Because Jesus did. Jesus is always open and approachable. We, as Christian, individually and corporately, as the church, must be the same. We must ask ourselves what kind of church we really want to be: one that values all of God's children and delights in the blessing of PURE people or a prideful one concerned more with appearances and programs rather than with true ministry to real people.

- Making PURE ministry a *total church* ministry and a reality in the church.

As discussed previously, PURE ministry within the local church is very unique. Though every member in the church may not be directly involved, we who are involved must lovingly and constantly continue to make all Christians aware and sensitive to PURE people and their families in our midst, welcoming them warmly into our fellowship. This goal is not theological or mythical, but must become a reality. Inclusion of the PURE person and family in the life and fellowship of the church requires consistent and diligent attention. We must help the family maintain their church activities:

  o Do they need transportation to or from church and church activities?
  o Are our buildings, doors, and rooms totally accessible? If not, how can we assist the family?
  o What about training of their peers as peer advocates?
  o Are all family members included in the life of the congregation?
  o Are all ministry opportunities open to all PURE people and family members?

- Respite care.

Ask any PURE parent what they need most and, if they are honest, most likely all will tell you the same thing: a *break*. In fact, the number one need of PURE families is respite care or, more put more simply, a *break*. Though we at *PURE Ministries* are very careful not to dictate to any church what their own PURE ministry should involve, we do believe that respite is the most important component of any church-based PURE ministry. The typical Sunday morning hustle and bustle of people coming and going to church simply does not afford the PURE family enough time and opportunity to get to know people and form friendships. However, the relaxed atmosphere, less hectic environment, and longer respite care event allows the PURE person and family more time to build relationships. A typical respite event in a local church has the look, feel, and warmth of a 3-4 hour Vacation Bible School. It is organized and manned by church members and other interested helpers, not PURE parents! Age appropriate activities are provided for both PURE people and their siblings so that the PURE parents have a welcomed and rare time out. Since the respite care event is typically held on a Friday or Saturday, there is much less crowd and commotion than on Sunday morning. As PURE parents bring and pick-up their children, they have time to fellowship with everyone involved. The church has a wonderful opportunity to meet this number one need of PURE families. Virtually any church of any size in any area can help meet this need by providing respite care in the church facility on a regular basis.

• Financial support.

Regardless of the type of disability, raising a PURE child is an expensive proposition! Knowing that most families will not openly discuss their financial needs with others, friends of the PURE family within the church need to be proactive in confidentially making the financial needs aware to the church leadership.

- Accessibility of church buildings.

  As a church body concerned about PURE people, constant attention needs to be given to *all* building access in and around the church. Attention to these details is not a one-time event, but a constant mindset.

- Help locate or begin an appropriate support group.

  Particularly helpful to PURE families is sharing their experiences with others in similar circumstances. Commit to becoming aware of and locating existing support groups in your community. In most larger cities in the U.S., support groups exist for PURE families with a child with a particular disability. In some cases support groups are organized by specific disability while others are more general. Regardless, sharing common experiences, concerns, and challenges is cathartic, therapeutic, and most helpful to PURE families. If support groups don't exist in your community, offer the use of your church building to be used in forming one. Contact support groups and other organizations for helpful information in starting and growing a support group. We can help by arranging childcare for the family to be able to attend.

- Medical and educational advocacy.

  If, and only if, asked by the PURE parents, some trained medical and/or educational members can be of great assistance in helping the PURE parent in these areas. When a PURE child comes of age and enters the public school system, all too often the PURE parent begins a long-lasting battle with school teachers and administrators concerning the education of their child. Issues with insurance companies, therapists, and others can tax even the most knowledgeable PURE parent. Again, the world of disability is confusing at best, and a person with knowledge is often welcomed by a stressed and beleaguered PURE parent.

- Provide *practical* support.

No other way of showing that we care is better received than doing practical things around the house for PURE families. In PURE ministry training sessions with *PURE Ministries*, we often joke that the most useless statement ever made to PURE families is, "If we can do anything to help, let us know!" We go on to ask those in the training session, how many times they've heard the very same comment and actually *told* someone what they needed! The point is no one ever *tells* us what they need - we must *anticipate* and, because we know them as *friends, know* what they need! We need not be overly assertive or offensive, but we need to be willing to do what needs to be done *without being specifically asked to do it.* We recall many stories of PURE parents telling us of returning home from the doctor's office or hospital stays to find their grass cut, clothes washed, or a cooked meal on the table - without asking anyone to do it. Be creative – simply do for these families what you would want to be done for you if you were a similar situation. Some ideas:

- o Do the grocery shopping
- o Provide family meals
- o Assist with housecleaning or laundry
- o Provide transportation
- o Take care of lawn maintenance and home repairs
- o Assist with personal care
- o Help with writing letters and paying bills
- o Provide child care

- Parent support.

  PURE parents will normally be the first to tell us that they
  are unequipped and unprepared to deal with being a PURE
  parent. So many times those of us on the outside looking in
  think that these parents are superhuman and must know what
  they're doing. They don't – they are just like most of us who
  parent. There is no parenting handbook, especially for PURE
  parents! Along with the extra anxiety of raising a PURE child,
  comes a whole host of additional issues. How do we discipline
  a PURE child? Are there community resources to help us?
  Why do I have these feelings of guilt and blame? Though we
  obviously do not know the answers to all of these questions,
  we can assist the PURE parents in locating resources and
  support groups. Further, we can encourage them and pray
  with them and rejoice with them as we watch God answer the
  unanswerable.

- Sibling support.

  A church concerned with PURE families must be especially
  attuned to PURE siblings. As stated earlier, because in most
  cases their parents must spend an inordinate amount of time
  and attention with the PURE child, the siblings sometimes
  suffer. Christians sensitive to these issues can make a world of
  difference in the lives of siblings of PURE children. Offering
  to care for and keep siblings while parents are concerned with
  the various demands associated with a PURE child can be a
  great help. Making special effort to include siblings of PURE
  children in other families' activities, having special events just
  for them, or simply taking them to get ice cream, to the park,
  or to a ballgame can mean everything to these children.

- Camp/retreat opportunities for the family.

  Helping the family locate and attend camps and retreats for PURE families and individuals is normally well-received. Some camps are targeted for specific disabilities while others are for PURE children in general or for the entire family. Financial assistance in attending these camps and retreats is also usually very welcomed.

- Transportation to medical appointments and to other activities.

  A wonderful way for Christians (especially those sweet saints who are a bit shy but want to do something) to become initially involved with PURE families is simply to volunteer transportation. PURE children typically require frequent visits to a variety of doctors and therapists. To have a friend volunteer to drive mom and the child to the appointment is a great way to help in a practical way - and many friendships have been developed simply while driving to doctor's appointments.

Youth

As PURE children grow into their teenage years, an entirely new set of issues arises for the PURE parent. Like other teens, issues related to sex education, socialization, and preparation for adulthood can be particularly challenging for PURE families. Intellectual, cognitive, and developmental awareness of the PURE person in relating to his or her peers is particularly crucial for the PURE young person. The church can and should be a safe haven for the PURE family as these issues are encountered and addressed.

What We Can Do:

• Make *certain* that *all* activities and events are open to and accommodating of *all* PURE young people.

As for PURE children, unless special attention is given to PURE teens and their needs, they too will be excluded from the youth group. The example of the youth leadership team purposefully making allowances in activities so that the PURE teen can participate will make a giant statement that the non-PURE teens can't miss: we understand. It's okay to be different and unique! The resulting empathy and sensitivity to PURE people and the challenges they face will not only encourage the PURE teen, but have a positive impact in the lives of the entire youth group. As a general rule, show me a youth group who seamlessly includes PURE teens in their group, and I will show you an exceptional bunch of teenagers.

• Assist the PURE teen and family with the transition from children's ministries to youth group.

It must be noted that even in the best PURE ministries, the critical transition from childhood to teenager within the church fellowship is often very difficult for the PURE person and family. The PURE person functions well in many cases in children's classes and activities but sometimes struggles when confronted with teenage activities and relationships. Sensitizing and educating the youth group to PURE youth, specifically, helpful information about each new PURE teen as he or she enters the group, can and will ease this transition greatly. Knowing that many teenagers (like many adults) are uncomfortable and awkward around those they deem *different*, a small group of committed and loyal friends of the PURE person can often make the difference between success and failure. Prior to the very first interaction in the youth group, identify and approach some of the more mature teens and ask that they make a special effort to welcome, make comfortable, and befriend the new PURE youth. This small group (even if there is only a single person) of accepting teens, looking out for and making sure their new friend is included in the group, can make all the difference.

- Provide ministry opportunities for PURE teens.

Like most all young people growing into adulthood, PURE teens not only want acceptance, but they also want to serve. However, once again, we, the church, must be very *creative* in identifying and matching PURE teens with ministry opportunities. Depending on the different disability issues, some PURE teens can minister in common ways alongside their peers (ushering, visiting the elderly, or working in nursery) while others can't. For these PURE youth, opportunities may need to be thoughtfully *created*. Additionally, age is not the primary factor for determining when PURE teens begin formally ministering. In fact, most PURE teens are beautiful, living examples and witnesses of the love, grace, and watch care of our Savior just by being here. Who are we to say that a high-functioning, thirteen-year-old PURE boy can't safely assist the teacher in a 8-year old class if that is where he is comfortable and what he wants to do? Or isn't it good if a fourteen-year-old girl with autism enjoys working in the church office and feels that she is serving by being there? Getting outside our preconceived notions as to what is age-appropriate or *normal* is a necessity if we are to truly allow PURE people to serve Jesus in our churches.

- Assist family in preparation for young adulthood.

As many PURE young people grow through the teen years, many normal issues and other PURE-only concerns arise. Like all teens, PURE young people must deal with socialization, sexuality, striving for independence, and other common milestones of growing into an adult. Also, moral decisions regarding virtually all aspects of life lurk around every corner. Many PURE young people, however, and their families must face preparation for young adulthood and a variety of new issues. Is further education or training a possibility? Will/can the PURE young person work? What type of work? Will the PURE young adult continue to live at home? Or alone? Or in a group home? As you can see, there are many decisions that must be made regarding the PURE young adult. Friendships with other PURE families who have lived through these experiences can be a great help to the family in this preparation time. Facilitating and possibly even hosting meetings among PURE parents going through this process is an excellent opportunity for the church to be involved. Though we may not be experiencing what the PURE parent is experiencing, the need for us to express our care and support verbally and, most of all through prayer, is never more evident or needed.

Adulthood

In the best of cases, the PURE teen grows from his teenage years into young adulthood, completely independent and self-supporting, with most of the same dreams and visions as his non-PURE peers. However, this is not always the case. Though the church's direct impact and involvement in the day-to-day lives of most PURE people change as they age, there still exists many opportunities to help and be blessed by the PURE adult. Though physical, intellectual, cognitive, and behavioral disabilities will normally determine the level of independence a PURE adult might be able to attain, they really have little to do with the church's ability and opportunities to continue to positively affect and encourage them.

What We Can Do:

- Support the PURE adult in their lifestyle situation regardless of what it may be.

  Given the fact that some PURE young adults and even older adults will be living in group homes perhaps far away from the local church, a special effort will be required to keep the PURE person connected to his church family. It is hoped that the PURE person will become involved in another church perhaps, but if not, the need to maintain ties with friends with whom they are familiar is extremely important. Phone calls, e-mails, and letters can help but personal contact is always best. For those PURE people living at home, independently, or in a group home nearby, the church body should continue to be *home* and hopefully more new friends will be made along the way. Though inclusion is the watchword today in Christian education, many churches have discovered that Sunday school classes and/or home fellowship groups formed specifically for PURE persons with developmental disabilities foster a wonderful environment for close friendships to occur within that group.

- Counsel with regard to marriage and family.

  For some high functioning PURE adults, dreams of marriage and having a family can and do become a reality! Just as we would do with any adults anticipating marriage, counseling particularly tailored for the PURE person and adapted for his/her particular issues can be extremely helpful and beneficial.

- Insure *full* integration into the church body.

  Regardless of the disability, living situation, or virtually any other reason, we, the church, must do everything within our power to fully integrate the PURE adult into the life and fellowship of the body. This effort must be real and not just philosophical. For example, it is one thing to say that we should do it and another thing entirely to actually invite a PURE adult to your home or to a social event with your friends. Our words become genuine when we lovingly welcome a PURE adult into our Sunday school class as a peer and not as a *mission project*. Full participation, as the PURE adult is led to serve, minister, and fellowship, is the goal.

Training: Myth vs. Reality

The Training "Myth"

Undoubtedly as PURE ministry is contemplated and discussed in any local church, variations of the following statements will be offered far and near by many well intentioned people: "I would get involved in disability ministry, but I'm just not trained," or "I would help in a special needs class but I'm not a special education teacher." The underlying perspectives embodied in these simple statements comprise the greatest myth in the world of PURE ministry. This myth is mistakenly and commonly believed by most people (yes, even Christians).

The Myth:

To be involved with PURE people, one
must first have *special needs training.*

If the statement above is true, then call the police: because literally every parent of a PURE child, or *any* parent for that matter, is unqualified and incompetent to raise that child! The truth of the matter is that parents of PURE children receive *no training* - period! As we often do in PURE Ministry training, we ask everyone to use his or her imagination and figuratively go and observe a PURE mom leaving the local children's hospital with her recently diagnosed PURE baby. Further, I attempt to illustrate the scenario by having someone come up and play the PURE mom. I then take a doll and state that it represents the PURE baby. At this point I take the doll and hand it to the PURE mom volunteer saying, "Here's your baby - Good luck. Don't call us; we'll call you." We do all this to simply emphasize the fact that PURE parents receive *no* special training for their PURE child. The PURE parents must deal not only with the heartbreak, broken dreams, and realization that their lives are forever changed - they must also figure out how to care for their PURE child, not only medically, but in a variety of unfamiliar ways in which they have had *no* training.

If parents of PURE children receive no *special needs training*, how can we as concerned Christians believe the myth? If PURE parents, with no special needs training, can care for, teach, and interact with their PURE children, who are we to say we can't come alongside and help these precious people? Frankly speaking, most people believe the myth out of ignorance while others unknowingly and perhaps, unaware, use it as an excuse or cop-out not to get involved. Beloved, it is imperative that we gently dispel this myth among not only our brothers and sisters in Christ but all people whom God brings into our path. If we fail to do this, to make the truth known, PURE people and families will remain more or less alienated and isolated, and we will miss a special blessing.

In stark contrast to the training myth, is a proven truth.

The Truth:

Special needs training is not required to love, engage,
and be involved with PURE people.

"Wait," you may ask, "Surely you are not saying there's no such thing as special needs training - what about our wonderful special needs teachers and their training?" No, we are not saying that special needs training doesn't exist, but we are definitely stating that what is commonly accepted as special needs training is not a *requirement* for involvement in PURE ministry. Many define or think of special needs training as the conventional training commonly received by special *education* teachers in our educational systems. This specialized training entails primarily the methodology, techniques, and processes involved in the formal *teaching* and *educating* of special needs children and adults. Special education teachers are uniquely trained and equipped to *teach* special needs children and adults. We obviously are not all special education teachers, nor need we be! Special education teachers are specifically trained to teach - we need not all be formal teachers. However, we *all*, who name the name of Christ, are called to be involved, to engage, and most importantly, to love.

No type or amount of training can enable us to love and engage others, whether PURE or not, save the love of Christ in us. God has given unto us through His Son, all that we need - we are able. The Apostle Paul confirms this truth many times in Scripture:

> *Who also made us sufficient as ministers of the new covenant, not of the letter but of the Spirit; for the letter kills, but the Spirit gives life.*
>
> *II Corinthians 3:6*

> *And God is able to make all grace abound toward you, that you, always having all sufficiency in all things, may have an abundance for every good work.*
>
> *II Corinthians 9:8*

> *Now to Him who is able to do exceedingly abundantly above all that we ask or think, according to the power that works in us,*
>
> *Ephesians 3:20*

The *Real* Training Need

If formal *special needs training* is not a requirement for PURE ministry participants, then what is the real need? This very real and genuine need to know enough to feel more *comfortable* and *confident* is the grounds for and constitutes the primary PURE ministry training need. Some people who volunteer for PURE ministry have some experience with PURE people, but many do not. Even people with PURE experience want to know something about what is involved in PURE ministry. As God moves and people's hearts are warmed toward becoming involved in PURE ministry, some degree of anxiety is not uncommon: what do I say and what do I do? Again, this apprehension is to be expected of people whether they have experience or contact with PURE people or not.

Whereas formal *special needs training* is concerned with teaching and educating PURE people, *PURE ministry training* is concerned with equipping people with practical information that will allow them to better relate to PURE people and their families. *Special needs training* concentrates on educational methods, while *PURE ministry training* concentrates on removing barriers and obstacles that hinder us in relating to people.

It is advisable to offer PURE ministry training sessions periodically so as to afford new volunteers opportunity to be trained. *However, even PURE ministry training is not necessarily a requirement for each and every person.* For example, a sibling with a PURE brother/sister most likely would not need to be *trained* - in fact, they may be more qualified to lead training. In addition, it is perfectly acceptable and encouraged for new volunteers to begin *even before* working in a Sunday school class or as a respite care volunteer *even before* they attend a PURE ministry training session. In many cases there is no substitute for on the job training and simple observation of peers relating to PURE people.

So, what exactly is PURE *ministry training?* PURE ministry training is simply sharing information that will help normal people better interact with and befriend PURE people. It is basically the "Cliff Notes," or broad summary, of this book with an emphasis on information that will help us all become friends with the PURE person and family. A typical PURE ministry training curriculum would include such topics as:

- The Biblical Reasons and Mandate for PURE Ministry
- Basic Facts About Families Experiencing Disability
- Common Questions Families Ask
- Overview of Needs of Families with a Child with a Disability
- How the Church Can Help
- Dealing with Feelings: The PURE Person, Parents, and Siblings
- How to Talk About Disability
- How to Talk To a PURE Person
- Let's Do Respite Care!

Obviously, the topics at any given PURE ministry training session may vary as needs change. But, as you can see, the subject matter is extremely practical and should help anyone better understand how PURE people and their families live and the challenges they face. Equipped with this useful information and the resulting deeper appreciation and respect for PURE people and their families, we are better able to minister, relate, befriend, and love.

Ready for PURE Ministry?

Who or what is really the key to PURE ministry in our churches? For those of you who have heard me speak publicly (or privately for that matter), will have probably heard me utter the words, "The greatest single barrier to special needs ministry is pastors. The second greatest barrier is children's pastors." These are pretty strong words and not something that will win friends and influence people among our spiritual leaders. Unfortunately, it is the sad truth. However, I always go on to say that pastors and children's pastors aren't uncaring people. On the contrary, they're wonderful people, but there are no "Special Needs Ministry 101" courses in seminary - yet. They just don't realize what special needs folks and their families can do to bless their own congregations. The inescapable truth is that they don't feel PURE ministry is really *worthy*. In fact, these pastors are just like the rest of us. By being in positions of leadership in our churches, however, they set direction, focus, and priority of ministry for that local body. They simply have more influence. If they are unaware, fearful, apathetic, or ignorant of special needs ministry, it just isn't going to happen in their churches.

I hope that if you've read this far, you're interested in reaching out to PURE people and their families. But is *my* church ready? Am *I* ready? Is PURE ministry worthy of my personal and my church's time, money, and support? Maybe the following will help.

As we have now seen, PURE people are out there and in great numbers. Our dilemma is how do we draw them into our churches? Or maybe the question should correctly be stated as, "How do we show the love of Christ to PURE people and their families *through* His church?"

The Current Situation in Churches Today

Just what is the current situation in churches in the U.S. today? Unfortunately, the situation is disappointing. PURE ministry or even an awareness that there is a need for ministry to people with disabilities and their families is nowhere to be found in the average American church. However, as Christians gain some awareness of the needs and blessings of PURE people and their families, God presents a time to lovingly confront and, we hope, minimize the attitudes that inhibit the ministry and the resulting blessings.

Attitudes That Stand in the Way

What are the attitudes that are typical in today's local church congregation concerning PURE people and their families – attitudes that can stand in the way of, hinder, or even extinguish ministry before it even begins?

Apathy

Webster defines "apathy" as *lack of feeling or emotion* – or lack of interest or concern. Apathy in the church regarding PURE people can best be summarized by a common, all encompassing statement: "I'm not a special needs parent or a special education teacher; therefore *anything* having to do with disability does not concern me." Apathy concerning the very existence of PURE people and families is at its worst when we, the church, don't even know enough to care, or to realize that we don't care at all.

Excuses

As we have discussed earlier, we normal folks are pretty quick to excuse our behavior around PURE people. Because PURE ministry, when proposed to the church, is typically viewed by most as threatening or even scary, people are quick to offer reasons (*excuses*) why it should not be done. Again, such excuses as "We don't have anyone disabled in our congregation anyway," or "We don't have room," and "We can't afford another ministry" are commonly made. These are some of the more common excuses and there are many more plausible-sounding ones. But, with very few exceptions they are excuses. When all things are considered, they are not valid reasons that would realistically prevent us from loving on PURE people and their families. Frequently, insurance concerns for the church are mentioned as a valid reason for not offering into PURE ministry. Though we recommend reviewing the church insurance policies as part of the planning process for beginning PURE ministry, it is extremely rare, if ever, that any church requires more or different insurance coverage for PURE ministry.

Ignorance

Most typically if we look seriously behind the root of the excuses, we will find a gross lack of knowledge (or ignorance) of PURE people, families, and the entire world of disabilities. The fact that PURE ministry doesn't require much room or cost much money must be lovingly communicated to church leaders and members who are unaware of PURE issues.

Pride

This is a very subtle and rarely verbalized area. Even though we as Christians would be slow to admit it, most of us normal people believe we are somehow *better* than PURE people. For example, though most of us would not verbalize it, we *assume* that a person with cerebral palsy is also intellectually inferior and somehow less of a person than we are. Pride in all forms is sinful and will consistently take us to places that we would rather not visit, much less reside. Making assumptions about people's relative worth is an affront to our Creator Father who has made us all just the way He desires and for His purposes. Just who are we to make a judgment of worthiness? Worse, who are we to view and treat people poorly because of such bad judgment?

Pity

The one single attitude that PURE people and family members most ardently reject is pity. Furthermore, the one single attitude that PURE people and family members don't need or want is pity. Regardless of how expressed and though not intended by the giver, more often than not the PURE recipient of pity does not hear, "I feel so sorry for you." Rather the message received is "I am so glad I am not you." Pity always has disheartening and demoralizing consequences for all involved.

Helplessness

In many seemingly impossible circumstances, a common human cop-out is helplessness. It is far too easy to do nothing, when confronted with the awesome challenges we see. Often we exaggerate these in our imaginations and simply declare ourselves helpless and the situation hopeless. For the Christian, this situation *is never true*. Yes, we are helpless in our own strength and efforts, but we are *more than conquerors* in the strength of Christ. This spiritual truth is never truer than when we reach out to PURE people in our weakness and trepidation only to find strength and confidence provided by the Holy Spirit.

Insensitivity

Often church leaders, when made aware of the need for PURE ministry in their congregation, will make an obvious, but totally insensitive ministry decision: "Since we don't have any experience or *training* with this kind of thing, let's just ask Mary, the special needs mom, to do it!" The one thing the average PURE mom does *not* need to be doing is leading PURE ministry and the one thing the average church does not need is to have a PURE mom leading PURE ministry! One of the main goals of PURE ministry is to care for the PURE person so that the PURE parents and siblings can participate and enjoy the fellowship, worship, and life of church. Insensitivity in this area has unfortunately resulted in anemic ministry and has frustrated PURE families in far too many situations.

Fear – The Greatest Attitude Barrier

As we briefly touched on before, without question, the number one barrier and inhibitor to PURE ministry is fear. Though in some cases we might see actual physical fear of a particular PURE person or situation expressed, more commonly, however, the *fear* that paralyzes most of us is reflected in these statements: "I don't know what to say or do. I'm afraid that I'm going to say or do the wrong thing. I just won't say or do *anything*." It is obvious in the church in America today as evidenced by the scarcity of PURE ministry that many, make that most, of us have at one time or another taken this self-protective position, and self-righteously felt justified in it. However, also obvious is the fact that if enough of us take that position, the PURE persons and their families are left alienated and isolated. As a major theme of this book, getting past our preconceived notions regarding PURE people and PURE ministry in our churches, we have stated repeatedly the necessity of our own personal involvement as crucial to it all. If every church thinks the church *down the street* is *better equipped* and supposed to be doing PURE ministry (yet very, very few churches are), then our individual fear has aggregated and amassed to our corporate church fear and has resulted in little PURE ministry getting done. If we could only understand that PURE people genuinely appreciate *any* attempt we make to communicate and interact with them! They do not expect us to be familiar with disability. They do, however, expect us Christians to be respectful, non-judgmental, and most of all, loving. Even the most awkward and ill-at-ease conversation we might attempt will be lovingly welcomed by the PURE person. "This person actually cares enough about me to talk with me!" This is something that happens far too infrequently in the life of the PURE person.

I submit that it is now time for us to get past this paralyzing fear that inhibits us as Christians, not just as it relates to PURE ministry, but in all areas of our lives. It's time we start caring more about the other person (whoever it is) than we do our own self-image and comfort. It's time to extend our miniscule comfort zones to God-sized ones. It's time to let God grow us by allowing Him to put us in places and situations where we have no control. Finally, it's time to stop trying to limit God in His plan to change us into people more like His son, Jesus.

As outrageous as it all sounds, all of these things can begin as we simply commit to becoming friends with PURE people. Of course, God can grow and change us in a fathomless number of ways, but as we will see later, PURE people have special power in this area. First, how can we communicate with PURE people?

Becoming Friends with PURE People

If it is true (and it is!) that the most common barrier keeping average Christians from approaching and relating to PURE people is the fear that they will say or do something wrong or inappropriate, then what are we to do about it? We certainly can't become friends with people with whom we are afraid to talk. So, what do we do? We commit to swallow our pride, put aside our awkwardness and apprehensiveness and *just do it*. All the while and in every situation knowing that *we can do all things through Christ who strengthens us! (Philippians 4:13)* Remember that usually PURE people are happy and thankful that you are even trying to talk with them in a loving and respectful way. Below are some suggestions that should help.

How to Talk *About* PURE People

As Christians living in a culture that has consistently marginalized PURE people with our terminology, we, the church, have not remained unaffected. The culture's terminology and negative presumptions about PURE people have permeated the church and left us much like the society in which we are called to be *salt - You are the salt of the earth; but if the salt loses its flavor, how shall it be seasoned? (Matthew 5:13)*

Below are some easy guidelines to follow as we talk about PURE people and disabilities. Most are just plain common sense, while others address issues most of us have most probably never even thought about. Hopefully, as we begin to be more respectful and loving in our conversations regarding PURE people and issues, we can begin to change our world around us.

Some suggestions:
- *Use PURE or the word "disability" rather than "handicap" to refer to your friend's disability.* "Handicap" is the correct word to use when talking about being hampered by architectural barriers or attitudes. For example, "Those steps are a *handicap* to any person using a wheelchair," or "He is *handicapped* by the low expectations of his parents."
- *Use PURE and/or people first language.* Use PURE wherever possible to describe people with disabilities. Don't say "the disabled," "the retarded," "the cerebral palsied," "a paraplegic." Rather say, "Bob *has* cerebral palsy." "The child *has* autism." "Lynn *has* a vision problem." Or better yet, "He/she is a PURE person!"
- *Avoid the words "cripple," "crippled," "deaf and dumb," "slow," "crazy," "invalid," "acts funny," and other insensitive, archaic descriptions of disability.* In the same vein, expressions like "afflicted with," "a victim of," and "suffers from" lead to pity and sympathy, not respect and acceptance.
- *Don't describe your PURE friend as special, overly courageous, exceptionally brave, or superhuman.* Most likely they are, but these

words ring hollow when constantly used to describe any person with disabilities that we encounter. Often in our nervousness, awkwardness, and desire to say anything, we make such statements. However, this kind of heartfelt praise coming from a good friend (that is, us, after we made the effort and have taken the time to become friends) can mean everything to a PURE person.

- *The language of assistive devices, mobility, and adaptive equipment should be kind and gentle.* Choose "Amy uses a wheelchair" rather than "Amy is confined to a wheelchair;" "Joan uses sign language" instead of "Joan talks with her hands;" "Walt communicates with an electronic machine" (or the specific name of the assistive device) instead of "Walt uses a machine to talk."

- *In ordinary conversation when conveying that someone does not have a disability, stay away from the word "normal" as much as possible.* Though we have used "normal" in this book for the sake of clarity, the terms "typical" or "a person without a disability" are more accurate and appropriate in common conversation.

- *Don't overdo such concepts as "Well, we all have a disability of some kind."* The person who is dealing with the loss of one of his five senses, or a physical problem that impedes his mobility and/or requires assistive devices will not find this comforting.

How to Talk *To* PURE People

Not only are we to begin a new way of talking *about* PURE people and disabilities, but we also need a new and better way of talking *to* PURE people. If we are to change the way the world views and interacts with PURE people, we must drastically change the way *we* interact with PURE people.

The first and perhaps most important step in relating to and befriending PURE people is communicating with them. Below are some suggested guidelines to help as we enlarge our comfort zones and approach PURE people that God brings into our path.

Some suggestions:

- *Just do it - TALK!* Don't ignore them and don't let your uncomfortable feelings stop you! Always acknowledge their presence just like you would anyone else's. A warm smile and even an attempt to communicate will always be appreciated. This is a truth applicable at church, at the grocery store, on a plane, or wherever.

- *Talk directly to the person and not through a companion or a family member.* A common mistake most people make with PURE people is the assumption that PURE people cannot communicate. Based on this erroneous assumption, we then ignore them and speak to whoever is *with* them - bad idea! Speak to the PURE person first and, by this simple act, you can greatly encourage the PURE person and any family members or friends present.

- *If a child is with a parent, always speak directly to the child, first, then to the parent, just as we would do with any typical child.* Exercising this common sense approach and suggestion can greatly encourage, cheer up, and give hope to a discouraged and frustrated PURE mom. Just try it the next time you are waiting in line to check out at the store or shopping at the mall. We can never underestimate the power and impact of such seemingly insignificant acts.

- *Don't necessarily expect a normal or age appropriate response, but don't be surprised by one either!* As we approach PURE people, it is normally best to expect some type of response; that is, we should expect to *communicate with* and not *just talk to* the person. However, don't be surprised by a normal response. Be flexible and go with the flow of the exchange. Like normal children, PURE children can be shy, too, or it may take them some time to process what you have said and to form a response.

I must share another learning experience that God used as the proverbial spiritual "2x4" to make this point with me. For many years I have been a strong supporter, advocate, and board member of one of the most wonderful and unique ministries anywhere, Southwest Christian Care, in Union City, Georgia.

It was begun as a vision of one of the most godly men I have ever had the privilege of knowing, Pastor Jim Dyer. Along with his good friend, Dr. Byron Harper, "Preacher Jim" led his church in first offering in-home hospice care which shortly led to the construction of what we know today as Southwest Christian Care. The campus of Southwest Christian Care has a beautiful, state-of-the-art facility in which residential hospice care, respite care for medically fragile PURE children, day care for seniors, and other spiritual resources and counseling services are provided. One of my very best and dearest life-long friends, Mike Sorrow, for over 20 years, has been the executive director of this amazing ministry that is totally like no other. One of the things that makes Southwest Christian Care so unique is that *all* of their services are provided free of charge; they take no insurance, government subsidies, or any other type payment. They exist solely on the gifts from churches and concerned Christians and have done so for 28 years. Anyway, back to my story. Several years ago at the annual Christmas party for the PURE children who attend respite care, I was standing by Santa Claus as all of the precious children were coming by to see him. I talked to the parents and children while they were in line; some responded in ways that I could perceive and understand, and others couldn't. It didn't really matter, because we were all enjoying ourselves. However, I received quite a shock as I began talking with a little nine-year old black girl in a wheelchair and her mother. The little girl had some severe issues and only looked at me with a blank stare as I talked to her and gently rubbed her head. I am embarrassed to admit my assumptions and thoughts at the time: based on a total lack of response, I concluded that this little girl was so *disabled* that she could not respond in any way to my attempt to communicate with her. Or so I thought! In the awkwardness of the moment, one of the nurses, who the little girl obviously knew, walked by. If she had been physically able, this little girl would have literally jumped completely out of her wheelchair - and she tried! A giant smile came on her face as she reached to grab the nurse's arm, making loud sounds of obvious delight as she hugged her friend. I just stood there with my wrong assumptions, feeling foolish. Then it occurred to me what had just happened. I ask you: what would a normal little nine-year old black girl do when confronted with a stranger - an older, balding, white man who was trying to talk to her? Nothing, that's what; and that's exactly what this little PURE girl did. It wasn't a racial thing. It wasn't even a disability thing. It was simply that she really didn't know me or who I was. Her response to me, or rather lack of response, was, in actuality, perfectly normal for the situation! She knew her nurse friend and responded normally to her as well. I learned an important lesson that day.

- *If possible and appropriate, get on the same physical level as the person with whom you are talking.* With a PURE child, this point is very important. It makes it easier on the PURE person to look straight ahead as opposed to always looking up!
- *Don't hesitate to use words such as "see," "walk," or "listen."* Relax and don't feel as if you must "walk on eggshells," afraid you may say the wrong word as you speak. More than likely, the person with whom you are speaking will use these words too!
- *Be careful of tone and choice of words.* If our speech is affected, it can come across as demeaning or condescending. For example, when meeting a PURE adult who is obviously cognitively impaired, it is common for our speech to become childlike as we attempt to communicate. It is important that we remember to treat PURE people as age appropriate as possible, particularly when conversing. We can learn to make our words plain and simple without treating PURE youth or adults as if they are children.
- *Be careful of non-verbal language.* Our facial expression, the way we are standing, and other nonverbal language can say more than our words in many situations. The common inconsistencies

between what we say and how we come across will disappear the more comfortable we become in conversing with PURE people.

- *Don't assume that a PURE person, other than those with a hearing loss, can't hear.* Often we respond to a person with a disability, any disability, by talking louder. Our assumption is that if we can see a disability, we wrongly assume it is accompanied by a cognitive disability as well. We then think (wrong again) that if we can just talk louder and slower, somehow they will understand! Have you ever caught yourself doing this very thing perhaps to someone who speaks another language? Same problem here.

Here's another funny story to illustrate this point. My good friend and former pastor, Dick Hester, would always approach and speak to Zach very loudly and slowly. He just did what most of us do as he loved all of our family and wanted to include Zach. One day, my son-in-law and Zach's dad, Kyle, was holding Zach when the "preacher," as we lovingly call him, walked up and started talking to Zach with his customary loud voice. Kyle then uttered those words which we still laugh about when our families get together today, "Preacher, he's blind, not deaf!" The preacher, like all of us have done, was operating on wrong assumptions, and he has been kidded about it ever since.

- *Don't assume that people with speech, hearing, or physical problems have cognitive problems as well.* In other words, don't treat them as if they are less intelligent than you are. I cannot tell you all of the sad stories I have heard and continue to hear illustrating this problem. Once again, often in our anxiety in being with a PURE person, we will do almost anything not to address them directly, particularly if there is someone else with the PURE person that appears normal. Our good friends, who have an adult son who is a quadriplegic share with us how they constantly are faced with this issue. Many times, they have had their wonderful, bright, and witty thirty-something year old son in the hospital emergency room only to be asked by a nurse or doctor, "What is wrong with him today?" Their reply is always, "Why don't you ask him? He's right there." Assuming *all* PURE people have cognitive issues is *always* a bad idea.

- *Normally, touch is very important and appropriate.* Offer to shake a hand, gently clasp the person's hand, or maybe even a "fist bump" for PURE guys if they are unable to lift their own. If you sense someone is touch-adverse, be sensitive and accepting - just use warmer words.

- *If the person is blind or visually impaired, be sure to identify yourself.* We often forget that the blind or visually impaired person must remember everyone they meet only by the sound of their voice. This point is particularly pertinent when first meeting a PURE person or if they are not familiar with you.

- *If the person is deaf or hearing impaired, try to stand in front of the person, look directly at the person, and speak expressively.* Don't over exaggerate, but remember body language, gestures, and facial expressions will help in communicating. Also, if the person is significantly hearing impaired, he/she might just be reading your lips to understand what you are saying.

- *Don't apologize for not understanding their speech.* Just ask the person to repeat what he said. Don't say you understand their speech when you don't. Develop a friendly response: "My ears aren't working right today—will you say that again?" or "Run that by me again, please." One of the worse things we can do is say we understand what a PURE person has said when we don't. We must keep trying to understand or bring someone else into the conversation that might be able to help.

- *If the speech is difficult to comprehend, learn to listen for the subject of the conversation.* Words like "Mom," "Dad," "store," "school" will focus your understanding; then listen for action words like "went," "walked," "saw." If push comes to shove, use pencil and paper, or gesture wildly. Work to get the message!

- *As you learn your friend's world, the communication problems will diminish.* After a while, the comprehension level will increase and the friendship will grow. You may be able to recall first trying to talk with someone with communication difficulties: at the beginning, you could understand very little, but as you became accustomed to their speech, you soon could *hear* and understand much better. Your PURE friend won't have changed or gotten better speaking, you'll just have learned to listen better. The PURE person is doing his/her best to communicate and we must do our best to understand.

So we now know a little about how we can each in a practical way reach out to become friends with PURE people and their families. But, what are our churches doing collectively in PURE ministry? It might just surprise you.

Doing PURE Ministry *On Purpose*

There is some definite GOOD news today concerning PURE ministry and the local church; however, there is also some BAD news! First, the GOOD news:

> Most churches in America today are currently already ministering to PURE people in some form.

Most local churches across the U.S. will have one or two PURE people who have, most commonly, been born into the congregation and grown up there. The PURE family has remained in the fellowship of the church, necessary accommodations and adaptations have been made for the PURE person, and church life goes on. The good news is *this is* PURE ministry. So, in some sense, churches are already involved in loving on these people. So, what's the issue?

Well, here's the BAD news:

> Most churches in America today, though currently ministering to one or two PURE people in a very limited way, *have no organized, functioning, intentional PURE ministry.*

Though the rare PURE family has remained in the local church after a PURE birth or accident resulting in disability, intentional or *on purpose* PURE ministry in most churches languishes or simply doesn't exist. It would be logical to question a church's reason for existence if it would be content with a children's program, for example (or any church ministry program, for that matter), *only* for those children or youth *born* into the fellowship. Would such a church be content in never evangelizing the surrounding community to win the lost and include others into their fellowship? By New Testament church measures, such a church would be considered essentially lifeless. Are we not called to evangelize, take the Gospel, and minister to *all in Jerusalem, and in all Judaea, and in Samaria, and unto the uttermost part of the earth? (Acts 1:8)* How then can we *not* include PURE people and their families *intentionally* in our efforts to be Christ in our communities?

It is encouraging that many churches *are* touching the lives of PURE families. However, when we consider the number of PURE people and their families in our communities, we fall far short given the aforementioned statistic that 50 - 60 million Americans (depending on definition of disability) are disabled. As we mentioned earlier and would like to reiterate, if we use our very conservative estimate of 5% of the population as PURE (not the conventional statistic of 15-20% of the population), the scarcity of PURE people in our churches becomes clearer. Using conventional numbers, approximately 1 out of 6 people in our churches *should be* PURE! Using the 5% number is statistically defensible as extremely conservative. 5 out of every 100 people in *our* church *should* be PURE.

Please now join me on an imaginary trip on any given Sunday morning as we walk through the halls of a local church - maybe, your own church. Let's look in the nursery, in the toddlers, in the elementary school classes, in the youth room, in the young marrieds, the adults, and finally, the mature adults' classes. Did we see PURE people making up 5% of our church or 4%, 3%, or maybe 2%? Was there even 1%? Unless you just walked through a very, very unique church, you saw less than 1% PURE people!

Though there are 50+ million PURE people in the U.S. today, we find relative few of them and their families in our churches. As mentioned earlier, when we include immediate family members in PURE families, 25 – 35% of our population is *directly* affected by disability and constitutes the largest unreached people group by any method of measurement. Disability knows no socioeconomic, racial, ethnic, gender, or national origin boundaries - it affects all types of people. Despite the overwhelming statistics and the virtual absence of significant numbers of PURE people in the church, the church in America has essentially never purposefully sought after PURE people in any organized way. How do we reach out to PURE people and their families?

What if someone came up to you and made an unbelievable offer - one that would truly impact the church in America today by stirring Christians? What if that offer promised to meet the needs of, and, for the first time in modern history, target the statistically largest unreached people group in our culture, a virtually forgotten people in our midst? What if this offer incorporated a ministry to and with a people who have neither asked for their situation in life nor have committed some sin that has caused their circumstances? What if this offer could also guarantee to energize believers who have become, perhaps, apathetic and lethargic, into enthusiastically ministering in the name of Jesus in new and exciting ways? Further, what if this offer would place the modern-day Christian church in a positive, public high-profile position? What if rather than taking that judgmental position of typically telling people the things that we are *against*, we lovingly tell and show them the things that we *support*? Finally, what if that offer, when accepted, would result in drawing closer to Jesus Christ not only the people who are the beneficiaries of that ministry, but also those that tenderly minister? Would you be interested? Would you consider it worthy?

We have that wonderful opportunity today! This is the challenge – the offer is simple and the time is now. The church today is receiving a wake-up call. Will anyone answer? We can choose to ignore the opportunity, look the other way, and go on as if these people don't exist. Or, we can choose to be the generation that answers *yes* to this, the purest of ministries. If we choose incorrectly, we will have only man's empty promises. If we choose correctly, we will have Jesus' guarantee: we *will be blessed*. We will truly be demonstrating the PURE love of Jesus Christ to a lost and dying world.

Bringing it All Home: The Power of the PURE

And He said to me, "My grace is sufficient for you, for My strength is made perfect in weakness." Therefore most gladly I will rather boast in my infirmities, that the power of Christ may rest upon me. Therefore I take pleasure in infirmities, in reproaches, in needs, in persecutions, in distresses, for Christ's sake. For when I am weak, then I am strong.

II Corinthians 12:9-10

Prologue to the Conclusion

Here we come to the close of the book. I hope that something in here has resonated with you. At the least we all now have some idea and appreciation of the why, what, where, when, and the who of PURE ministry. We've looked at the Scriptures, have examined the need, described our practical response, and, if any of this has somehow touched and inspired you, you're now waiting expectantly for the Lord to make PURE ministry part of your life.

Perhaps nagging questions remain: What does all this *mean* to *me* in how I live my life today? How does all of this really *affect me*? How do I engage in PURE ministry and what does it look like in my life? What exactly do I actually *do now* – just wait? All are good questions.

On the other hand, some of you may remain largely unaffected and unconvinced still. You may need more persuading and you just aren't won over quite yet. Maybe you see the need, but are just not very sure you can do anything to positively change things. I ask only that you read just one last chapter as I attempt to bring this all home – personally, to where we live.

So, as we begin this last chapter, I will attempt to crystallize my thoughts into something that will stay with you after you have finished reading. At this point though, I am again painfully reminded of my own prideful nature. When any of us are about to say something that we think is profound (perhaps in a gathering of family, friends, or business associates), we want people to listen. Particularly we writer-wannabes want to think our profundities are timeless and transcend the mundane aspects of living. You'll rarely see authors referring to things occurring to them in real-time, while they were writing what you are reading. Since I am a "rookie" writer, I can now violate this unstated tradition just as I have already violated and shattered most other commonly accepted rules and standards of writing correctness!

God knew I needed one more trip to take and one more message to hear before He was ready for me to quit writing.

Two things have happened to me recently (within the last week as I write this) that I know the Lord wanted me to experience before I ended this book. Before these two unrelated events occurred, I had found myself struggling to put into words exactly what final truths I wanted you, the reader, to take with you. All the while the Lord was telling me to wait; He had more to share with me.

This past weekend Lee and I returned again to Eagle Eyrie for the annual Virginia Baptist Retreat for Youth and Adults with Special Needs. You will remember from an earlier chapter how powerfully the Lord used this event years ago in the formation of *PURE Ministries*. The retreat was again fantastic. We renewed old friendships, met and made new friends, and were again literally blown away with how the Lord is manifested there in new and exciting ways. Coming home on the airplane, I realized that as nice and beautiful as Eagle Eyrie is, it is not the thing that makes the retreat so special. It's not the program, though it, too, is excellent. It's not the time of year, food, or even the worship, praise, and fun-filled time – even though I love it all. So what is it that makes it unique, I thought? The answer is obvious: the people! Right at the top of that list of people are my PURE friends. It is the relationships with people that make it what it is. We could have this retreat in a stifling hot warehouse in the middle of summer with no fans or air conditioning in any big city in America and it would still be wonderful!

Further, it is not just *this* retreat or any *retreat* per se. It is still relationships that make the time and experience what it is. The retreat atmosphere just eliminates many of the daily distractions and obligations we have so we can concentrate on the relationships. Finally, it is not just any *people* either. It is the PURE people that I know and have come to appreciate that affect me so. Some I can talk with, while others I only observe and exchange smiles, but all affect and touch me in a meaningful way. I have to admit to myself these are not the same emotions I have when I am with other groups of people. I am blessed with a wonderful family and many good friends. I am blessed to have opportunity to find myself constantly in various kinds of Christian groups with these friends and others during any given week. Though I always enjoy the people, am occasionally challenged or emotionally moved in some way, I am *never* as profoundly affected as when PURE people are involved. As I was thinking about this on the flight home from Virginia that Sunday night, I kept asking myself how and why is this so. What is it in PURE people and how is it that they affect me, or any of us for that matter, so?

We are blessed at my church, Blackshear Place Baptist in Gainesville, Georgia, to have a young, great teaching and preaching pastor, Jeff Crook. God has truly gifted this young man with a unique ability to share the Gospel. He teaches in a direct, meaningful, and insightful way. Mingled with a great dose of humor and a constant sense of humility, Jeff expounds on the Scriptures each week.

One of my favorite times, though, is our men's Wednesday morning Bible study. Each Wednesday morning at 6:00 AM, Pastor Jeff teaches the Word to a large group of men - both from our church and many visitors. As I have shared with Jeff, I'm not sure how he does it, but he is wound up, ready to go, and *on* each and every Wednesday morning! Jeff has been teaching through the beatitudes (*"Jesus Really Said That?"*) and that Wednesday morning, he taught on *Matthew 5:8 - Blessed are the PURE in heart: for they shall see God*. Once again, sitting there at that early hour, things that had been a bit perplexing to me suddenly came into focus. In a biblical context, Jeff explained what *pure in heart* actually means in a way that was unique and perfectly applicable to this PURE discussion. When I got home, I immediately sent him an email thanking him and telling him not to be surprised to see some of his words and thoughts in this book.

The Eagle Eyrie retreat and a men's Bible study lesson: the two final pieces to a puzzle in my mind finally were in place. So, ready? This is it:

If we choose, God uses PURE people to
profoundly and deeply change us.

PURE people *can* actually *change us*. This thought may not be revolutionary to you, but, I can assure you it is to me; at least to see it written down as a statement. You, friend, family member, or passerby, can influence me or maybe you can inspire me temporarily. You might even frustrate or make some impression on me. However, you can't really significantly *change* me like PURE people can.

One of the clearest illustrations of this God-given ability of PURE people to change others was recently described to me by Jacque Daniel, our Executive Director of *PURE Ministries*. Though I, too, have seen the same phenomenon occur in other places and at other times, her experience paints a picture truly worth a thousand words.

Besides her role with *PURE Ministries*, Jacque also has her own ministry (*ConnectAbility*) that she manages for some 70 PURE adults. Recently, she was asked by the head of a children's home in a small town nearby, if some of their children could come to a respite night as a way of getting involved in the life of the community. This isn't your typical children's home for orphans, but one for very rebellious teenage girls who could no longer function in their own homes. Jacque, with no small amount of trepidation, told the lady to send some of the girls over for the next respite night. Concerned about just how disruptive these girls might be, she decided to have them help serve the snack for the evening. What could they do to cause problems there?

What Jacque did not anticipate was what happened there that evening. This particular respite night was actually a talent show featuring the PURE folks themselves. If you have been around PURE adults for any amount of time at all, you know that most PURE people *love* to get on stage and entertain. As we talked earlier about the enthusiasm at the Eagle Eyrie talent show, Jacque's group was no different. So get this picture: as the talent show begins in the auditorium, the girls from the children's home saunter into the back of the room to watch. Hearing and seeing Jacque's description of the scene is priceless. Obviously, having been a teenage girl earlier in her life, and an animated person as well, she can momentarily transform herself into one of these sullen, gum-chewing, insubordinate, defiant, with a "What am I doing *here* with *these kind* of people on a Friday night when I could be out partying?" girls as they entered the room. What happens next is utterly amazing.

As different PURE people went on stage to perform, the girls' appearance and attitude slowly began to change. The girls became involved in cheering on and supporting each PURE person and soon after, went and sat among their new PURE friends. By the end of the show, the once rebellious girls actually went on stage to perform themselves! Can you imagine such a thing: troubled, insecure, self-conscious, image-conscious, identity-seeking teenage girls becoming sufficiently uninhibited to perform in front of a group of PURE adults? And loving it? For the rest of the night, the girls were kind, considerate servants. They had been transformed – at least for a little while – by being in the middle of a group of PURE people.

The turnover in the children's home is rapid, so Jacque could not follow-up on any enduring or long-term effects of this night on these girls. It may have been just this one night that they felt free, secure, and worthy enough to get outside of themselves and think of others for a while. Jacque did tell me that after that first talent show, one of the staff members wanted to make sure she could bring the girls each month to respite. More revealing, she told Jacque that being with the PURE people at the respite evenings was "the most meaningful and important activities that the girls do" while they are at the home. Some of the girls' lives may have been significantly changed that night. We will never know, but the Lord does. What we do know is that, at least for a little while, a group of hardened, tough, and cynical teenage girls became softer, kinder, sweeter people.

Think about this: you could gather a room full of psychiatrists, trained on the behaviors of dysfunctional teenage girls, to plan an evening specifically to accomplish this kind of dramatic transformation. They would fail miserably. Or, we could locate the girls' frustrated and depressed parents and coach them on traditional "parenting techniques" that *work*. Finally, armed with this information, they could deliver, for the 200th time, that sermon they have preached to their daughters so often about how they were ruining their lives and had to change or face destruction. They would have failed, too. So please explain to me how a group of PURE adults accomplish this impossible thing, seemingly without any effort and certainly with no intent of trying to *change* them! No, the PURE adults didn't get together before the show and discuss how they would pull it all off. They did what trained professionals, well intended parents, or anybody else couldn't do *and* they didn't even purpose or try to do it. *This* can only be explained by the power of God working through PURE people.

I am certainly not saying that other people, non-PURE people, don't change us profoundly and deeply in some ways as well. I am loved by my wonderful wife of forty-plus years and love her more than my life itself. We have been blessed with three great children who have brought me joy, made me proud, and made me look like a better dad than I really am. I get to be Granddad to nine (as of this time) fantastic grandchildren – each totally, wonderfully unique gifts from God. Moreover, I have been blessed with more godly, good friends than I could ever deserve. However, there is something different even here. Even in a child/parent scenario, the one relationship where we as parents are responsible for loving, teaching, admonishing, and raising our children and intentionally set out to do so, we discover that *changing* them is still virtually impossible. I can love you, teach you, and pour out my heart, even begging you, but I really can't *change* you. Through the love, commitment, sacrifice, and devotion developed and refined in these relationships with those we love and who love us, family and friends have certainly changed and formed me in some ways. Yet, it was still that one little PURE boy, Zach, that God used late in my life to change the very direction and focus of all that I am. Incredibly and more miraculous still, PURE people never intentionally try or purpose to do it! They aren't even aware of their ability and power to change those of us who enter their world. Most probably like you, I have tried to change people I love and over whom I have had some influence and authority. I was completely and totally incapable of doing it, no matter how hard I tried or how righteous or justified I thought I was in doing so. The result was absolute failure each and every time. How then, is it possible that people who can't talk or can't even so much as utter a single word can so profoundly change us? Yes, I may be able to influence you. On a good day, I might inspire you. I definitely can find a way to make you angry. I might even impact you in some way, but, I can't really *change* you. But, PURE people can, or rather God can change me through a PURE person, *if* we allow them to.

We have a choice. We choose whether we will be changed by people. This is true as well in our relationships with non-PURE people, but perhaps harder to discern. Do we *choose* to be faithful to our wives, to be loving, attentive parents and grandparents, or, to be loyal, good friends? Or, are we simply slaves to our own and others expectations and sense of responsibility and obligations? Just what motivates us, in these relationships that are so precious to us, is a hard and sticky question. The answers are even harder and stickier. Further, how does this all relate to PURE people?

I have concluded that the profound depth and insight of the statement "PURE people can change us," lies not so much in its blatancy but more subtly in its apparent lack of any underlying logic or rationality. Just as I considered myself sufficiently wise, mature, logical, etc., before God gave me Zach as my grandson and threw me into the PURE world, I realize in retrospect and as I've said earlier, I was clueless! I am not unique because many others have had similar experiences. What previously was thought to be required for happiness and to have a fulfilled, rich life was summarily replaced with a totally different perspective: a different perspective about everything! Incredibly, I was unaware most of the time that I was being changed. I was, and am, profoundly and deeply changed now. I found that allowing ourselves to be in a position to be transformed or changed is not something we do haphazardly. Real PURE ministry is not a spectator sport. Sure, we can watch from a distance, but it will not change us.

Before we look at this *power* PURE people have to change us, let's get real. I am basically selfish and prideful and if you're breathing right now, so are you. As Christians, we have power over our flesh *not* to be selfish and prideful, but our flesh still thinks, operates, and acts only for itself. In my fleshly pride I arrogantly ask, "What can a ten-year-old girl with Down syndrome really do to or for me?" In my ever-present selfishness, I reluctantly and superficially agree with the premise that "everybody has something to offer"; but then ask, "What then is *in* it for me – what is the benefit for *me*?" I don't know if you already have been, or someday will be, changed by a PURE person in your life, but I do know it is a choice. If a PURE person is born into your family or an accident leaves you or someone you love disabled, you'll have a choice to make. With clinched fists you can scream and ask God, "Why?" and "Why ME?" and remain unchanged, or worse, become angry and bitter. Or, you can choose to allow God to draw you and the PURE one you love closer to Himself through it all: to be fundamentally and forever changed. We have the choice.

Just how does God change us through PURE people? The answers to this simple question are as infinite as the goodness of God. However, in the remaining words of this book I will address three of the most common ways I know God has and is moving through PURE people. Like so many others, my earthly and spiritual eyes are much clearer and, though I fail miserably, God has definitely worked on me in some major and rather unique ways. I implore you not to stop reading just yet. I pray God speaks plainly to you in these last paragraphs.

How Did You Like Your Heart Attack? Transforming Tragedy into Triumph

Strange question, right? However, for many important reasons, I can remember well the story behind this peculiar question, and it is very applicable here to our discussion of PURE people and their unique, transforming, and God-imputed power. To set the stage, it was a fall weekend and the year was 1978. I was attending the annual men's retreat of the United Methodist church at beautiful Rock Eagle, a camp in Eatonton, Georgia. With me were my pastor, Larry Rary, a wonderful godly man, and a group of good friends from our church. The speaker for the weekend was Bob Benson, a gifted writer and speaker. Bob is in Heaven now, but if you ever have a chance to pick up one of his books, you will never regret it. Bob, then President of his family-owned Benson Company Christian publishers, was a very quiet, unassuming man who spoke softly and very articulately about the Lord he so obviously loved and with whom he was well acquainted. I remember it all so well, because it was this quiet man that God used that weekend to awaken me to the Gospel, resulting in at least one very religious, but lost person – me – being saved. A great story in itself (at least to me), but I digress. Bob Benson was a great story teller, and he used his stories to make his points in ways that really touched people. Bob also used humor very skillfully and aptly as well and combined those wonderful abilities to tell this story on Saturday night that weekend. Here's the story as I recall it:

> *Jim, a good friend of Bob's, had recently suffered a serious heart attack and was slowly recovering. In the days during his rehab and up until the conversation recounted here with Bob, Jim*

talked incessantly about his heart attack. As Bob said, "He talked about his heart attack a lot. In fact, his heart attack, his brush with death, and his recovery were all he could or would talk about." Having heard enough, Bob approached his friend one day and asked him how he was doing. Jim immediately began his usual discourse regarding his recent heart attack. Before his friend got too far, Bob interrupted him with the question, "Jim, how did you like your heart attack?"

Jim, dumbfounded, responded, "Why, I didn't like it all! Why would you ask such a stupid question?"

Bob then replied, "Well, that is all you ever talk about and I thought since you obviously enjoyed your first heart attack so much, you might like another!"

Confused, Jim stared silently at Bob, who asked him another question, "Well, would you like another?"

Jim exclaimed, "Of course not! Why are you asking such questions?"

Bob continued to probe, "Well, could I ask you something else then? Don't you really cherish and love your kids more today, than you did before you had your heart attack?"

Jim responded, "Sure."

Bob queried, "And don't you just love your grandkids just a little bit more when they crawl up in your lap and call you granddaddy now, than you did before you had your heart attack?"

Jim, "Yeah."

Bob again, "And don't you hold Mary (his wife) a little closer each night, enjoy walking hand-in-hand, and love her even more today, than you did before you had your heart attack?"

Jim, "Yes."

Bob, finally, "Well, then, how did you like your heart attack?"

Jim, no answer.

The point is all too clear - and convicting, is it not? What we experience on this earth that we might at first call tragedy or disaster becomes something entirely different when we see it as given to us from our loving Heavenly Father. When the *bad* comes, at first we don't want to be reminded of Scriptures like these:

> *In every thing give thanks: for this is the will of God in Christ Jesus concerning you.*
>
> Ephesians 5:20

> *Giving thanks always for all things unto God and the Father in the name of our Lord Jesus Christ;*
>
> I Thessalonians 5:18

In our anguish, the words are more like sawdust on our tongues before they become the cool, refreshing waters to our hurting hearts.

How do we give thanks for something so obviously *bad*? Do we really have to thank God for *this* happening? Though many godly people have attempted to rationalize these verses by reasoning, "We aren't really to thank God for actually *everything* like it says, but are simply to have a *thankful spirit*." Sounds good, except it's wrong. It isn't what Paul said nor is it what, I believe, he meant. Perhaps a better question is, "How can we have a *thankful spirit* without being, in reality, *thankful*?" These verses say we are to *literally* thank God for *everything* – not just for what we recognize as *good* with finite eyes or can justify as *good* with human logic. *Everything.* Deaths, divorces, disease, disaster … and, yes, even PURE people. We don't know if God is protecting us or someone else from suffering through a painful death, or laying a foundation for something that will occur generations ahead in time through a divorce, or drawing people we don't even know to Him through some disaster.

Scripture teaches us that God uses these *bad* things in our lives for various purposes – God has His purposes:

To bring glory to Himself:
> *When Jesus heard that, He said, "This sickness is not unto death, but for the glory of God, that the Son of God may be glorified through it."*
>
> John 11:4

To teach us the consequences of our sin:

> *For the creation was subjected to futility, not willingly, but because of Him who subjected it in hope; because the creation itself also will be delivered from the bondage of corruption into the glorious liberty of the children of God. For we know that the whole creation groans and labors with birth pangs together until now.*
>
> *Romans 8:20-22*

To teach us of the broad, long-lasting effects of living in a sin-sick world:

> *that you may be sons of your Father in Heaven; for He makes His sun rise on the evil and on the good, and sends rain on the just and on the unjust.*
>
> *Matthew 5:45*

To build us up and make us grow:

> *through whom also we have access by faith into this grace in which we stand, and rejoice in hope of the glory of God. And not only that, but we also glory in tribulations, knowing that tribulation produces perseverance; and perseverance, character; and character, hope.*
>
> *Romans 5:2-4*

To show us the cost of belonging to Him:

> *So they departed from the presence of the council, rejoicing that they were counted worthy to suffer shame for His name.*
>
> *Acts 5:41*

> *For to you it has been granted on behalf of Christ, not only to believe in Him, but also to suffer for His sake,*
>
> *Philippians 1:29*

To teach us patience:

Blessed is the man who endures temptation; for when he has been approved, he will receive the crown of life which the Lord has promised to those who love Him.

James 1:12

To show His strength:

These things I have spoken to you, that in Me you may have peace. In the world you will have tribulation; but be of good cheer, I have overcome the world.

John 16:33

To teach us the value of suffering:

And not only so, but we glory in tribulations also: knowing that tribulation worketh patience; And patience, experience; and experience, hope: And hope maketh not ashamed; because the love of God is shed abroad in our hearts by the Holy Ghost which is given unto us.

Romans 5:3-5 (KJV)

To teach us that our suffering here is minor compared to what we will enjoy in Heaven:

and if children, then heirs—heirs of God and joint heirs with Christ, if indeed we suffer For I consider that the sufferings of this present time are not worthy to be compared with the glory which shall be revealed in us.

Romans 8:17-18

Yea doubtless, and I count all things but loss for the excellency of the knowledge of Christ Jesus my Lord: for whom I have suffered the loss of all things, and do count them but dung, that I may win Christ,

Philippians 3:8 (KJV)

To be able to comfort others:

Grace to you and peace from God our Father and the Lord Jesus Christ. Blessed be the God and Father of our Lord Jesus Christ, the Father of mercies and God of all comfort, who comforts us in all our tribulation, that we may be able to comfort those who are in any trouble, with the comfort with which we ourselves are comforted by God.

II Corinthians 1:2-4

To teach us the cost of following Christ:

For this is commendable, if because of conscience toward God one endures grief, suffering wrongfully. For what credit is it if, when you are beaten for your faults, you take it patiently? But when you do good and suffer, if you take it patiently, this is commendable before God. For to this you were called, because Christ also suffered for us, leaving us an example, that you should follow His steps:

I Peter 2:19-21

To strengthen our faith:

And we know that all things work together for good to them that love God, to them who are the called according to his purpose.

Romans 8:28 (KJV)

I can do all things through him who strengthens me.

Philippians 4:13 (KJV)

To teach us of our total dependence on Him:

And He said to me, "My grace is sufficient for you, for My strength is made perfect in weakness." Therefore most gladly I will rather boast in my infirmities, that the power of Christ may rest upon me.

II Corinthians 12:9

And my God shall supply all your need according to His riches in glory by Christ Jesus.

Philippians 4:19

To teach us the value of tested faith:

My brethren, count it all joy when you fall into various trials, knowing that the testing of your faith produces patience. But let patience have its perfect work, that you may be perfect and complete, lacking nothing. If any of you lacks wisdom, let him ask of God, who gives to all liberally and without reproach, and it will be given to him. But let him ask in faith, with no doubting, for he who doubts is like a wave of the sea driven and tossed by the wind. For let not that man suppose that he will receive anything from the Lord; he is a double-minded man, unstable in all his ways.

James 1:2-8

That the trial of your faith, being much more precious than of gold that perisheth, though it be tried with fire, might be found unto praise and honour and glory at the appearing of Jesus Christ:

I Peter 1:7 (KJV)

These are just some of the many Scriptures that help us understand the connection between *thankfulness* and *suffering*. However, there is a problem: we seldom know at the time of suffering *why* we are suffering. Sometimes we know immediately; sometimes we know later; and sometimes we will not know until we reach Heaven. Like everything a sovereign, loving God does, He uses even these things – these things that are painful - to grow, shape, and transform us as He desires. The simple truth is that we really don't know enough to *know* whether something is truly *good* or *bad*, but we do know God and He tells us to thank Him.

If we are truthful with ourselves, we must admit that we certainly don't *like* the deaths of loved ones, sickness, or car wrecks. However, we sometimes get confused; we equate *thanking* God for something as opposed to *liking* or even *enjoying* something. God does not say we necessarily must *like* everything He does. He says we are to *thank* Him for it and there is a big difference between the two. When that tragedy comes, we obviously don't like or enjoy it. However, since we trust God to use it in our lives for good and His glory, we can and must thank Him for it. Our thanksgiving, in reality, *validates* our trust we have in Him. Peter tells us:

> *Beloved, do not think it strange concerning the fiery trial which is to try you, as though some strange thing happened to you; but rejoice to the extent that you partake of Christ's sufferings, that when His glory is revealed, you may also be glad with exceeding joy.*
>
> I Peter 4:12-13

In other words, we might not like or enjoy our trial, but we know God will use it to grow and teach us and, someday, we will actually rejoice because we are counted worthy to suffer as Jesus did.

In fact, when we do acknowledge His divine intervention in *all* things, those same tragedies and catastrophes turn out to be life-changing, but certainly not in the way we feared. Those very things that happen that we think we cannot live through or endure are the very same things we often look back on as *good*, even blessings directly from the Hand of God! How can this be and how does it apply to you, me, PURE people, and their families? This is the primary way I believe PURE people actually change us:

> PURE people have the power to *teach* us that we really don't know or understand how God is using the events of our lives for our good and His glory.

Good or Bad? We Get to Decide.

I think I knew the answer before I even asked the question, but once, when I was speaking to a Sunday school class of people around retirement age, I asked, "Besides your salvation and your marriage, what single event has impacted your life most?" I received answers to that innocent, yet explosive, question from virtually every person in the room; everyone wanted to share. Their answers? They were gut-wrenching: the death of a parent, the death of a spouse, the death of a child, the death of a grandchild, a divorce, an abandonment, a rape, a failed business venture, a job loss, a wayward son or daughter, and other similar events. Notice anything similar about the answers? Not one of the answers given by the people in any way described what we would normally call a *happy* event - not one of the over 30 responses. Yes, as far as I know, everyone who responded was a Christian and, as it turns out, that's really all that matters.

What does this say about us as Christians? That we love heartache and pain and sorrow? No, it's simply a matter of trust and in whom we place our trust. As Bob Benson's funny story and the answers given by the members of the Sunday school class can attest, we Christians have the power to choose to look at God's involvement in our lives differently than unbelievers. That is not to say, though, that we, at times, don't briefly panic when faced with an unexpected (as if any disaster *is* expected) disaster. The major difference is that, even in the midst of *tragedy*, we as Christians are blessed with the power in the presence of the Holy Spirit, once again, to choose how we view what God is doing in our lives. However, like me, you may still have difficulty thanking and praising God nearly as much *during* the *disaster* as we do looking back at the experience. However, isn't it interesting that most of us still recognize that it is during the worst times that we grow most and experience the love, grace, mercy, and sufficiency of God more deeply?

The famous English preacher of the 1800's, Charles Spurgeon, addressed this perplexing topic of why we grow in times of pain and suffering, in one of his sermons:

> *The farmer does not sift his wheat because he dislikes it, but just the opposite—he sifts it because it is precious. And you, child of God, your trials and changes, and constant catastrophes and*

afflictions are no proofs of lack of affection on the part of the Most High, but the very contrary. "As many as I love, I rebuke and chasten." It is because you are gold that you are in the crucible! And it is because you are wheat you are put into the sieve.[1]

We discussed this before, but we really need to grasp the situation in which typical (if there is such a thing) PURE parents find themselves. Unless we are a PURE parent who, in the excitement and euphoria in the hours after having a child, has been stunned and shocked with the news that there is "something wrong" with their baby, we probably cannot properly place this experience in the correct spot on the hurt, pain, and shock spectrum. It is plain to see how this ranks pretty high on the scale. I have experienced this only as a granddad. I don't pretend to know what a PURE parent feels completely when the diagnosis comes in, but I have observed and been told these things. Questions are asked and then answered guardedly. Imaginations and perceptions of the future run wild. Emotions waver drastically minute to minute from "We can do this" to "What are we going to do?" "We don't know anything about this." "How are we going to care for our little baby boy/girl?" "Will they ever be able to walk, talk, or get married?" and a million other questions are asked. Further, and virtually in every case, PURE moms and dads can immediately think back to something in their past that they did, that caused *this*. From the moment of the first diagnosis or as the emergency room doctor reveals the prognosis resulting from the accident, the PURE parents are thrust into a strange and frightening world. They must quickly transition from bringing the baby home to consulting with many doctors, hearing insufficient explanations and projections, getting little sleep, and caring for a new baby or child in an entirely new and unfamiliar world. As they love and get to know their precious baby, they confront and begin to learn to deal with their ever-present nemesis: broken hearts, shattered dreams, and anxiety about the future. Plus, they must learn all they can so they can care for their child who is diagnosed with something about which they knew nothing only hours and days before.

Yes, life is changed forever from that moment on. Yet, most PURE parents will tell you that having their PURE child is the greatest experience of their lives. Even with all the heartache, suffering, and disappointments, they still say this! How and why does happen? God, through their PURE child, teaches them that.

I have seen this transformation in others. I have experienced it myself, and I live it today.

Tragedy Transformed

I remember it like it was yesterday: the night Zach died. Lee and I were visiting my mother who was recovering from back surgery in a hospital in Roswell, GA. Zach had spent about a week in intensive care at Scottish Rite Hospital (now Children's Healthcare of Atlanta) undergoing tests and recovering from yet another shunt revision. He had been at home for just a few days and was doing great. At about eight that evening, Katie called on my cell phone and began crying, "Something is wrong with Zach, the EMT's are here and the ambulance is coming to rush him to the closest hospital." I could tell from Katie's voice it was not going to be just another emergency room visit. I tried to comfort her as we ran out of the hospital to go be with them and Zach, "He'll be ok, baby; he's stronger than all of us."

"No, Daddy, this is different," she cried as the line went dead. We literally flew up the highway and ran into the emergency room only to find Katie, Kyle, and Zach's little 2 year old brother, Ben, sitting alone in the waiting room.

As we rushed in to embrace them, a doctor suddenly appeared asking if we were Zach's family. He simply said, "Come with me." We ran down the halls and entered the room where Zach was being cared for. We were all unprepared for what we saw in that treatment room. There were doctors and nurses all around this little boy. Tubes and needles and machines were everywhere. Somehow we all knew this was it. This was the moment that we had never even allowed ourselves to think about. We were losing Zach. The scene was horrible: all of us crying and trying to get a glimpse of Zach, or maybe hold his little hand. I can't really explain how I felt as I watched all of this transpiring.

In tears and knowing how close I was to him, Katie cried to me, "Daddy, talk to him - tell him how much you love him." I did. I spoke into his ear telling him how much I loved him and what he had meant to me - everything. I thanked God for giving him to us. As I looked down toward the foot of the bed, I witnessed a scene I will never forget. Kyle, who is my hero, a wonderful dad to Zach, and is today a wonderful dad to Zach's brothers and sister, was saying his goodbye to his son. As he lovingly held Zach's little feet, almost as if he were making a vain attempt to keep him from going, he cried and kept saying, "I love you, Zach. All I ever wanted to do is just be your Daddy."

Time stood still and was impossible to measure in that room, but I think we were in there for ten to fifteen minutes and it was obvious even to me that Zach had not responded to the valiant efforts of the doctors and nurses. I asked the doctor in charge, "Are you waiting on us to tell you to stop?"

He spoke quietly, "Yes." I looked at Katie and Kyle and they tearfully nodded their agreement. The machines were turned off, the tubes removed, and the doctors and nurses all backed away from his bed. It was all surreal and my memory fades a little here, but I do remember holding this precious little boy for a few minutes longer. We all remarked as we each took turns holding him in that room that, freed from the effects of his cerebral palsy, it was the first time we could remember that his little body was relaxed.

In our family even today, this night remains tender and raw in our memories. But, God in His goodness, reminded us what had really taken place that night with a most unexpected blessing. After Zach, died, I left the room to go call family members and friends. When I entered the room again, I found Zach's little brother, Ben, sitting on the gurney beside his big brother's little body. Katie and Kyle have always been great parents and even in such a moment, they had used this as a teaching moment. Ben exclaimed, "Granddaddy, Zach's not here, this is just his body – he's in Heaven with Jesus!" Such truth coming from the mouth of a two year old helped us all focus on what had really happened that night in that room.

The next morning, after a sleepless night, our family (Lee, Katie, Kyle, Anna Lee, our youngest daughter – Gabe, our son, had not yet arrived) was sitting around on the floor trying to process it all and beginning to make funeral plans. After completing this heartbreaking and surreal job, we continued to sit in Katie and Kyle's bedroom talking and reminiscing. After a while, I asked Katie and Kyle, "If you had the power to do it all over again, would you do it the same way? Would you want Zach just the way he was or would you want him normal?"

They both looked at me and responded almost simultaneously, "Except for the suffering that Zach had to endure, we would do it exactly the same way – we would want Zach just the way he was." Again, I'm not exactly sure how this happens. But, I witnessed something there that morning that was so profound, so real, and so astonishing. Something we just can't miss. Katie and Kyle had been just a typical young married couple. They had experienced the birth of their first child, who just happened to be PURE. Though all parents' lives change with their first child, because Zach was PURE, Katie and Kyle's lives were *really* changed. They had changed in ways that weren't entirely evident even then, but they knew they had grown much deeper. At this moment they were PURE parents who had just lost their precious son. Through all their heartache, suffering, and pain, they understood in ways unknown to most of us that their blessing of a PURE little boy, their Zach, was not a tragedy to them. No, Zach, a little boy who never took a step alone or said a single clear word, was the *greatest thing* that had ever happened to them.

But, what if *you* are the *tragedy*? Most of the bad things we tend to think about are events: something happens and, though consequences occur as the future unfolds, the event is over. Now, imagine being a PURE person and being looked at by others, friends and family, as the actual *calamity* and *heartache* that was inflicted on your family. How would that make you feel? How would you respond to a world that completely ignores you, or worse, won't even acknowledge your existence? "Oh, they can't process or understand that – they're developmentally disabled and can't sense our attitudes." You wanna bet? PURE people are much more tuned in and sensitive to their surroundings, especially our attitudes toward them, than we can possibly imagine. Despite all that, they survive, and most flourish! Despite all, they live. They must deal daily with the difficulties and limitations inherent in their disabilities. They must deal with a world full of people who don't or won't recognize their very presence, much less worthiness. They must deal with that constant, ever-present realization that "I am not like everybody else." They live and have so much to teach us about life.

The typical PURE person (now that's a paradoxical and ironic description for you!) has insights, techniques, and experiences about loving, living, perseverance, toughness, forgiveness, and acceptance that we normal people can only dream about. PURE people live it and will share their lives with us if we'll only get to know and love them.

A young PURE mother described this reality as she wrote about the experience in, *A Different Kind of Miracle*, with her PURE daughter:

> *Last January, the halls of Duke University Hospital teemed with friends and family anxiously awaiting the birth of our precious daughter, Claire. Just months earlier, we had learned that she would be born with severe hydrocephalus and that she likely would never walk, talk, eat, or breathe on her own. While we knew that Claire would have challenges, we fully expected that she would surpass the doctors' grim predictions. Quite frankly, we expected a miracle. To us, that meant that she would meet and exceed all of her therapy goals with ease and would be running marathons, reciting Shakespeare, and doing quantum physics by Kindergarten.*
>
> *Claire, however, had other things in store. Within just a few hours of birth, Claire developed seizures and spent five days hooked up to a continuous video-monitored EEG while doctors tried one medicine after another to get them to stop. A few months later, we learned that Claire was visually impaired. Then, after we noticed she did not seem to respond to sound, we had her tested for hearing loss and learned of yet another obstacle Claire*

would have to overcome. Finally, just as we seemed to have found our rhythm, Claire developed infantile spasms, a "catastrophic childhood epilepsy" with a poor prognosis.

With each new challenge, the miracle that we were hoping for seemed more and more unattainable. Yet, through these experiences, my husband Brad and I have grown and changed. We have had to pull together as a team in order to keep up with Claire's ever-changing medicine, feeding, and sleep schedules and her numerous doctor's appointments, tests, and therapies. We have had to learn to communicate better to coordinate her care and help make difficult decisions about which treatments to pursue. We have had to recognize one another's strengths and weaknesses to delegate duties and have had to swallow our pride every now and then and admit that we might not know everything all of the time. We have pushed our own abilities beyond limits we never knew existed and have done things we never thought we would be capable of doing.

In the nine short months since Claire's birth, we have learned a lot more about one another and about ourselves than we had in the previous ten years of courtship and marriage. We have laughed harder and cried more violently, but have also loved more deeply than either one of us could have expected. We have brought out the best in one another. We have learned the humility of relying on others for love and support and the beauty of feeling that love and support. I have been overwhelmed by how my heart just swells with pride when someone pays a compliment to Claire.

As I recently reflected on the past nine months, I realized that even though Claire has faced a number of challenges in her short little life, we still got our miracle. It just didn't manifest itself in the way we expected. The miracle is not what Claire can do, but how she has transformed us.[2]

So, the real question is this. Are heart attacks, divorces, death, and the like, good or bad? How about having a PURE child, being a PURE friend, brother, or sister, or actually being a PURE person:

good or bad? You decide – and we do and we will. PURE people help us see everything better. Perhaps more than anything else, they teach us that our words or *labels* for things, events, and even people that God chooses for us, are most often inadequate, if not downright wrong. Unbeknownst to them, PURE people have a unique ability to teach us this profound truth. They don't sit us down and preach to us, for many can't speak. They don't pridefully say, "Follow me," for many can't walk. They don't say, "Watch me," for many have never even seen themselves. But, in their usual quiet, unassuming way of living, they change us - if we let them. Every breath a PURE person takes is turning what some might think of as tragedy into triumph. PURE people *are* living and breathing *tragedies*, as the world sees them. Yet, it is PURE people, by God's miraculous power, that can change us to live a better way.

Gently Smashing Our Idols

Normally we use the word *economy* to refer to financial matters. Throughout the Bible and culminating in the New Testament, we have been given a new *economy*, one drastically different from the world's understanding. Merriam-Webster defines a more generic, not exclusively financial economy as *the arrangement or mode of operation of something.* This Biblical economy is definitely a new way of operating; though not just of *something*, but in *everything* if we are indeed Christians. If we look at the *economy of God* as described in the Bible, none of it makes sense on the surface. Oh, we'll agree with it with our Christian friends and we might even "Amen" it when we hear it in a sermon. However, what do we do in the quiet of the night when our heart is breaking and the other side of the bed is empty? When we would give anything and everything we own just to hold our son or daughter and tell them how we loved them one more time? When the night is not so quiet and the physical pain in our bodies is so bad we don't care if we ever take another breath? Or when we watch and listen to our child suffer unbearable pain, and we are powerless and can do nothing to ease it. It is times like these where either a superficial faith in a superficial God or real faith in *the* God is revealed. Pat answers or simple platitudes are like chewing tinfoil. Our hurting hearts bleed. It is these times, the *bad* times, that we must dig deeper or be buried ourselves under our doubt, lack of trust, and self-reliance. Strangely enough, PURE people can help.

God's Upside Down Economy

When we speak of idols, we speak of things we *value* above other things. When we speak of valuing, we must look at the perspective by which certain things are judged to have greater or lesser values. This perspective is based most prominently on a system that ranks the relative value of all things. This system in a financial sense is called an economy. As with the financial economy, God's economy has its own *fundamentals*: the basic truths and principles on which the economy is based. Jesus Himself spoke of His economy's fundamentals as He walked this earth. Here are some samples from Scripture:

> *But many who are first will be last, and the last first.*
> *Matthew 19:30*

> *And whosoever will be chief among you, let him be your servant*
> *Matthew 20:27 (KJV)*

> *For whoever desires to save his life will lose it, but whoever loses his life for My sake and the gospel's will save it.*
> *Mark 8:35*

> *We are fools for Christ's sake, but you are wise in Christ! We are weak, but you are strong! You are distinguished, but we are dishonored!*
> *I Corinthians 4:10*

> *Blessed are you poor, For yours is the kingdom of God*
> *Luke 6:20*

> *And again I say unto you, It is easier for a camel to go through the eye of a needle, than for a rich man to enter into the kingdom of God.*
> *Matthew 19:24 (KJV)*

In these and so many other verses, Jesus states concepts that are foreign to us in the flesh. We must *die* to *live*? How in the world does one become *first* by being *last*? Tell that to an NFL football coach and you will be helping him find a new job by the middle of the season. What about this *servanthood* thing? Jesus says to be a *leader* we must become *servants. Saving* our life by *losing* it? *Strong* when we are *weak*? *Honored* when we are *despised*? Even in our present world of economic chaos, Jesus tells us that when we are *poor*, we somehow *possess the very kingdom of God*? In fact, He tells us that it's easier for a camel to go through the eye of a needle than it is for rich man to enter into His kingdom.

Let's take a closer look at one of these *fundamentals*, the needle and the camel. Some theologians have tried to explain away this verse about the camel and the needle. Most of us are still trying to get *rich*, even though Jesus is telling us it will be difficult to enter the kingdom if we are. We intellectually convince ourselves and justify our life's priorities by agreeing with others that say that the *needle* is really the "needle gate" around ancient Jerusalem. Supposedly this needle gate was a smaller gate with a smaller opening that required that the camel stoop down to get through. We understand not only that wonderful metaphor, but additionally all the baggage the camel was carrying had to be removed or it would not pass through the gate. Now with this explanation, Jesus' words make some sense and have some great spiritual truth for us. We conclude that this is another of Jesus' wonderful parables: we only enter the kingdom on our knees with all of our *baggage* removed. What a wonderful truth and good material for many a sermon! Unfortunately, it's not what Jesus was talking about, and neither is there any proof at all that a needle gate ever existed! And why would the architects of the great wall around Jerusalem ever design and build a gate where a camel, the common mode of transportation in those times, could not pass through easily? It makes no sense.

No, we must take what Jesus says. *Exactly*, for what He says. Do you know how hard in actuality it is for a camel to go through the eye of a needle? It is impossible. It's not just hard, it's impossible! No, we can't reduce a camel down to its atomic size and shoot it through the eye of the needle either. It's impossible. So now, what is Jesus saying to us? He is not saying anything new here that He has not said and explained to us before. Only with Jesus is the impossible, possible.

In the account recorded in *Mark 10:17-31, Matthew 19:16-30*, and *Luke 18:18-30*, Jesus is speaking to the rich young ruler who came to Him asking what he must do to *enter into the kingdom of God*. Unfortunately, the young man comes to Jesus not with humility but pride, fully declaring his own righteousness. Knowing his heart, Jesus simply reminds him of the Ten Commandments. The young man incredulously replies, *"All these have I observed from my youth."* As an aside, I personally think here is one of the greatest confirmations recorded in Scripture that Jesus is God: only Jesus, the God-man, could respond to such an arrogant person with such compassion. I know if it would have been me responding (maybe you, too), I would've probably said something like, "Reeeeally? Liar, liar pants are on fire! You've done no such thing!"

Back to our story. Jesus calmly and simply replied, "Oh yeah, there's one more thing: go sell everything you have and give it to the poor." This stopped the young man in his tracks for he was rich. Did this rich young ruler go away sad because he was rich? I don't think so; it was simply that he loved money and the things that it could buy more than he loved Jesus. He liked being rich more than being a child of God. He went away sad, not because he was rich; he went away sad because Jesus asked him to give up the one thing in his life that he loved more than Jesus – his money and his things,

I think all of us in America can identify with this rich young ruler, or I believe we should. Don't think you're rich? Go to any Third World country, live with the people there for a day or two, come back, and then we can talk. By virtually any standard, *everyone* in America is rich. Yet, none of us would ever come right out and say we love money. It's not the money we love – it's the stuff it buys that we really love: comfort, security, emotional peace, freedom, conveniences, safety, and pleasures. In my heart of hearts, I know this to be true, so Jesus is in fact talking to me in these verses. In fact, I have to fight this thinking daily (no, make that minute by minute) lest I, too, walk away sadly loving my stuff more than Jesus.

Could there possibly be other *things* as well that you and I might be loving more than Jesus? Perhaps, more troubling, are we even aware of these things that so subtly deceive us? More importantly, how might our lives and perspectives literally be changed by the PURE people God brings into our paths?

When Identities Become Idols

If we were to take the time to examine all of Jesus' words relating to His economy, we would discover that what appear to be paradoxes or contradictions are really something else entirely. By using these worldly and illogical comparisons, Jesus points out what I believe is the identity crisis we all face as humans. Who are we? Further, who are PURE people and how can they help us here?

I must tell you that I get the biggest kick out of watching people identify with different groups. If I weren't guilty of the very same thing in my life, I would probably enjoy it even more. But, if we look around our culture, we will see some strange happenings. In many ways, we base our identity on different groups with whom we identify. We are in essence the sum total of the various identities we assume.

How do we do this, you may ask? Are you an Apple or PC person? Are you for Alabama or Auburn (or a million other college rivalry football teams)? Braves, Yankees, or Cardinals baseball fan? Rotary or Kiwanis club? Who's your favorite NASCAR driver? What kind of car do you drive? Where do you live? What church do you go to? What's the logo say on that jacket you wear? How about the brand name on that shirt or blouse? Do you think advertising affects you? Why do you buy what you buy? It's not just that we have likes and dislikes, preferences, and favorites, but *we are who we identify with*. I can't just like my college team; I have to wear their jerseys or at least their colors. I can't just live in a community; I have to put a tag on my car announcing it. I just can't believe in a cause; I have to have a bumper sticker (make that many bumper stickers) that says I do. I can't just go to any church; I have to go to *the biggest*, most popular church where all the *in* people go. Sometimes we don't even *officially* belong to the groups with which we identify, but we want other people to *think* we do! Some groups with which we associate and identify aren't really groups at all. These are people who wear the same type shoes, drink the same kind of energy drink, and buy the same brand of furniture. We get some kind of identity boost just knowing we are in the group together. How crazy is this? We indeed live in an image oriented world. We are infatuated with *belonging* or identifying with the right groups.

As you probably know, I live in the South and football, particularly college football, is big in the South. If you need further proof of our identity obsession, you need only join me to spend an autumn weekend in the South. Also, let me admit that I am a college football fan, too, though I don't think (hope) I take it quite this far. College football stadiums are sold out with enthusiastic, sometimes even fanatical, fans. Many drive hours to get there. There is no parking to be found around the stadium. They come early and tailgate hours before the game. Fans are dressed in their school colors, they wear the team jerseys, and some have even painted their faces and/or bodies with school colors or mascot symbols. Many are inebriated before the game even begins. They stand with tens of thousands of other like-minded people and yell their lungs out for three to four hours for young men eighteen to twenty-two years old that they idolize for no other reason than they play for *their* school's team. Crazy? Insane, even? Maybe so, but you can find literally millions of college football fans all over this country whose weekends are deemed good or bad solely on whether their team wins or loses. A win means smiles all around, and all is at peace with the world, at least for the weekend. A loss and you don't even want to go near the person until he (or she) puts on their game face for next week's game when redemption may be won. It would be difficult to find more passionate people on the face of this earth than college football fans, especially Southern college football fans.

However, the contrasts and craziness doesn't end there. If we visit that same college town on the Sunday after the game, we'll not find the same numbers of fans and certainly not the same enthusiasm and passion in the local churches. Many Christians will have gone to the game only to be too tired to attend worship the next day. Even the talk at church is about yesterday's game. Maybe it's better to just sleep in this Sunday morning. We certainly don't want to be too tired to watch the pro games on TV Sunday afternoon, do we? Passion for church? Not very much.

Now, this identification thing we do, in and of itself, is not such a bad thing. But, as Christians, our identity crisis can become an identity *catastrophe* if we're not careful, and we haven't been careful. In our "search for significance" we've come up empty so we've defined our own significance and shortened the search.

Pastor David Nasser describes this situation beautifully in his book *"A Call to Die."* After his Damascus road experience, Paul writes:

> *But what things were gain to me, these I have counted loss for Christ. Yet indeed I also count all things loss for the excellence of the knowledge of Christ Jesus my Lord, for whom I have suffered the loss of all things, and count them as rubbish, that I may gain Christ.*
>
> *Philippians 3:7-8*

Pastor Nasser goes on to reflect on Paul and his new, better way of thinking:

> *But something happened to Paul. He met Jesus.*
>
> *In this letter Paul reminds the believers where he came from: "If anyone else thinks he has reasons to put confidence in the flesh, I have more." Then he lists his impeccable credentials. "circumcised on the eighth day, of the people of Israel, of the tribe of Benjamin, a Hebrew of Hebrews; in regard to the law, a Pharisee; as for zeal, persecuting the church; as for legalistic righteousness, faultless" (Philippians 3:4-6). If anybody had reason to trust in his family position, Paul did. If anybody had reason to boast in his success, he did. If anybody could point to radical commitments and a faultless lifestyle, Paul could. He had it all!*
>
> *And it was all worth less than nothing.*
>
> *Paul and others had thought all these things were "profit" to him because they gave him position and clout, but when he experienced "the surpassing greatness of knowing Christ Jesus my Lord," all those things paled into*

insignificance. But that's not quite accurate. Paul said that those things that had seemed so important before are now considered "rubbish." The Bible translators looked at the word Paul used in the original language and said, "Nah, we can't use that word. It's too vulgar. We'll use 'rubbish' instead." Unless you are British, you probably don't use the word "rubbish" much. Frankly, I feel uncomfortable using the literal translation in my book. But you do the math. You know what he's talking about. Let's just say "waste."

When you see a pile of dog waste (or "rubbish") on the sidewalk, you don't stop and admire it saying, "Oh, Helen, look at that! Isn't it lovely?" (Well, some guys I know might …) No, you say, "Don't step in that!"

Paul was saying the prestige, possessions, and power he enjoyed were actually hindrances to him, and he was going to be careful not to step in them! Dietrich Bonheoffer said, of this realization: "The call of Jesus teaches us that our relation to the world has been built on an illusion." The promise of the world is an illusion. We thought the promises and the substance were real, but they aren't. We thought those things would satisfy, but they can't. We thought they were treasures, but they are "rubbish." They are, indeed, waste, when we compare them to "the surpassing value of knowing Christ Jesus my Lord."[8]

Why do we do this? Why do we identify with groups and use our roles to define ourselves? Why do we define ourselves in terms of the amount of *rubbish* we have accumulated? Perhaps we could blame it on our culture, saying, "Everybody does it." Or maybe in our competitive world, we must appear a little more connected, a little smarter, a little more *in* than our competitors. All plausible reasons for non-Christians, but implausible for us Christians. However, I fear we, too, have fallen victim to the real reason why we choose to project ourselves in terms of our identities: we are not satisfied and content with who we are. Think about it. If we were satisfied and content with ourselves, would we really spend the time, money, and effort that we do in trying to appear to be something greater and more impressive than we believe ourselves to be? I believe it is an inescapable truth that even as Christians, we don't seem to *be* enough, *do* enough, or *accomplish* enough. We are not content with who we are and must wear masks that tell others that we are *somebody*.

In the Old Testament we have a virtual nonstop account of God's chosen people, Israel, serving false gods, recommitting to return to follow Jehovah God, only to fall away again to seek after other gods. Back and forth they went, God to idols; from idols back to God. As we read, we take a collective thankful breath that *we* are too sophisticated, enlightened, and educated today to actually worship idols. You know, those idols made of gold or some other precious metals. Just who are we kidding? Our idols today are not made of gold, but they are just as real and just as prevalent today as with the Jews coming out of Egypt. I ask you: With apologies if you are someone who does these kinds of things, just how much religious fervor, passion, dedication, and commitment to a cause is required to make grown men and women wear plastic "cheese" triangles on their heads, dress up like a Viking or a dog, or don hats that look like eagles, dogs, or tigers – out in *public*? And feel proud, fulfilled, and loyal in the process?

Our idols today in America could be described on one level simply as our pleasure, our security, our happiness, our contentment, our status, our comfort, or our _____ (fill in the blank here as what is important to you). Note the key word: *our*. Our idols in reality are ourselves. Think about it. What are our priorities? Who is really #1 if we objectively look at how we spend our time, money, and effort? Pastor Adrian Rogers remarked once about how our priorities and labels have become so confused in our present day culture in America:

> *We live in a day where a hero is a sandwich, life is a magazine, power is a candy bar, joy is a detergent, sin is a perfume, a star is an actress who's been married three times, and the real thing is a soft drink.*[4]

Dr. Rogers had it right. We've gotten things really messed up. In a very real way, since we are more concerned with how others perceive us, our identities themselves have become our idols. Most of us would find it very difficult to define ourselves without mentioning our *membership* in various groups or roles we play in life. Not unlike our always identifying with the *good guy* in Scripture (as we talked about earlier), I find it interesting that we *always* identify only with groups that we think, in our judgment, to be good or worthy. I mean, if you lose enough games for enough years, the group identifying with and supporting that team will shrink drastically. Nobody wants to identify with the losers' group! We not only want to be identified with the *right* group, but we also evaluate others by the groups with which they identify as well. We want people to know about our power, our possessions, and our perceived prestige.

The world tells us to be strong, independent, and to rely on no one. We sing, "I did it my way" and "I've got to be me," yet we only can do it in a chorus of others exactly like us, or we don't feel secure. Why do we have to feel so accepted? Could it be that we really don't like what we see when we take off our masks?

It has been said, and I agree, that our identity or how we see ourselves can be best stated as:

We are *not* who *we think* we are.

We are *not* who *other people think* we are.

We *are* who *we think other people think* we are!

Pastor David Platt shares some real insight to this self-directed idol worship and takes it one step further:

> *Let's put ourselves in the shoes of these eager followers of Jesus in the first century. What if I were the potential disciple being told to drop my nets? What if you were the man whom Jesus told to not even say good-bye to his family? What if we were told to hate our families and give up everything we had in order to follow Jesus?*
>
> *This is where we come face to face with a dangerous reality. We do have to give up everything we have to follow Jesus. We do have to love him in a way that makes our closest relationships in*

300

this world look like hate. And it is entirely possible that he will tell us to sell everything we have and give it to the poor.

But we don't want to believe it. We are afraid of what it might mean for our lives. So we rationalize these passages away. "Jesus wouldn't really tell us not to bury our father or say good-bye to our family. Jesus didn't literally mean to sell all we have and give it to the poor. What Jesus really meant was ..."

And this is where we need to pause. Because we are starting to redefine Christianity. We are giving in to the dangerous temptation to take the Jesus of the Bible and twist him into a version of Jesus we are more comfortable with.

A nice, middle-class, American Jesus. A Jesus who doesn't mind materialism and who would never call us to give away everything we have. A Jesus who would not expect us to forsake our closest relationships so that he receives all our affection. A Jesus who is fine with nominal devotion that does not infringe on our comforts, because, after all, he loves us just the way we are. A Jesus who wants us to be balanced, who wants us to avoid dangerous extremes, and who, for that matter, wants us to avoid danger altogether. A Jesus who brings us comfort and prosperity as we live out our Christian spin on the American dream.

But, do you and I realize what we are doing at this point? We are molding Jesus into our image. He is beginning to look a lot like us because, after all, that is whom we are most comfortable with. And the danger now is that when we gather in our church buildings to sing and lift up our hands in worship, we may not actually be worshipping the Jesus of the Bible. Instead we may be worshipping ourselves.[5]

Pretty heavy stuff. Lost in our identity crisis, we have molded Jesus into a comfortable version of ourselves and thereby, are in actuality worshipping an idol – our *self* – even though we think we are worshipping Jesus! Could this really be true? Have we gone so far as to re-doing, an "extreme makeover" if you will, of Jesus Himself into a more comfortable image to coexist and remain in harmony with our own identities?

The words of Jesus are in stark contrast to this phenomenon of identity so prevalent in our western culture. To belong to Him, He says, we must: be poor, not rich; weak, not strong; servant, not leader; dead, not alive; last, not first; slave, not master; and despised, not honored. Jesus tells us, as He told the rich young ruler, if you are Mine, you must *acknowledge* and *accept* that you are *not* in the rich, strong, leader, alive, first, master, and honored groups. Rather, we must reckon ourselves in the poor, weak, servant, dead, last, slave, and despised group. And guess what? This latter group is really where we belong. In ourselves, in our own strength, and in our own doing and being, that's actually who we are. We may have a million friends on Facebook and followed by millions of others on Twitter, but it just doesn't matter in the long run. Our works won't save us and our group identifications won't either. The images of ourselves that we so meticulously craft, protect, believe in, and on which we base our significance, are just that: images, illusions, false. Just who is beneath the trademarks, brand names, and team jerseys?

A most frightening aspect of our identity infatuations is that we actually believe it really doesn't matter to God. He still loves us even when we are more busy preserving our self esteem and masquerading around His creation than we are with serving Him, doesn't *He*? Yes, He does, but that doesn't mean He likes it or will tolerate it in us for long. As Pastor Francis Chan says:

> "*The core problem isn't the fact that we're lukewarm, halfhearted, or stagnant Christians. The crux of it all is why we are this way, and it is because we have an inaccurate view of God. We see Him as a benevolent Being who is satisfied when people manage to fit Him into their lives in some small way. We forget that God never had an identity crisis. He knows that He's great and deserves to be the center of our lives.*"[6]

No, God has never had an identity crisis: He has always known who He is and He has always known who we are, too. How can PURE people help us rediscover who we are in Christ?

"And the Walls Come Tumbling Down"

Before we go any further, I must caution you and also add that we must be very cautious here. If we are not careful, we will simply shift our worship from one false idol to another. What I am about to say about how God helps us "break our chains" through our relationships with PURE people could be wrongly interpreted if taken out of context.

Though I have said this repeatedly before, it deserves to be said again: I am not in any way implying that *all* PURE people are *without sin*. I am not talking about that kind of purity. However, I must add too, that many PURE people have such severe intellectual disabilities that, though they indeed have been born with sin natures the same as you and me, they are incapable of *understanding* sin. It is the same situation as with babies and very young children who are incapable of sinning because they do not even know what sin is. They may do what we think are sinful things, but they don't *understand* that what they do is sin. Again, not all PURE people are without sin; but, some are. But even if not PURE without sin, all PURE people have something to teach us about being *pure in heart.*

PURE people with minor or major disabilities can have a relationship with Jesus Christ that we normal people cannot always comprehend. To think in any other way is to put the Lord in a box and denies His ability to choose and use whoever He desires. Because someone cannot recite the 4 spiritual laws, carry on a normal conversation, or even read does not mean that the person is not a Believer. In fact, I truly believe Jesus has captured the hearts of many PURE people that I know personally in such a profound way that I find myself envious of their relationships. If we can return to Eagle Eyrie one last time, I think I can clearly demonstrate this. A friend of mine who always brings a group from his church to the retreat shared with me something that had happened that morning. At first it had caused him great panic, but within minutes turned to great inspiration. Normally, caregivers share rooms with one or more PURE people. On this morning, my caregiver friend awoke at daybreak to find one of the PURE young men from his room, missing. This young man was non-verbal, had significant intellectual disabilities, and was generally non-responsive, so my friend was particularly concerned. Alarmed, he started searching up and down the hallways in the lodge for the missing PURE man. At the center of the lodge is a grand meeting room with an enormous glass wall facing east towards the mountain tops surrounding Lynchburg. It is a spectacular view at anytime of the day, but it is awe inspiring at dawn. As my friend entered the vast great room of the lodge on his search, his eye suddenly caught a glimpse of the silhouette of his PURE friend standing in front of the glass wall facing the rising sun over the mountains. Greatly relieved, he walked towards the young man and, for the first time, clearly heard the young man saying something. As he inched closer to the young man, not wanting to startle him, my friend was both astonished and humbled. The young man was smiling as he was repeatedly pointing to the sunrise and then touching his heart and saying, "My Jesus, my Jesus." My friend simply stood behind this young man and joined him in silently worshipping their amazing God. Do PURE people have relationships with Jesus? Yes. Is there some minimal intellectual level that a person must attain for the Lord to be able to save him or her? I don't think so. Can Jesus move in ways and in people without our being aware? Most definitely.

My intent here is not to focus on the PURE person at all and certainly not as the epitome or some embodiment of what it is we are to be if we are become more Christ-like. This is true even if our PURE friend or loved one happens to be one of these truly PURE folks (not mentally able to perceive sin, therefore not accountable). Even like our Zach. No, my focus is not on the PURE person. The focus is the Jesus who *made* them and *whom we find and grow closer to in our divine appointments* with them. Jesus and a closer relationship with Him is the goal and PURE people can help us get there. This is the point of a better way.

In Matthew, chapters 5, 6, and 7, Jesus preaches His greatest sermon, the Sermon on the Mount. In Chapter 5 and verse 8, Jesus says *"Blessed are the pure in heart for they shall see God."* Maybe like me, you read this verse and though it is beautiful, you're not exactly sure that you understand the depth of what Jesus meant, and simply hope that you are sufficiently *PURE in heart* so you can see God.

Jeff Crook, in his morning Bible study that I mentioned before, said some things that helped me understand what *pure in heart* really means. I hope it helps you as well. Jesus was talking about a *purity* that is first, *perfect.*

> *Beloved, now are we the sons of God, and it doth not yet appear what we shall be: but we know that, when he shall appear, we shall be like him; for we shall see him as he is.*
>
> I John 3:2 (KJV)

Since Jesus is perfect, and we will be like Him, we will be perfect only as we live in Jesus and He in us.

Secondly, a *purity* that is *positional.*

> *For He made Him who knew no sin to be sin for us, that we might become the righteousness of God in Him.*
>
> II Corinthians 5:21

We are not pure in and of ourselves, but only as God sees us through the filter of Jesus. No "Jesus filter," no purity for us.

Finally, a purity that is *practical.* Though our *perfect* purity will be realized only in the future in Heaven and our *positional* purity is real today, Jesus is saying that through Him, we are to live lives characterized by purity. We do this by choosing to guard our eyes:

> *Turn away my eyes from looking at worthless things, And revive me in Your way*
>
> Psalm 119:37

To guard our mind:

> *Finally, brethren, whatever things are true, whatever things are noble, whatever things are just, whatever things are pure, whatever things are lovely, whatever things are of good report, if there is any virtue and if there is anything praiseworthy—meditate on these things.*
>
> *Philippians 4:8*

And to guard our feet:

> *Let your eyes look straight ahead, And your eyelids look right before you. Ponder the path of your feet, And let all your ways be established. Do not turn to the right or the left; Remove your foot from evil.*
>
> *Proverbs 4:25-27*

James, the brother of Jesus, tells us in *James 4:8 - Draw near to God and He will draw near to you. Cleanse your hands, you sinners; and purify your hearts, you double-minded.* We will see and experience God only when we choose to be drawn to Him. Further, we must be clean and have again chosen to pursue purity in our hearts, minds, and lives. Because of our sinful natures, we are double-minded (or maybe even ninth or tenth-minded)!

Here is when the lights came on for me in how PURE people can help us somehow become more *pure* ourselves. I knew it, had seen it, and even experienced it, but had not perceived it exactly this way. We can think about something being *pure* in one of two ways. First, something or someone is *pure* because of what it *is*. Secondly, something or someone is PURE because of what it *is not*. In other words, a piece of gold is PURE if it is 100% gold or it is PURE because it is gold and has *no* impurities, in other words. *Pure is not the presence of something, but rather the absence of something.* These two perspectives are similar but have very different implications for us as we examine PURE people.

In an earlier chapter we talked about the *limitation of life options* for our PURE friends and their families. That is, inherent with any disability (physical, intellectual, cognitive, emotional, or any combination), a PURE person's life's options are limited in some way when we compare them to the common, though fictitious, norm. We can understand this more readily when considering one of the more common developmental disabilities, e.g. Down syndrome. Regardless of the severity of our friends with Down syndrome, there exists some degree of what appears to be a lack of complete awareness, perception, discernment, and understanding of their surroundings and what we would commonly label normal responses to many of life's situations.

More easily recognizable still is the PURE person with only a physical disability of some kind with no other cognitive, intellectual, or emotional impairment (e.g. paralysis, mild cerebral palsy, etc.). Though that PURE person is totally aware and involved in his/her world, he or she is more or less (once again, depending on severity) limited in their mobility, speech, vision, etc. These physical only limitations are just as real as the developmental limitations, but they involve a different set of problems and hurdles for the person, family, and for us, their friends.

However, much more common are the limitation of life options of PURE people with multiple disabilities. Though to us interested onlookers, a PURE person may appear to have *only* a cognitive disability or a physical disability, it is rare that a PURE person is singularly affected. Let me explain. Though the official diagnosis for a PURE person is X, most likely, one or more related or collateral consequences of X, will result in Y and maybe Z. For example, a PURE person with a birth defect resulting in the loss of a hand or arm might well have some emotional issues as a result of living life without an important appendage. Similarly, that PURE person with Down syndrome will frequently have physical heart issues which can reduce their physical activity and longevity. We think we can distinguish and identify the PURE person's limitations, but usually they are beyond our comprehension and understanding.

With this appreciation of the PURE person in mind, let's now consider why a PURE person is in fact PURE, in light of our definitions from above, and what that means to us.

A PURE person is *not* PURE for *what they are*, but for *what they are not*.

Regardless of the number and severity of disabilities, each and every PURE person must deal and come to grips with who they really are. Though we normal people must do the same, we have the skill and capability to mask and hide our flaws and shortcomings behind our multitude of identities. PURE people can't. More importantly, we, in our attempt to impress others, assume all of the identities we can muster to project ourselves a certain way. Again, PURE people can't and don't do this. Most PURE people don't have the awareness of the need to do such a thing or the ability to do it even if they did. This is the beauty and magnificence of it all.

PURE people are PURE because they are who they are. They are simply and marvelously the way God made them - with *no* pretense. Perhaps the really scary part to us is that, unlike you and me, PURE people do not have or need identities to hide behind. What you see is what you get! Pretty scary thought, is it not? Maybe scarier still, is that they are happy that way and see no need of trying to be something other than who they are.

Approach the typical PURE person, and he or she won't care what you look like, what you have on, where you live, or what you drove to get there. They just don't care about such trivial things which don't determine or define who we are in their eyes. Think about this and honestly tell me that you or I don't do this very thing. We make snap judgments about people based on these and other temporal and worldly criteria. For example, don't you think *more* of a man wearing a suit than a man with tattered, dirty clothes? Well? Of course, one does. PURE people don't do this! Most PURE people don't even have the capacity to do this and, in their world, certainly don't see the need or value in doing this which we so easily and unconsciously do. They seemingly don't even recognize personal appearance or group allegiances as even factors. Status, education, job, and credentials of success may be important to us, but they mean nothing to the PURE person. All they care about is me or you. Oh, we may see a PURE person with a pro football jersey on, but it won't be to identify with some team; it will be to identify with us, their friends.

PURE people are also PURE for what they *are not*. They are not encumbered and hindered as we are, with the perceived need to be *something else* to really be accepted. PURE people don't see the need to belong to certain groups – again, most couldn't even if they wanted to. Most PURE people will never be a college graduate, so they would have difficulty understanding why we would put such importance on such a relatively unimportant identity. Many PURE people will never be a husband, wife, dad, mom, granddad, grandmother, or be in a family anything more than the roles into which they were born. Very few PURE people get the opportunity to choose a mate and have a family. Further, most PURE people will never be a deacon, basketball star, teach a class, or run for public office. Most PURE people will never do or be many of the things on which we hang our proverbial hats, and, that's why they are PURE. It is what they aren't that makes them able to teach us what is really important. That's the better way God can teach us through them.

There is one last but very important identity I need to mention. When we identify and empathize with our PURE friends, we see the world differently. When we put ourselves in their shoes, with their perceptions, and in their relationships, our world begins to change. When we view the world through a new simplicity, total transparency, and absence of need for self-importance as they do, our worldview changes.

Just by being themselves and certainly with no intention to change us, they can and they do. God uses PURE people and they have the capability to:

- *Smash our identities*, because identities are valueless and meaningless to them.
- *Force us to cast aside our facades and disguises* we so skillfully use on each other – to be real, open, and honest.
- *Cause us, as Believers, to rediscover our real and only identity* as crucified with Christ (as described in *Galatians 2:20 - and the life which I now live in the flesh I live by the faith of the Son of God.*)

Our identities, which we think reflect our power, possessions, and prestige, are nothing when compared to who we are in Christ and, further, they get in the way of reflecting Him. Who are we in Christ? What are we in actuality when we belong to Him? By His grace, in Him we are His children *(John 1:12)*. We are Ambassadors for Him *(II Corinthians 5:20)*. We have been bought with His blood *(I Corinthians 6:19-20)*. We have been redeemed and forgiven of all our sins *(Colossians 1:13-14)*. We are already seated with Jesus Christ in the Heavenly realm *(Ephesians 2:6)*. We can do all things through Christ, who strengthens us *(Philippians 4:13)*.

If we can grasp and hang on to even one of these identities, it is enough. Why do we have so much trouble accepting what we have when we identify with Christ? It is only in Him that we can be truly who we are created to be. Only in the transparency that comes with Jesus can we reach out to others and really touch them and be touched by them. We can't just *add* Jesus to our identities; He *is* our identity, our *only* identity. Everything else only has meaning in this context.

From the PURE person with the most severe autism who will not so much as acknowledge our existence, to the PURE person so physically impaired he or she cannot move, to the PURE person seemingly devoid of any and all awareness, in them we see something very different from us yet common to each of them. Though everything may not be great, they deal daily with unbelievable obstacles, and they struggle in ways incomprehensible to us. Yet, despite everything, PURE people seem satisfied and content with themselves. Their disability is just part of who they are: it really doesn't seem to matter to them. They see it and accept it as part of who they are. More astonishing still, God uses them each and every one. Every PURE person can teach us something. And, they do all this with absolutely no awareness that they have such an ability or power to do so.

A good pastor friend told me about an experience he had recently with a teen friend who volunteered to care for his PURE son at a church respite care time. At the end of the night, he asked the young high school girl, "What did you learn in caring for my son?"

Her reply, "I learned what it was like to have a person totally dependent on me."

"Anything else?" he asked.

The young girl looked at this dad and said, "Yes. I learned I need to be a lot more like your son."

As I said earlier, we must be careful here not to, in error, transfer our worship from one idol (i.e. us) to another idol (PURE people). Ironically, just being around and becoming close to PURE people will keep us from doing this very thing. Unlike us, they don't pretend. If we only intellectually accept this unique blessing of PURE people as a gift from God and never experience it for ourselves, we might indeed view these PURE people around us as endowed with some mystical, angelic presence. Getting to know them will do just the opposite; we will love them for simply who they are and be drawn closer to the God who made them. Remaining aloof from and uninvolved with PURE people prevents us from experiencing this transforming power from God that flows through them. We must glory in the Creator and not the created.

I wish I had the ability to magically make myself more like my PURE friends: to be more transparent, accepting, non-judgmental, and less temporal and materialistic. I want to be more concerned with the interior as opposed to the exterior. In and of myself and in my own power, I can't. However, it is God, and only God, who can and will do this *if* I draw closer to Him; like James said in *James 4:8, Draw near to God and He will draw near to you.* How do I actually draw closer to Him in my daily life? What can and must I do?

Jesus tells us Himself in *Luke 11:9, And I say unto you, Ask, and it shall be given you; seek; and ye shall find; knock, and it shall be opened unto you.* But, how do we seek? The Bible tells us how: we pray; we serve; and we see His hand in everything and all things. He tells us we draw closer to Him in the most unusual places, in the most unusual circumstances, and with the most unusual people: *Verily I say unto you, Inasmuch as ye have done it unto one of the least of these my brethren, ye have done it unto me. (Matthew 25:40)* Yes, we seek Him in prayer, in serving Him, in sensing His Hand, and here, unexpectedly, in strange places and with *strange* people. PURE people are some of these *strange* people that God uses to draw us closer. Again, they are not even aware of how God is using them to draw us, but Jesus says we encounter Him when we encounter them. Slowly, maybe even imperceptibly, He uses them, PURE people, to gently smash our idols; in reality, it is *us*. He uses *them* to teach *us* to be content with how He has made us, to help us focus on the eternal, and, in the process, to draw us to Himself. Only God would choose this way. Amazing!

A Better Way to Live

It was a cold winter morning and I remember I couldn't sleep, but that's not too strange for me as I have gotten older. Always an early riser, I got up this particular Saturday in the early wee hours. I was driven to write something: something that would express what my grandson, Zach, meant to me. Though I knew he would never be able to see it, let alone read it, it didn't matter. I had to put it down on paper if for no one else but me. I really didn't understand then the total impact of Zach's life on me, but I knew it had and was changing me. In retrospect, the fact that God would take him home one year later was obviously unknown to me that Saturday morning, for I thought we would have him for at least my lifetime.

The title, theme, and truth were and are that Zach had taught us all *"A Better Way"* to live:

A Better Way

Living life through touch from those who love and are loved,
Not seeing as the world sees, little body so stiff,
What to think, what to do, where am I, what is that?
His short life, a better way, an example to really live.

How does one begin to do it — see life anew, without vision, with hardened touch?
When we had it all down so pat, so ordered, so clear?
Working, spending, gathering, thinking, we really thought life was such —
And then, God sends this little boy, is the world now to be feared?

We could see, we could move our limbs exactly
When and where and how we want, the world moves our way -
We could do it all and see it all and feel it all,
And yet, we were the ones who really were blind and lame.

313

How much life can God pack in a three-year-old, imperfect shell?
How can those who love him, and be graced with knowing him
Only come to see real life after his birth?
We just thought we understood, but our view of life was deadly dim.

How much difference in living can a single smile make?
True meaning and purpose to those a gift,
Nothing asked in return, save time and closeness,
Just to touch a face or catch a spoken drift.

How is it to know and be denied the expected reply?
How hard to feel so deeply and be bound so,
Some things must be told and heard now with ways not known,
To only be able to say "I love you," "My head hurts," "Can I go?"

Little boy so cute, so beautiful, handsome, yet something different -
Others look, so unaware of failing to hide their stare,
The power of cruel comparisons, the glare of the "normal,"
Can never hurt this one so strong, the others the unknowingly unaware.

For to really see and feel those around us requires a special gift,
We learn to see through different eyes and feel through unresponsive fingers,
To eternally impact those who love and are loved,
Requires concern and loving care only when expressed and then received,
Is a presence that truly lingers.

He touches me in ways I can never explain, to any but him or Him -
God has given us "words" and "sights," a better way I've never had -
To communicate with such depth of love, unconditional - as only on the Cross,
A gift to share and cherish forever,
Between a special grandson and blessed granddad.

It is definitely the curse, burden, and yes, even obligation of a poor poet (me), that I feel compelled to explain the poem for it to be understood. Some of it is understandable on the surface while other parts do seem a bit vague and confusing, I know. Let me attempt to make it clearer.

Zach was born with a host of issues. His diagnosis, like many PURE children, evolved and was revealed over a period of time. We first learned that he had hydrocephalus and would require a shunt in the inner part of his brain to properly drain the spinal fluid and reduce pressure. At two days old, he survived the surgery and did well, thanks to a gifted pediatric neurosurgeon, Dr. William Boydston. Just as an aside, he loved Zach, was an integral part his and his family's life, and even served as a pallbearer at Zach's funeral 4 ½ years later.

Over the next few months my daughter (a very smart registered nurse) began to notice that Zach's eyes weren't tracking or following correctly. I must confess here that being an ignorant, non-medical lay person was a blessing during this time. Katie, Lee, also a very smart registered nurse, and my younger daughter, Anna Lee (now a practicing physician) all knew too much, medically speaking, and were aware of things that I did not notice in Zach. Sometimes not knowing is better than knowing. A traumatic visit to a pediatric ophthalmologist left us with a diagnosis of an improperly formed optic nerve: Zach was essentially and effectively, legally blind. His vision issues were related to his original neural issues, and there were more issues to come.

The women of the family knew that cerebral palsy was most likely probable for Zach and, as expected, it soon started to show its effects on him. His little body became more stiff and inflexible as the days and weeks passed. Yet, all the issues were still not known.

Lee and I were keeping Zach for Katie and Kyle to take a much needed and first short getaway trip since his birth. I was holding our one year-old Zach just after we had fed him lunch on the first day. Zach suddenly started hitting me repeatedly and rhythmically in my side with his little arm. My wife immediately recognized it as his first of many seizures. This first seizure continued after we rushed him to the hospital and lasted for over twenty-four straight hours. Zach now had seizures to add to his growing list of medical issues.

So, this is the situation: here we have a beautiful little boy with big, beautiful brown eyes who, if just by looking at him, you would not think there was anything medically wrong with him. But there were. As he grew older and therapies began, the combination of his issues made everything very difficult for Zach. If he were only blind, the therapies involving motor skills and touch would help, but the involvement of cerebral palsy in his whole body made those therapies virtually impossible. If he had only cerebral palsy, the therapies for it would help, but his vision impairment was an even greater hurdle and worked at cross-purposes to his development. As a result of all this, Zach had other collateral issues: speech - he couldn't really talk, but could make sounds; eating - he couldn't handle certain textures or tastes of most foods (he pretty much lived on a few favorite baby foods and Krispy Kreme doughnuts!); walking - he couldn't alone, but he loved standing and movement and would "walk" for hours if we held and assisted him. Life was difficult for Zach, to say the least.

Yet, except for the shunt cloggings (he had many shunt revision surgeries in his four and a half years), and his seizures, he was always happy and an encouragement and joy to be around. How does one explain this? I can't, but he and I were close! Despite what his mom and dad might say, don't believe them. I was his favorite person in the entire world! I loved him and he loved me. We had our own communication, void of words, yet better than words. Yes, I used words, he used sounds, and we both used body language with lots of hugs. Why, he could even smell me! One of his therapists even made me leave the house one day, because, though I was careful to be absolutely silent, Zach was aware of my "scented" presence and wouldn't do what she wanted because, obviously, "Granddaddy was there" to play instead!

In fact, if you and I ever meet face-to-face, I will most probably be the only man you will have met or will ever meet named *after* his grandson. Yes, you read that right; I am named after and in honor of my grandson and not the other way around. Zach was named after his dad, Zachariah Kyle Emerson (for the record, my second grandson is named after me, Benjamin David Emerson, but I digress). After Zach died, I wanted to do something to honor him and the effect he had on my life. After asking for and receiving the blessing from Katie and Kyle, I legally changed my middle name to Zachariah.

Got a better picture? Maybe the poem makes a little more sense now. I hope so. Zach did, in fact, live his life through those whom he loved and those who loved him. In the physical realm, he literally had nothing else. He was content and satisfied with that. He really did teach us "a better way to live."

However, if the truth be known and though I don't want to necessarily admit it with all my grandfatherly pride, as I have gotten to know more and more PURE people, I have learned that Zach wasn't that unique after all. Yes, his combination of disabilities, his personality, and his uniqueness as a person were real all right, but his ability to teach those around him a better way to live was not. I've seen it over and over in a myriad of PURE people: different disabilities issues; different levels of severity; and different ages. None of those things seem to make a difference. Each PURE person possesses this ability.

When I talk with people about extending their comfort zones to include PURE people, I can relate to them in their feelings of awkwardness, anxiety, insecurity, and feelings of being uncomfortable in doing it. However, I never had that problem with Zach. Though he was only minutes old when I first met him, he was family, my first grandbaby, and I loved him unconditionally at first sight. That didn't change when we became more aware of who this little boy was. As I look back now, I don't remember making a decision to love him; I just did. I think the difference in the way I felt then, and the way we might all feel as we approach that PURE stranger is simple: I loved him even before I saw him and nothing could make me stop. The love I had for Zach – and he for me - was resident *in* me, but not *of* me. I did not engender, cause, or create it – it was just there. It was the love that God had placed in me for this special little boy and it is that same love He makes available to us to love others.

A *New* Way to Live

That is perhaps the most important life lesson we can learn from PURE people: if we wait on PURE people to do or be something that will draw us to them or make us love them, we will wait a long, long time. In fact, the PURE person may actually be repulsive to us physically in some extreme cases. How long must we wait then, for them to become physically attractive, witty, or be other things that naturally attract us on a human level? No, PURE people will force us to make a decision. As Christians, we will either appropriate, that is put it in action in our everyday lives, the love of Christ *in* us, and freely give it to each and every person He brings across our path, regardless. Or, we won't. It is as simple as that. We must make the decision and I truly believe God places PURE people in our lives to force us to make it. PURE people help us validate the love of Christ in us. We can wish the Great Commandment had some qualifiers about who we don't have to love, but it doesn't. If we reserve our love for just the people that we think deserve it, are worthy of it, or are sufficiently like us, it isn't really from Christ, is it? If Jesus had the same criteria, none of us would be loved by Him. PURE people teach us to love with the love of Jesus Christ in a way no others can.

In what other ways can PURE people show us a better way to live? Glad you asked, for my good friend Colleen Swindoll Thompson, daughter of legendary pastor and author Chuck Swindoll, and PURE mom herself, has beautifully captured another perspective of the PURE person in her poem, *"Most Blessed."*

Most Blessed

Courage is not natural to one's character. But it can appear when a person is forced to face fears and depend on Christ. My suffering with a disability has cultivated within me courageous character. I am blessed. My struggle with being misunderstood because of my disability has cultivated within me grace and mercy. I am blessed. Being hearing impaired has caused me many sorrows. Yet, I am able to hear God's voice without distraction. I am blessed.

Those who are visually impaired cannot see God's creation—the beauty
of nature, the joy of a smile, the sadness of a tear, the fascination of
colors, nor the uniqueness of another person. However, my perspective,
my imagination, and my need to touch reach to the core of my soul.
I am blessed.
People who suffer with pain or disabilities depend on others. Over time,
this has revealed my pride, transforming and humbling my character.
I am blessed.
I know my disability might cause others to feel awkward, uncomfortable, and
even fearful. Yet, because of this distance, I am vastly aware of God's presence.
I am blessed.
The parking sign for the disabled that hangs in every lot bothers many
non-disabled people, but they may miss the wonderful truth that Christ
welcomes us all to the throne of grace, which is never far away.
I am blessed.
Most people who suffer or are disabled need help each day to do what
most people do without thinking. In this dependent state, I am deeply
connected to all God's promises for those who depend on Him.
I am blessed.
Few disabilities are curable, yet because of my struggle, I am acquainted with
humanity's broken condition and not bound by shame or fear. As a result, my
soul is filled with authentic freedom and God's unconditional acceptance.
I am blessed.
The challenges I face in this life have allowed me to recognize how
profoundly I am blessed by Jesus Christ, my Savior and Lord.
Yes, I am most blessed.[7]

This is so good and so simple to understand. Unlike me, Colleen is
a very gifted writer and wordsmith. Her writings need no explanation
or clarification. Where do you think Colleen gained such insight? I can
tell you that it wasn't from some mountaintop, blissful revelation. No,
it was from living life with her precious PURE son, experiencing great
joy and great pain. That's how she learned it.

As you read this poem, did it make you think differently? Honestly,
have you ever thought that a PURE person might think, view life, or

be blessed in this way? They might not be able to verbalize it or they might not be aware of it, but their lives reflect and give evidence to it. Again, not all PURE people are this way, but most are.

As I have explained to people over and over again how Zach taught me a better way to live, I always try to relate it to the real, nitty-gritty issues of life where we daily live and with which we all struggle. For it is in those things that PURE people teach us best.

As we have said before and bears repeating again, we first must be willing to adjust to PURE people before we can learn from them. We must meet them where *they* are and *how* they are or we never will connect with them at all. They're not being selfish or inflexible; it is just simply who they are and they have no other option to be something or somebody else. I can assure you they would love to speak plainly, shake hands with us, or walk around the room to see something; they just can't. It's not that they necessarily want to be the way they are; they just are. We must adapt to communicate with and love them in ways meaningful to them and not necessarily, at first, to us. Then and only then, will our communication and love become meaningful to them, and ultimately to us as well. Only after we have sacrificed our self-esteem, sense of worth, and self-importance, can a new and better perspective be gained.

Need patience? Watch a PURE person deal with life day in and day out and you'll learn patience like you've never experienced before. Watch as they struggle with everyday tasks that we take for granted. Watch as they are ignored or stared at by people. Watch and you will gain that patience.

Want to be more thankful? Persistent? Have more courage? Accepting of others? Sensitive to the really important things? Less fearful? More joyful in the simple things of life? Just watch, love, and live with PURE people.

Now let's go even a little deeper. Do you and I sincerely want to be more transparent, more authentic, and less inhibited? Do we want to be more PURE, in other words? PURE people can teach us how to become this way as we actually become more like them. PURE people put an actual face and life to words that many times to us are but ideas and concepts. Words like transparent, authentic, and uninhibited come alive when they are attached to real people. In a narcissistic culture, PURE people can teach and show us how to get outside ourselves. As we come to the end, let me say again: PURE people aren't necessarily without sin, but they are simply more *pure* than we are, and they can teach us much about the love of Christ.

A Better Way to Minister

A few years ago, I found myself in a church service for PURE adults at a community center in Daytona Beach, FL. It was wonderful. PURE people did everything in the service except preach the message. In reality they did that, too, but not in the way we customarily think. The prayer time was sweet as two PURE people stood up front to take prayer requests. Each PURE person waited patiently in line to approach one of the prayer leaders, and voice their requests. The prayers that we prayed were unlike most you've ever heard before: honest, without pretense, and pleadings for each and every request. Requests you and I would never reveal in public were offered without reservation. The offering was meager by the world's standards, but as the plate passed somehow my thoughts kept going back to the widow's mite.

Finally, the non-PURE group leader began preaching and as the poorly dressed, middle-aged, PURE man beside me listened, he started to mumble something to me. I couldn't quite understand him and leaned closer as he kept repeating the same, unintelligible phrase. I listened to the preacher to see if I could make some sense of what he was saying. The preacher was talking about people in our human state; that we are naturally sinful, selfish, and prideful. It was then that I heard the man next to me clearly for the first time. He was smiling broadly and looking back and forth at me and the preacher. He knew something and he was saying it out loud. With a sense of security and confidence in His Jesus that he so obviously knew intimately, he was telling me, over and over again as he pointed his finger at his heart, "That was me, that was me, that was me ..." Would you or I have ever been so open, honest, and uninhibited? I can truthfully say that I desire to be more like that PURE man. I know that when I do, I will be more like Jesus.

As I contemplated this PURE man in that service, God began revealing one final power that, through His grace, God has given PURE people. It is perhaps a power you might first think totally improbable. However, if you think more about what I am about to say, it not only makes perfect Biblical sense, but, again, in God's economy, it also makes perfect sense. Where, but the most unlikely place, would God put something so special?

This power is being manifested every second of every day by PURE people right before our eyes. God is not only teaching and showing us a better way to live by His blessing us with PURE people, but I believe He is doing something even greater to His church now in the twenty-first century, particularly through them. Is it conceivable or plausible that, simply through PURE people, God is actually demonstrating a *new* and *better way* for us, His church, to minister and win people to Christ? I think He is and they are.

When we look at the personal evangelistic style of PURE people, that is, how they relate to people, we see something remarkable. First, consider PURE people who are cognitively aware of their relationship with Christ. These PURE people typically have no status symbols to display, no buttons to wear. They don't drive up with a Christian fish emblem on their car. They have no impressive credentials to parade and they don't recite a long list of worldly successes with which to try to impress us. They may not even know the *right* Christian words to use. They probably won't talk about doctrine. More likely they will talk freely and sincerely both with people whom they know as well as with complete strangers. Their goal in the relationship or encounter is not to impress, but to get to know you better and tell you about their best friend, Jesus. Though speech and communication is often a problem, it doesn't slow them down. They are not very likely to complain of their situation, but may stop you in midsentence to pray for you if you mention something bothering you. They are real, sincere, and authentic. If you are like me, you can appraise yourself more honestly and objectively after being with such a PURE person. You'll probably appear a little more inhibited, insincere, or guarded when comparing yourself to them, and this is beneficial for us. We can start to see them for who they are and how we don't measure up very well normally in the open, authentic, and transparent categories. They have taught us this simple truth, not by rudely pointing it out to us, but rather by just being themselves.

Even the PURE person, who is perhaps too physically or cognitively impaired as to be unaware of their relationship with Jesus, or a PURE person who seemingly has no relationship with Jesus at all, has a personal authenticity and sincerity so lacking in most of us. An important aside here, though, is that we must be very careful in judging the spiritual condition of any person, and we must be even more careful with PURE people. Who are we to say that a person doesn't know Christ or already belongs to Jesus just because they cannot verbally explain it to us or are too physically or intellectually disabled to respond to us in any discernable way? God will and does what He will do, and we do not know how God has worked or is working in that person's life. Again, not being judgmental is important with all people, but even more critical with PURE people. But, we must never assume that salvation is unimportant because we know there *are no disabled souls.*

So PURE people are more open and honest in their relationships than we are? Is that all? No. Ready for a drastic and sweeping statement? *Ministry to and with PURE people is the model of ministry that can change the world for Christ.* In fact, and even more revolutionary, it is not only a better way; it is the *only way!* Though this claim and entire subject of the PURE ministry model is too extensive to cover in detail here, I believe there is a Bible's worth of proof that will substantiate it. Also, I personally have hundreds of examples of how God is using PURE people to bring others to Himself.

Further, this power that PURE people demonstrate among us even today can be the model of ministry to reach *any* group of people. This new ministry model we see in PURE people is particularly applicable to disenfranchised or alienated groups of people. These are groups of people in our culture that, for all intents and purposes, are ignored by the church as "too difficult" to reach. These groups can be identified by their collective *sin* (adulterers, homosexuals, criminals, etc.) or other demographic groups traditionally sparsely present in our churches (college age, young singles, divorced men, etc.). This revolutionary ministry model or method of ministry not only works in our culture, but it works in all cultures and in all countries. It is not limited ethnically, racially, economically, or in any other way.

What is this *new* and *remarkable* method of ministry which cannot fail? It is amazingly simple and perfectly visible to any of us willing to open our eyes to see it. However, in our humanness, shaded by our misconceptions and through the dimness of our pride and because it makes no sense in our logical thinking, too often we just can't bring ourselves to see it, or admit it even if we do see it. The model is not actually new at all; it has been around since Jesus came to earth. The better way to minister can best be summarized this way:

> We must disappear. Not just symbolically or allegorically, but literally disappear just like PURE people do. We must in essence, become more like PURE people. Until we love Jesus more than we care about how we are perceived, until we love others more than ourselves, until our only identity is that we belong to Jesus, our lives will have little lasting impact. This will happen only when we disappear; when we become invisible; when others see and experience in us His qualities, His character, and His love superseding and prominent over our human ones; and, when our only objective in living is to be instruments of grace in bringing others to Christ. This is the reason we were created: to reflect Christ.

Though I obviously don't presume to speak for God, I think it is entirely possible that one of the reasons that He has given us disability in this world is to change the life focus of not only PURE people, but also to change the life focus of the rest of us as well. Because PURE people don't normally fit our church demographics, programs, or focus groups, they are left to their own devices. In their brief encounters, casual friendships, and deep relationships with others, all PURE people have to offer are themselves. This is just the way Jesus wants it, for this is when He is there in all of His glory. It is in this atmosphere of humility and love that Jesus has the words of comfort, hands of help, and the embrace of love. We are simply instruments of grace in His hands, but only if we get out of the way. Only if Jesus has us completely, can He use us completely.

Whether PURE people can articulate it or not, and whether they understand it or not, they are used by God to reach others. Because of their simplicity and sincerity in not trying to mask who they are, Jesus can be preeminent in them and in their communication. This is even if they can't pronounce the word *Jesus*, even if they cannot even utter a single word, or as much as lift their head. People come to Christ and find Him real in personal relationships with PURE people and that is what *we normal people*, who name the name of Jesus, are to be doing as well.

PURE people seem so much better at this than we are. Living lives of isolation, pain, loneliness, hurt, disrespect will do that to you. It will also make you humble, dependent, and usable. Though the twelve disciples weren't PURE as we define it, they were certainly nothing out of the ordinary. They just had this understanding that they weren't anything and Jesus was everything, and they went about sharing Him with everyone they met. And totally and forever changed the world in the process. Always one-on-one, without big buildings, giant crusades, standing committees, choirs, or whatever else we can name and think is necessary. Just a few *disappearing* people living life so that others can see and experience Jesus in them. That was the secret two thousand years ago and that's the secret today.

Improbable and implausible as the world might think, that's where PURE people come in, and that's where they shine. They might not even know they are being instruments of grace. Pharaoh didn't. King Darius didn't. Herod Antipas didn't. Even Saul before he became Paul didn't. All of them were used. You see, God does use anyone and everyone according to His purpose. More importantly, He uses even PURE people for His glory and we can learn so much if we just open our eyes and observe. Even the PURE person who never speaks, walks, or moves can be better instruments of God's grace just by breathing another breath than many of us lukewarm Christians hiding behind our multiple identities. As St Francis of Assisi once said, and is so very true and descriptive of most PURE people, *"Preach the Gospel at all times and when necessary use words."* PURE people do in fact preach the Gospel of Christ with their lives; few are able to use words. The PURE person with awkward gait or slurred speech is beautiful to Jesus and is often more effective in His work on earth than we are as able-bodied believers, too comfortable in our own self-righteousness.

PURE people are who they are, and Jesus can and does use them. If we watch them, we'll get to see the secret. They might not use the "Roman Road," correct Scripture verses, or words at all. They might not know much about formal evangelistic methods, the four Spiritual Laws, or other techniques. They don't have to. They let Jesus do the talking through their lives. Jesus knows exactly what to say to every person, every time, and in every place.

This is what PURE people are teaching us about ministry. It has never been, is not now, and will never be grandiose plans, new programs, or innovative techniques that win people to Christ. It always has, it is now, and it will forever be one person sharing Christ with another. The *new* model of ministry that PURE people teach us is not new at all. PURE people simply give evidence to, manifest, and validate what Jesus said and did two thousand years ago. It's just that PURE people, stripped bare of the very things which most of us use to define ourselves, must use this divine method of ministry of care, love, and being an instrument of grace in the Hands of Jesus. They have no other option.

It is only after we have lived with and among PURE people that we can see this lived out in their lives. We see PURE parents who once cried to God, "Why me?" later praise and ask God, "Why did you *choose* me for such blessing?" We see PURE moms and dads, PURE brothers and sisters, PURE aunts and uncles, PURE grandmas and granddads, come to Christ as a result of living with their PURE family member. We see friends of PURE people and their families come to Christ through their PURE friends. In the process, all of us are drawn closer to this remarkable and loving God.

The power of PURE people? My good friend, Helen Heard, told me about something that happened to her one Sunday in her church, North Point Community Church in Alpharetta, Georgia, that says this better than I ever could. Helen, no stranger to suffering herself, is a wonderful godly woman, is the best friend of my sister, Lynda, and has been a friend of our family for more years than any of us wants to remember. Helen volunteers each Sunday morning in the PURE ministry at her church. This particular Sunday she saw a young boy about six years old being brought into the room in a wheelchair. Though busy at the time, a few moments later, Helen read the information sheet on the new young PURE boy. Helen learned that the young boy had severe cerebral palsy and could not so much as lift his head or utter a sound. Checking further the things his mom had written that he "liked," she noticed at the top was "He likes to be held." Helen's response was quick and sure, as she proceeded to lift the young boy out of his wheelchair and began holding him; in fact, she held him for the whole hour.

This is when the story gets really interesting. Helen was telling me the story days afterwards and, after she was about one sentence into it, she was barely audible through the tears as they ran down her face. They continued as she told that story. More significantly, she reflected about her experience, "I cried for the entire hour that I held this precious little boy. I couldn't stop. Not tears of sadness, but tears of joy and thanksgiving!"

Joy and thanksgiving? I asked her, "Why?"

She replied, "I felt like I was so privileged to be holding him. I felt God was there!" She continued crying even after she had finished with the story. I think I know where she is on this.

Helen was tremendously moved by this experience. She has been around PURE people before and enjoys her relationships with them and their families. Did I tell you that Helen was a wonderful help and encouragement to our family with Zach? Did being around Zach influence Helen to be who she is and do what she does now? I believe it did, for I believe Zach taught Helen a thing or two as well. She knows God's blessing when she sees it.

However, the main thing to understand here is this: *regular, normal* people cannot invoke this kind of thing in us, but PURE people can and regularly do it when they aren't even aware of it. No matter how cute or darling a baby is, we'll not normally be moved like this. Know this: this young boy did not cause Helen to focus on him and his difficulties. No, somehow he, without saying a word, responding in any way, was simply the instrument of grace that God used that morning to draw another person even closer to Himself. To encourage and inspire her and us in ways that we cannot. Only God can, through PURE people. This is the secret: it is in our being more like them that God can use us to change the world.

Ministry to other groups of people is less complicated when we approach them with love and acceptance rather than our expectations. PURE people teach us this. It is only when we become more like PURE people that we can minister with love and without pretense. It is only then that we can be the church that Jesus desires of His people. All because Jesus has given us His best example in the weakest of the weak – the *least* residing on His earth. PURE people will increase our impact and our capacity not only to evangelize, but to also love and minister in new, meaningful ways to anyone as they do. Lifestyle Christianity, I think they call it.

A new model of ministry? One-on-one relationships? And we learn it from people of great worth that the world deems worthless? In reality, it is when we can identify with our PURE friends, that God can do His divine and best work through us. Sounds exactly like something God would do.

So, The Next Time You're in Wal-Mart ...

If you have been to one of our PURE Celebrations you've already heard me say this, but I will end this book the same way I end the Celebrations, with a simple challenge. If you will just do this one thing, I will leave you alone. This one thing will prove to yourself, not me or anyone else, that you are serious about loving the way Jesus loves. It may not at first seem easy, but it will with practice. The one thing I know is that it is the kind of things that Jesus wants us to be doing.

How do you prepare? Simply this: First, pray and ask God to remove your ego, sense of pride, and fear. Secondly, ask Him to open your eyes to people around you that you may have never seen before. Finally, ask Him to help you do it:

Here is the challenge!

> The next time you're in Wal-mart and you see that group from a home, a PURE family with a PURE family member, or a PURE person by themselves: walk up and talk with them.

That's it. If you do this simple thing, God will bless it because He says in His Word He will. What He does with this simple encounter is up to Him and you. This may be a *first* for you in doing something as bold as this. It may be a big stretch for your comfort zone. Or, for others, it may be as ordinary as breathing. Whatever it is for you, if you are willing to *disappear* and let God work through you, I can promise you this: you will meet Him there in that encounter with that *invisible* person, you will be blessed, and you'll never be the same again. This truly is a better way.

About the Author

David, an ordained Minister of the Gospel, is President and Founder of *PURE Ministries*. David holds a Bachelor of Industrial and Systems Engineering degree (1970) from the Georgia Institute of Technology in Atlanta, Georgia. He and his wife, Lee, are both native Atlantans, but currently live in Dothan, Alabama. They resided previously in the north Georgia mountains in Gainesville, Georgia for 25 years. They are the parents of Katie, Gabe, and Anna Lee, and grandparents of Zachariah, Hunter, Benjamin, Madison, Landon, Riley, Josiah, Anna Gracelyn, Reagan, River, Waverly, and Ezra. While in Gainesville, David and Lee were active members of Blackshear Place Baptist Church in Flowery Branch, Georgia. They now are members of Calvary Baptist Church in Dothan, Alabama. David was instrumental in the founding and development of several technology companies: as Senior Vice President at Stockholder Systems, Inc. (SSI), co-founder and Chief Operating Officer of First Bankcard Systems, Inc. (FBS Software), and co-founder of ITManna, Inc., an IT consulting firm. David currently serves (or has served) on the boards of directors of: ITManna; Southwest Christian Care (a hospice care facility and a respite center for medically fragile children); Fellowship of Developmental Disabilities (a national association of disabilities ministries, homes, and organizations); and Happy Acres Mission Transit Center (a missionary support organization). David has also served as National Consultant for Disabilities Ministries for NAMB (North American Mission Board) of the Southern Baptist Convention.

You can contact David through the *PURE Ministries* website, www.PURE-Ministries.com, or directly via email, david@pure-ministries.com.

Notes

Chapter 1 - An Introduction to PURE Ministry

[1] *"Somewhere in the Middle"* by Mark Hall Copyright © 2007 My Refuge Music (BMI) (adm. at CapitolCMGPublishing.com) / Be Essential - Mark Hall (BMI) All rights reserved. Used by permission.

Chapter 2 – What is PURE Ministry?

[1] Bob Russell, Bob Russell Ministries. Used by permission.

[2] Corrie ten Boom, *The Hiding Place*, Copyright 1971 and 1984 by Corrie ten Boom and Elizabeth and John Sherrill, (Ulhrichsville, OH: Barbour Publishing, Inc.), 231.

[3] From the *International Standard Bible Encyclopedia*, Edited by James Orr, published in 1939 by Wm. B. Eerdmans Publishing Co., Website HTML © 2011.

[4] Francis Chan, *Crazy Love: Overwhelmed by a Relentless God*, Copyright © 2008 David C. Cook, (Colorado Springs, CO: David C. Cook), 86-87.

[5] John MacArthur, *Safe in the Arms of God; Truth from Heaven About the Death of a Child,* Copyright © 2003 by John MacArthur, (Nashville, TN: Thomas Nelson), 6.

[6] *Comparative Mortality in Cerebral Palsy Patients in California*, 1980-1996, Richard B. Singer, David Strauss, and Robert Shavelle.

[7] *Woman's Day,* April, 2009 edition.

Chapter 3 – Truth Cloaked in Irony

[1] Vance Havner, (n.d.). BrainyQuote.com. Retrieved October 2, 2011, from BrainyQuote.com Web site: http://www.brainyquote.com/quotes/quotes/v/vancehavne401703.html.

[2] David Platt, *Radical: Taking Back Your Faith from the American Dream*, Copyright © 2010 by David Platt, (Colorado Springs, CO: Multnomah Books), 48-50.

[3] Boyd Bailey, *"Wisdom Hunters"* Devotional, from *Strength in the Lord*, March 10, 2010.

[4] David Nasser, *A Call to Die*, Copyright © 2000 by David Nasser, (Redemptive Art Publishing), 166-167.

[5] Wilbur Rees, Leadership Magazine, Winter edition 1983, *$3 Worth of God*, Vol. IV, No. 1, 107.

6   John Ortberg, *If You Want to Walk on Water You've, Got to Get Out of the Boat*, Copyright © 2001 by John Ortberg, (Grand Rapids, MI: Zondervan), 83-65.

7   Dr. Adrian Rogers, *Adrianisms: The Wit and Wisdom of Adrian Rogers*, Copyright © 2006 by Life Worth Finding Ministries, (Memphis, TN: Life Worth Finding Ministries), 18.

8   Chan, 29.

9   Dwight L. Moody. (n.d.). BrainyQuote.com. Retrieved November 6, 2011, from BrainyQuote.com Web site: http://www.brainyquote.com/quotes/authors/d/dwight_l_moody_2.html.

10 Vance Havner, *Hearts Afire*, Copyright © 1972 by Vance Havner, (Westwood, NJ: Fleming H. Revell Company), 77.

11 Christopher De Vinck, *The Power of the Powerless: A Brother's Legacy of Love*, (Grand Rapids, MI: Zondervan), 9.

12 De Vinck, 12.

Chapter 4 – Practical PURE Ministry

1   SBC reports statistical decline By Bob Allen Friday, June 10, 2011.

Chapter 5 – Bringing it All Home: The Power of the PURE

1   Charles Haddon Spurgeon, from sermon #825, Volume 14, *The Sieve*, Adapted from *The C.H. Spurgeon Collection*, Ages Software.

2   Amy Grynol, *FOCUS*, November/December 2011, Volume 28, Number 6, (Atlanta, GA: FOCUS).

3   Nasser, 108-109.

4   Dr. Adrian Rogers, *Adrianisms: The Wit and Wisdom of Adrian Rogers, Volume 2*, Copyright © 2007 by Life Worth Finding Ministries, (Memphis, TN: Life Worth Finding Ministries), 93.

5   Platt, 13.

6   Chan, 22.

7   *Most Blessed* by Colleen Swindoll Thompson. Copyright © 2011 by Insight for Living, Plano, Texas. All rights reserved worldwide. Used by permission. www.insight.org/specialneeds.

Printed in the United States
By Bookmasters